# MYSTICISM ACROSS CULTURES

Studies on Select Poets and Saints

# MYSTICISM ACROSS CULTURES

## Studies on Select Poets and Saints

A.N. Dhar

ATLANTIC
PUBLISHERS & DISTRIBUTORS (P) LTD

Published by

**ATLANTIC**

**PUBLISHERS & DISTRIBUTORS (P) LTD**

7/22, Ansari Road, Darya Ganj,
New Delhi-110002
Phones : +91-11-23273880, 23275880, 23280451
Fax : +91-11-23285873
Web : www.atlanticbooks.com
E-mail : info@atlanticbooks.com

Branch Office
5, Nallathambi Street, Wallajah Road,
Chennai-600002
Phones : +91-44-64611085, 32413319
E-mail : chennai@atlanticbooks.com



ISBN 978-81-269-0145-6



Printed in India at Nice Printing Press, A-33/3A, Site-IV, Industrial Area, Sahibabad, Ghaziabad, U.P.

**DEDICATED TO**

*My Parents*

*and*

*to the hallowed Valley of Kashmir :*
*abode of saints and mystics*

# FOREWORD

In Professor Amar Nath Dhar's writing one notices a confluence of several traditions. There is the heritage of his birthplace, Kashmir — rich in philosophy, especially mysticism, and in sainthood. There is also the multicultural tradition of India. In addition, there is the tradition of English literature, especially that of the 19th century Romantics, which Professor Dhar studied and taught to generations of students.

The great variety of writings contained in the present volume bears testimony to Professor Dhar's versatility as a scholar, thinker, educationist, critic, as well as poet and translator. His earlier eminently scholarly book *Mysticism in Literature* (1985) had a Foreword written by the British scholar Ronald Tamplin, who wrote : "...It is one of the attractions of the present book that Dr. Dhar, writing from within the traditions of India, adds a further ring. Learned in his understanding of Christianity, especially in his sense of the central importance of the incarnation, he adds the insights of another spirituality, not dissonant but distinct and so additionally illuminating. It is a book much to be enjoyed and savoured."

*Mysticism in Literature* dealt particularly with the work of Coventry Patmore and Francis Thompson, poets of 19th Century Britain. The book, in its exceptionally wide scholarly range, also brings into discussion Eckhart, Dante, Jacob Boehme, Hegel, Newman, Emerson, T.E. Hulme, T.S. Eliot, Aldous Huxley and the *Gita* and the *Chandogya Upanishad* among the Indian philosophical and mystical texts.

Prof. J.R. Watson, who taught for years at the University of Durham in Britain, and is now Professor Emeritus there, impressed by Professor Dhar's grasp of the mystical texts he had worked on, wrote about the volume *Mysticism in Literature* : "...Mr. Dhar has studied the material with loving care, and has imposed his own insight quietly but firmly which can justifiably be commended as original work." Professor Dhar's originality is also to be seen in the book mentioned in his ability to relate and balance the Western and Eastern approaches. That quality of a mature and balanced critical approach marks as well the present compilation of writings titled *Mysticism Across Cultures* : *Studies on Select Poets and Saints*.

The reader will see in its contents no personal axe to grind on the part of the author, but a truly classical mind at work. Professor Dhar has attempted to put together several essays which indicate a search for his roots. Being displaced from home — the Valley of Kashmir — he finds that all modern Kashmiri writers are in a way reasserting their rich cultural past : researching and even reinventing its many facets. Kashmir's saint-poets and mystics *e.g.,* Lal Ded, Nunda Rishi, Rupa Bhavani, and Bhagavaan Gopinathji of the past century, will interest any reader, who is seeking to discover the glory of India's spiritual past. In fact, Kashmir did not remain as an isolated island in itself, so far as philosophy and spirituality were concerned. India, as a whole, from the Vedic times onward, has had a galaxy of philosophers, sages, poets, and thinkers, such as Shankara, Ramanujachari, Madvacharya, Kabir, Guru Nanak, Shankar Dev, Sant Tulsidas, Mirabai, Sri Chaitanya, Sri Ramakrishna, Swami Vivekanand and others, who have contributed to the country's great distinction as a leading country in world thought. Kashmir, as a part of India, has made notable contribution to the uniqueness of our cultural heritage. Professor Dhar's perception of this invaluable element in Kashmir's philosophical traditions is a befitting tribute to his native Valley.

Another feature of Professor Dhar's writings is the sense of stylistic discipline which he seeks to explore in every literary work. Trained in stylistics at the Central Institute of English and Foreign Languages, Hyderabad, from where he obtained a Diploma in English Studies, he has developed an acute sense of critical analysis which he applies to the study of any constructed artifact. This mental discipline I consider to be a mark of

Prof. Dhar's maturity as a critic. There is nothing mechanical about this kind of technical analysis of a work of art; such a method of reading and approaching a literary artifact is a balancing factor in literary criticism; it has a quality of impersonality which I consider essential to appreciation.

I had the pleasure of working together with Professor Dhar at the University of Kashmir during the years 1982-84. I went on leave from the University of Delhi to Kashmir to function as the Head of Kashmir University's Postgraduate Department of English at Hazratbal, Srinagar, at the invitation of the University. One of the boons of that short appointment of mine was knowing Professor Amar Nath Dhar and his family. Ever since we have been in touch. He headed the Postgraduate Department of English at Kashmir University for a few years after my return to Delhi. During that tenure, the Department made remarkable progress. After his retirement from there he moved to Jammu; it proved to be what he calls an 'exodus' from the Valley. Because of growing political turmoil there, he has stayed on at Jammu. But living outside of his native place, Professor Dhar continued to carry out his cultural pursuit vigorously. He was awarded a U.G.C. Emeritus Fellowship in English for two years (October 1990 to September 1992) and later a Senior Fellowship in Literature for another two years (October 1997 to September 1999) from the Department of Culture, Government of India. Some of the valuable work included in the present volume is the product of those four years of fruitful intellectual pursuit.

I am most pleased that Professor Dhar decided to put together all the essays in one published volume. Any reader will find material in it to read and enjoy. With the publication of this book Professor Dhar shows that the Indian scholar can do intellectual work comparable in merit to that of a mature scholar living a rewarding life in any part of the world.

**G.K. DAS**
Retired Professor of English,
University of Delhi.
Former Vice-Chancellor,
Utkal University, Bhubaneswar

# PREFACE

The present study has been conceived and planned as a fitting sequel to my earlier volume titled *Mysticism in Literature* brought out by M/s Atlantic Publishers and Distributors, New Delhi in 1985, which examines in fine detail the interrelationship between poetry and mysticism with particular reference to the poetry of Coventry Patmore and Francis Thompson, British poets of the mid-Victorian era. I planned this volume in response to the advice I was given, two decades back, by the late Professor Sisir Kumar Ghose, eminent scholar of English, known internationally for his special expertise in the area of mysticism. He desired that I should as well apply the critical tools I had acquired to the poets of my own region with whom I was conversant as a Kashmiri. With this aim largely in view, I remained occupied, during the past decade, with the works of the poets selected for the present volume — poets with divergent religious and cultural backgrounds. In fact, in pursuit of this aim I made the best use of the two national fellowships that I was awarded on my retirement from thc University of Kashmir : (i) Two-year U.G.C. Emeritus Fellowship in English held at the University of Jammu (October 1990 to September 1992) and (ii) Two-year Senior Fellowship in Literature from the Department of Culture, Ministry of Human Resource Development, Government of India (October 1997 to September 1999).

Some of the relevant material incorporated in the present book is derived from the papers and essays contributed by me during the past decade to standard journals and critical anthologies published in the country : A. (i) *Prabuddha Bharata,* (ii) *Bulletin of the Institute of Culture*, Ramakrishna Mission, Calcutta, (iii) *Jodhpur Studies in English,* (iv) *Koshur Samachar;* B. (i) *Twentieth Century Literature in English*, Vol. I edited by Manmohan K. Bhatnagar, Atlantic Publishers and Distributors,

New Delhi, 1996 and (ii) *Essays in Comparative Literature* edited by Sureshchandra of M/s Anmol Publishers, New Delhi, 1998. I make due acknowledgments here to the publishers concerned.

In the Introduction to the present volume, I have briefly discussed mysticism and its vital connection with poetry : how the latter serves as the most appropriate medium for conveying man's experience of a direct *encounter* with the Divine. Thus, the mystic poet, if he is creative enough, suggests the "mystical" through the use of apt images and symbols. The present study is focused on (i) the Kashmiri poets : Lal Ded, Nunda Rishi, Shams Faqir, Zinda Koul, Swami Govind Kaul and Bhavani 'Bhagyavaan' Pandit and (ii) British poets : Coventry Patmore and T.S. Eliot (besides the Spanish poet, St John of the Cross). The study seeks to examine their selected verse in some depth in order to highlight the universal bearings of mysticism, expressed poetically across cultures and faiths. I have also incorporated the essay 'Krishna and the Way of Love' as a chapter in view of its direct relevance to the main theme of the book.

The present writer had two difficulties to cope with : (i) to attempt acceptable English translation of the bulk of Kashmiri verse used, also to adopt or modify the translations that were available and (ii) to transliterate the verse into the *Devnagri* script found convenient for use in view of its being very phonetic (in preference to any other script). I hope I have managed to overcome the difficulties to an appreciable extent. There was another difficulty I could not, however, cope with fully : many relevant secondary materials available for study on the Kashmiri poets of my choice in the troubled Valley of Kashmir were hardly accessible to me as a displaced Kashmiri.

I pay my homage here to the memory of Professor Sisir Kumar Ghose under whose initial motivation I planned the present work. My wife, Rupa, has been a source of inspiration and strength to me in compiling this volume. I have great pleasure in acknowledging the fact here.

I am grateful to my young friend, Shri Sohan Krishen Khordi, for the kind help he rendered in going carefully through the contents of the book and offering valuable suggestions. I am specially grateful to Shri R.K. Abrol and his staff for preparing the typeset with loving care.

Finally, I am extremely grateful to Prof. G.K. Das, well-known and eminent scholar of English, for writing the Foreword to this volume.

**A.N. DHAR**

# CONTENTS

# 1
# Introduction

## Mysticism and Language

LIVING ON this planet, man has never been content with what he observes in the phenomenal world. It has always aroused in him an urge to know and seize the unknown, that is far beyond his immediate grasp. His spirit does not let him sit still; he has been ever restless to probe the mystery and immensity of the universe. As the scientific temper demands, he analyses and classifies the observed facts systematically, on the basis of which he arrives at theories and doctrines. His quest, however, does not stop at the theoretical and the empirical. This is because he is not merely a creature of reason; gifted with a soul, he is a conscious being — as is evident from his natural inclination towards reflection and introspection and also from his unbounded capacity for love. In its higher form, love embodies man's innate urge for union with the Divine which mystics speak of as the Substratum or the Ground of Being. They also characterize the Divine as the Transcendent, that is "beyond" the reach of the human intellect.

Not alien or opposed to religion, mysticism, as distinguished from orthodox creeds and dogmas, claims validity for itself in the emphasis it lays on man's *direct* experience of the Divine, which may be understood as an immediate apprehension of the Transcendent, or of the Reality behind appearances. Accordingly, the great mystics of all ages and climes could be classed with the founders of various faiths who "owed their power and originality to the fact of their direct personal communion with the divine".[1] Although most mystics known to history either conformed to the faiths they were born into or did not openly dissociate themselves from religious creeds, some, like the English poet William Blake and the Persian mystic Mansur-al-Hallaj, professed heretical views and stood away from organized religion. In the words of W.R. Inge, the English theologian, "institutionalism and mysticism have been uneasy bed-fellows".[2] In his eagerness for direct and personal contact with the Divine, the true mystic chooses to be unfettered, free from subservience to narrow dogmas. Freedom is the essence of his sense of 'closeness' to the Beloved, also reflected in his constant awareness of his own innate divinity.

Essentially, mysticism stands at the "heart" of all genuine religious experience. This is borne out by the intensity and authenticity of the mystic's experience, that invariably works a noble transformation in his or her personality, what religious motivation can achieve only at its best. Although mysticism looks beyond the empirical, it does not run counter to reason. Accordingly, the poet Coventry Patmore, who was revered by G.M. Hopkins as an elder contemporary and co-religionist, characterizes mysticism "as the science of ultimates".[3] It is "as incommunicable to those who have not experienced it as is the odour of a violet to those who have never smelt it".[4] Francis Thompson, the author of the well-known mystical poem "The Hound of Heaven", who looked upon Patmore as his master, is very articulate on the true character and ultimate goal of mysticism :

> The core of mysticism is a fact, not an understanding or feeling. Still less is it an *endeavour* after a something nameless and unattainable. All true mystics know well about what they seek, and that it can be gained or missed according to the fidelity of their own effort. The thing sought is *Union*.[5]

The *Upanishads* and Sufi mysticism lay stress on purification and contemplation as indispensable to the 'illumination' of the soul and as the only reliable means to the realization of the universal Self. Likewise, Christian mysticism also lays emphasis on hard self-discipline and inward purity as the essential prerequisites for 'illumination', which is followed by the soul's abiding contact with the Divine.

In the nineteenth century, the term 'mysticism' was suspect in the West as it was much abused and often confounded with sheer emotionalism; it generally suggested what is 'vague' and 'misty', reflecting a 'foggy' condition of the mind. While this trend continued into the 20th century, mysticism has in the last few decades been experiencing a "renewed interest and understanding".[6] The possibilities that lie beyond the empirical are not rejected outright by science today. At the same time, the unprecedented technological advancement that the modern world has witnessed, which we mainly owe to the growth of science, has displaced man's faith and alienated him from the Divine. The conflicts which afflict the world today and the tensions that plague man's *psyche* have bred in him a sense of waste and rootlessness. Consequently, sensitive souls have started looking 'inwards'; hence the revival of interest in what mysticism stands for and promises.

However, mysticism has never been suspect in India, a land noted for its rich cultural diversity, where freedom of belief has prevailed from time immemorial. Different faiths have co-existed here for centuries; saints and mystics of all hues have been venerated here. What mysticism means in essence was long back set forth in clear terms in the *Upanishads*. The *Gita*, which is characteristically a theistic Hindu scripture, mentions throughout the three well-known ways of approach to Reality — *karma*, *bhakti* and *jnana*. These correspond to the spiritual way of life respectively termed practical, devotional and philosophical mysticism by Christian scholars; this parallelism points to the proximity and compatibility between Hindu and Christian mysticism. Sufism, which had flourished in Persia as the "mystical dimension of Islam"[7], easily found a fertile soil in our country. In fact, it found another home here, and interacted with Vedanta and the Bhakti movement alike. The mingling of various faiths and philosophical schools in India has thus given rise to a synthesis which represents our composite culture unmistakably. This synthesis is ultimately traceable to the universal basis of mysticism in the East and the West.

What mysticism involves, in terms of the soul's encounter with the Divine, is best known to the practical mystic, the yogi who is well-established in the spiritual path. By its very nature the experience of the Transcendent defies expression and cannot be conveyed in plain language. Articulate mystics have, however, hinted at the experience through paradoxes and the indirect language of symbolism — poetic language serves the communicative mystic here as an appropriate tool. As a conscious craftsman, he shapes and accommodates language to his purpose : illuminating difficult and sometimes rare mystical concepts. In fact, there are devices and mechanisms available within language itself which the mystic poet exploits skilfully to bring the inarticulate within our apprehension. Thereby language performs the paradoxical role of suggesting experiences which belong to a world beyond itself, "the world of silence".[8] In the sacred writings of the East and the West alike, we often notice culture-bound symbols and images representing vital mystical concepts. The 'Lotus' in the sacred Hindu and Buddhist literatures, the 'Mole on the cheek of the Beloved' and the 'Rose-garden' in the *Secret Garden* of the thirteenth-century Persian poet Shabistari, 'the cloud of unknowing', 'the Divine Dark' and the 'Kiss of Christ' in Christian writings are some well-known examples. Drawn from diverse cultures, such symbols looked at as a group present a coherent pattern showing that there is a universal dimension to all human experience including the mystical.

It is relevant to add here that the mystical mode of communication is not restricted to verse; the mystics often resort to the aphoristic mode in communicating esoteric knowledge and experience. In fact, ancient wisdom, based on 'real apprehension', as distinguished from philosophical speculation, has largely come down to us in the form of aphorisms. Patanjali's *sutras* and the *vaakhs* of the celebrated Kashmiri mystic poet, Lal Ded, serve as fine examples. Coventry Patmore's prose work titled *The Rod, the Root and the Flower* deserves special mention as a rich storehouse of aphorisms, conveying valuable spiritual truths and doctrines related to the Christian mystical theology. These aphorisms occur as disjointed fragments presenting insights in a flash, expressing "the highest truths" better than "fine writing".[9] Here are some examples from Patmore's work mentioned, especially noteworthy for the significance most mystics attach to silence :

(i) A song
Loud with the tune which cannot be expressed.

(ii) I am
As one that knows a tune but cannot sing.

(iii) May I know by love and speak by silence.

Mysticism of all shades emphasizes man's innate divinity and sees the union of the soul with the Divine as the goal of spiritual life. Human pursuit of the Divine is often analogized in mystical literature to a journey marked by stages — termed purgative, illuminative and unitive stages of the Mystic Way in Christian mysticism. For the Sufis "the journey winds through seven valleys". In the Hindu system of yoga, the concept of spiritual progress is conveyed in terms of the 'ascent of the self' from the lower to the higher planes of consciousness.

In almost all cultures, sacred poetry involves a characteristic language use, deriving from the two seemingly opposed ways of approach to the Divine : *via affirmativa* and *via negativa*. The two ways are, in fact, complementary and point to the same goal; affirmations may alternate and sometimes mingle with negations. Strikingly, the Transcendent is best suggested by 'silence', signalling a breakdown of language, which assumes special significance in mystic articulation. The utterances of advanced mystics are often characterized by this feature, marking the culmination of their attempt to reach out to the Beyond. Both the ways of approach — *via affirmativa* and *via negativa* — associated with the spiritual pursuit of the divine occur as significant motifs in mystical literature in the East and the West alike.

**Spirituality and the Scientific Temper**

On thoughtful reflection, one doesn't see any basic or sharp opposition between what spirituality essentially is and what science stands for. It is quite tenable to conceive of a fair degree of compatibility between the two — the scientific temper is not alien to spirituality nor is a scientist necessarily an atheist or a person with an unspiritual outlook. To an appreciable extent, science and spirituality can be seen to have a common aim — promotion of human values and welfare of mankind in general. Just as disinterested curiosity for the unknown marks the scientific temper, the quest for Truth is often a strong motivation for the spiritual seeker. However, it is evident to all that science is not enough. Its practical applications may serve human needs, make life comfortable and enable man to achieve longevity through control on diseases. But too much dependence — as we have seen — on machines and other scientific gadgets has made life mechanical, not to speak of the havoc wrought on earth through the abuse of science.

Spirituality essentially aims at man's inward transformation, leading to the realization of the Self. This process involves cleansing of "the doors of perception", enabling the aspirant to see the Divine as the indwelling spirit of all creatures, inhabiting "a blade of grass", the stars above and "all that we behold". The truly spiritual person provides the best example of a noble human being, moral to the highest degree and "divine" to the core. Such a person is the friend of all, a well-wisher and benefactor of the whole world. The true scientist, likewise, pursues knowledge both for its own sake and for the welfare of mankind. We cannot blame him outright for how his research findings and theories are exploited by those who wield political power.

The boundaries of science and spirituality overlap : the scientist's intuition, at times, goads him on and steers his empirical investigations in the right direction. So do the thrilling accounts of the universe, given in science fiction and in works like the scientist James Jeans' *The Mysterious Universe,* sometimes awaken in the inquisitive reader "a sense of wonder". Such accounts may inspire the potential spiritual seeker, whose perception is fine, and awaken the 'sleeping' Kundalini in him. Something similar happened when Sri Ramakrishna was struck by the beauty of a host of cranes flying high up in the sky. He was instantly thrown into a trance-like state. There is as much of compatibility between the fine arts (including poetry and music) and spirituality as there is between pure science and the religion of man (transcending creeds and dogmas). Swami Vivekananda rightly visualized the future possibility of science coming close to religion and *vice versa* : extremes, he said, will eventually meet.

**Some Positive Trends**

In the contemporary world scene, we notice some positive trends too in spite of the disturbing trend towards terror and violence now rampant in many parts of the world. Thus movements concerned with the spiritual well-being of mankind and moves aimed at the resolution of conflicts through dialogue and mutual understanding are also gradually gaining momentum.

In this context, we may turn our attention to the prospects of global understanding growing gradually between various faiths, through what is referred to as "inter-religious dialogue" that has been encouraged through the institution of comparative studies in religion in various universities and other centres of learning in the West and the East alike. Hopefully, through the interfaith "encounter" the universal essence of religion that spirituality truly consists in will crystallize for us and come to the fore, making it possible for intellectuals to see how men can live in peace and amity. We come across very sound views on the significance and implications of the interfaith dialogue beautifully set forth by M. Darol Bryant in the illuminating little volume he has authored, titled *Religion in a New Key* (Wilney Eastern Ltd., New Delhi, 1992). However, it is pertinent to mention here that it was, in fact, Swami Vivekananda's historic address delivered at the first Parliament of Religions held in

Chicago in September, 1893 that set the tone for inter-religious dialogue and understanding in a significant sense. It was he who emphasized the universal basis of all religions at this international meet.

Another healthy trend contemporaneous with the interfaith dialogue is the perceptible change taking place in the thinking and outlook of some outstanding men of science today across the globe — in regard to the validity of the spiritual truths that have come down to us from the *rishis* and sages of the Vedic times. Consequently, the possibility and prospects of an accommodation between science and spirituality do not seem very remote now. Modern physics seems coming closer to a philosophical view of the world, akin to the views our *siddhas* have upheld from the ages past. It is heartening to hear men of science now raising their voice against environmental pollution and the destruction of forests and wild life : what our *rishis* said centuries ago is being reinforced in effect through the pronouncements of the environmentalists.[10]

Studies devoted to individual saints and mystics, and to the body of mystical poetry across cultures and religions, can be depended upon to explore the universal dimensions and bearings of mysticism articulated through language in its literary form. That is precisely what the present author has attempted to achieve through the studies undertaken in the chapters that follow. Such studies must complement and reinforce what is being aimed at by the scholars and intellectuals engaged in "inter-religious" dialogue.

## NOTES AND REFERENCES

1. William James. *The Varieties of Religious Experience* (New York : The Modern Library, 1929), p. 31.
2. S.K. Ghose in 'Mysticism', *The New Encyclopaedia Britannica* (Chicago : Encyclopaedia Britannica Inc., 1977), p. 786.
3. *The Rod, The Root and the Flower*, ed. Derek Patmore (1950; rpt., Freeport, New York : Books for Libraries Press, 1968), p. 50.
4. Caroline Spurgeon. *Mysticism in English Literature* (1913; reissued London : Keni Kat Press, 1970), p. 20.

5. Quoted in Everard Meynel. *The Life of Francis Thompson* (1913; London : Burnes and Oates Ltd., 1916), p. 20.
6. S.K. Ghose. 'Mysticism' in *The New Encyclopaedia Britannica*, p. 786.
7. Saiyid, A.A. Rizvi. *A History of Sufism in India*, Vol. I (New Delhi : Munshiram Manoharlal Publishers Pvt. Ltd., 1978), p. 18.
8. Ernst Cassirer. *Language and Myth*, trans. Susan K. Langer (London : Constable and Co., 1946), p. 58.
9. E.J. Oliver. *Coventry Patmore* (London : Sheed & Ward Ltd., 1956), p. 168.
10. The views expressed under the caption 'Some positive trends' are contained in the present writer's 'keynote address' presented at a seminar. See A.N. Dhar & Neerja Mattoo, Editors, *Bhagavaan Gopinathji Birth Centenary Volume : Our Spiritual Heritage* (Bhagavaan Gopinathji Trust, Pamposh Enclave, New Delhi-110048 : 2000), pp. 1-2.

# 2

# Aspiration and Fulfilment in *Lalla Vaakh*

THIS CHAPTER is devoted mainly to Lal Ded, the well-known mystic poet of Kashmir, and her *vaakhs*, that have come down to us as a rich legacy; I shall restrict my discussion to her standing as a mystic on the basis of what we gather from the *vaakhs*. In them, we have authentic evidence of her two striking qualities as a highly advanced mystic — firstly, the extraordinary intensity of her aspiration for union with the Divine, and, secondly, her assured sense of fulfilment in having found the Beloved close at hand, both conveyed in unmistakable accents. Uttered by the saint-poet in the fourteenth century, the *vaakhs* haven't, surprisingly, lost any of their freshness and charm for the Kashmiris today; they have perpetuated Lalla's memory, as a living monument of her literary achievement and of the heights she had scaled as a mystic. They range from the mature aphorisms of a seer, an accomplished mystic, to the spontaneous outpourings of a seeker (in the realm of divine love) : she speaks in the tone of a wise sage in one *vaakh* here, counselling self-restraint and avoidance of extremes, and conveys her anguished sense of separation from the Beloved in another *vaakh* there; many *vaakhs* have the preacher's tone and a good number of them breathe the confidence of a highly developed yogini who has tasted the final beatitude and now holds "infinity in the palm of hand". In view of these qualities, Lal Ded's verse-sayings can aptly be characterized as the poetry of direct mystical experience.

Though a literary study of Lal Ded has to base itself mainly on the solid foundation of her *vaakhs*, any adequate account of this great saint-poet cannot leave out the biographical aspect altogether. In her case, however, we have no authentic biographical details available and have nothing other than the *vaakhs* to fall back upon to draw useful inferences from. Several Lal-Ded scholars, notably Professor Jayalal Kaul, have raised the question of the authenticity of the *vaakhs* — Professor Kaul would depend upon the stylistic criteria in establishing the genuineness or otherwise of a *Lalla vaakh* and, at the same time, he accepts as valid the fact of linguistic change some of the *vaakhs* could inevitably have undergone across time. Given the severe handicaps of Lal-Ded scholarship, including the non-availability of a wholly authentic compilation of Lalla's utterances, except perhaps the earliest compilation of 60 *vaakhs* brought out by Rajanaka Bhaskara along with his Sanskrit translations over two hundred years ago, it is difficult to pronounce on the genuineness of a number of *vaakhs* with certitude and equally difficult to arrive at any biographical detail through mere textual analysis of a *vaakh*. Grierson and Barnett have done a commendable job in bringing out *Lalla-Vaakyaani*, which remains to this day the most valuable and dependable collection of Lalla's *vaakhs*; together with the elaborate commentary provided by the editors, it still remains an indispensable material for the Lal-Ded scholar.

Before I come to the particular *vaakhs* that I propose to discuss in the present chapter, I should like to draw attention to some opinions about Lal Ded which I consider untenable — based as these are on one-sided approaches and sometimes on misreadings of the text. Some scholars, for example, want to project Lal Ded mainly as a Saivite, a follower of the *Trika* (Kashmir Saivism);[1] others paint her as deeply influenced by Islam, particularly Sufism, while still others would characterize her teachings as an "admixture of the non-dualistic philosophy of Saivism and Islamic sufism".[2] One cannot deny the fact that much of the mystical terminology we come across in the *vaakhs* is very obviously rooted in Kashmir Saivism; such terminology is clearly traceable to her upbringing in a Kashmiri Hindu family. Some scholars, attaching significance to the interaction between Hinduism and Islam in Lalla's time, have been at pains to assert that her *vaakhs* have a marked bias of both Saivism and Sufism, or more precisely, owe their richness and power to the fusion of Yoga and *Irfan* that the saint-poet realized in her spiritual life. In the view of a scholar, "Lalleshwari...took the best of Islamic thought, and fused it with the best in her own creed."[3]

None of these approaches seem wholly valid. To see Lal Ded as just the follower of a particular religion or of a particular school of thought would only dwarf her spiritual stature, which is indeed among the loftiest in the recorded history of the saints and mystics of all time. When we study the *vaakhs* as a body of utterances and ponder over them seriously, we feel convinced of her uniqueness and of her extraordinary stature. Whatever she might have owed to this or that influence is far outweighed by her individual genius. Her perceptions are entirely her own, her experiences very acute and her poetic sensibility one of the finest we have known. All these qualities are immediately discerned by the perceptive reader. Men of all faiths will always derive satisfaction from Lalla's *vaakhs*; all will agree that her teaching approves of all faiths, rather than conflicts with this or that creed. This is because she has got to the root of the matter and realized the universal in its essence. Behind all religions, there is one Religion which belongs to all humanity — of which the *rinda*, the unfettered mystic, is the most legitimate custodian. Lal Ded, undoubtedly, speaks to us, in the *vaakhs*, in the confident tone of such a mystic.

Several Lal-Ded studies advocate the view that Lalla roamed about *vivasan*, without apparel, in a state of ecstasy after she had left her in-laws' house for good in search of God. There are, on the other hand, some scholars who reject this view partly. They seem to feel uncomfortable about Lalla's nudity, considering it incompatible with the spiritual height she had attained. They would argue that as a woman who preached self-control and moderation in life, she could not have moved about in a nude or semi-nude state in violation of social decorum. In this context, a suggestion has been put forth that the word "nangai" in one of her famous *vaakhs* (which will be discussed later) is a misreading or a corrupted form of the word "nonguy", a flower found in Kashmir, which could "rise up and dance" when "pressed between the thumb and the forefinger".[4] One fails to understand why scholars should read too much of biography into Lalla's mystical utterances though the biographical aspect can assume relevance in certain contexts. In the present case, the scholars concerned have got worried over the nude state suggested in the phrase "nangai natsun". Obviously, this lyrical utterance conveys the state of spiritual ecstasy Lalla must have experienced when she followed the secret doctrine imparted to her by her preceptor.

If we accept the fact that Lalla was a highly advanced mystic who saw the Self all around her as the Reality behind phenomena, then to expect her to have scrupulously followed social conventions or the dictates of a religious order is to shut our eyes to the greatness she had achieved.[5] True mystics tend to escape "the fetters of organized religion".[6] Lalla's *vaakhs* bear ample testimony to her mystic vision and to her state of spiritual exaltation. In them, we find "live symbols of a deeply felt experience",[7] which explain Lalla's extraordinary power and appeal as a mystic poet. It is to the *vaakhs* that we must now turn our attention, to the poetry of aspiration and fulfilment that they embody.

Lalla's *vaakhs* are an assemblage of her utterances handed down from generation to generation by word of mouth, not recorded in any authentic manuscripts during her life or preserved in writing posthumously. The order in which they occur in this or that compilation today has no validity beyond what suited the considered choice of the editor(s). It is not to be disputed that, if we arrange the *vaakhs* in accordance with a preconceived scheme, we can demonstrate a pattern in Lalla's spiritual development — a thing rigorously done in Professor Parimoo's *Ascent of the Self*. In this work, the *vaakhs* have been arranged systematically to show Lalla's progress in the Mystic Way : the stages she passed through as a yogini till she attained union with the universal Self. One could, however, have reservations about such an approach, though its usefulness cannot, at the same time, be disputed (as Professor Parimoo's lucid and pains-taking study bears out). It is very difficult to judge the actual state of mind of a mystical poet, precisely the level of his or her spiritual attainment, on the basis of isolated sayings or poetic compositions; no definitive arguments and interpretations can be offered in support of the views one puts forth in this regard. Secondly, we should not forget that the moods of a mystic are likely to vary from time to time, assuming that he feels impelled to communicate his experiences as a normal human being. So long as poetic communication belongs to the realm of art, it seems reasonable to expect the mystic poet to sing of pain and separation, and of joy and fulfilment, in the same breath at times, and in quick succession, too, all depending upon the social context of such communication. The accomplished mystic may, for example, look back and write faithfully of his former moments of poignant divine separation in moving lines. In the absence of any knowledge of the time-sequence of poetic utterances or compositions, the task of tracing the mental or spiritual development of a poet through sheer literary analysis seems a very difficult one, and the conclusions arrived at thus cannot be altogether unquestionable.

In Lalla's case, we hear the note of aspiration and anguish in a relatively small number of the *vaakhs*; on the other hand, the note of confidence and fulfilment is, on the whole, pervasive in a good number of them. This, however, does not in any way render her poetry of aspiration less significant or valuable than her poetry of fulfilment. A quantitative approach is bound to be misleading while one interprets or evaluates mystical poetry of diverse types and shades.

In the textual analysis of the select *vaakhs* that I am undertaking presently, I do not aim at unfolding a developmental pattern in Lalla's spiritual life. I have picked up the *vaakhs* of my choice here and there, and shall discuss them sequentially bearing in mind the precise title of this chapter.

I begin my examination of the *vaakhs* with the one I alluded to earlier in connection with Lalla's use of the word "nangai natsun" the authenticity of which has been questioned by some scholars. The *vaakh* is reproduced below, followed immediately by its translation :[8]

ग्वरन वो'नुनम कुनुय वचुन,
न्यबॅरुॅ दो'पनम अंदर अचुन।
सुय गव ललि वाख तुॅ वचुन,
तवै ह्यो'तुम नंगय नचुन।।

The Guru gave me but one precept :
"From without turn inward".
It came to me (Lalla) as God's word;
I started roaming nude.

This *vaakh* is very significant in that Lalla unfolds here a remarkable experience she had as she progressed in her spiritual quest. She indirectly acknowledges her indebtedness to her preceptor here, identified as Siddha Srikanth (Sedamol स्यदुॅमोल) by her biographers, who is believed to have been an advanced *yogi* of the *Trika* school. I have emphasized earlier that Lal Ded was a spiritual genius, who can be classed with the greatest mystics of the world. Yet, before she came out into the open and roamed about as a *rinda*, not tied to any dogma or religious order, she sought initiation from a Master in accordance with the tradition followed by seekers throughout all cultures. Having all the makings of a yogini (before she got initiated), Lalla took the Guru's precept as God's word; it worked an instant transformation in her. She was thrown into a state of ecstasy, often a sign of the seeker's intimacy with the Divine. In that state, she continued to move about god-like, forgetful of her physical condition and of how others regarded her in that condition.[9]

The *vaakh* conveys in brief the steps of the *sadhana* prescribed by Lalla's Guru — withdrawing the mind from the external world and directing its attention inward, on the Self. The

Trika school, no doubt, preaches this doctrine; but we find it as no different from the essential teaching of the *Upanishads*. In fact, it is the gist of what mysticism of all shades recommends as the technique of meditation, as a prelude to "Illumination". We can see that Lalla's mysticism, as conveyed so pithily in the *vaakh*, accommodates the essentials of mysticism across cultures. It is relevant to add that Guru Srikanth recognized Lalla's excellence in Yoga in these words : "गवति चाठा ग्वरस थो'दुय" (The disciple excelled the Guru), believed to have been uttered by him when he complimented her on performing a rare spiritual miracle, something that was far beyond his own capabilities.

Lalla expresses her aspiration for the Divine through the metaphor of one's being ferried across the 'ocean of *samsara*'. Through its use in several of her *vaakhs*, which are often recited and sung to musical accompaniment in Kashmir, the metaphor has assumed the character of a loaded symbol — a highly suggestive image that continues to impress the popular imagination. The *vaakh* given below employs this image in a crucial context, conveying a spiritual longing of great intensity :

आमि पनुँ सऽदुँरस नावि छस लमान,
कति बोज़ि दय म्योन म्यति दियि तार।
आम्यन टाक्यन पोन्य ज़न शमान,
जुव छुम ब्रमान गरॅ गछुँहा।।
I am towing my boat on the sea
With a slender thread;
Would that God heard my prayer
And ferried me across!
Like water vanishing
In plates of unbaked clay,
All my striving is proving futile;
How I pine to get back home!

The *vaakh* expresses Lalla's sense of futility of human efforts in general; in particular, it conveys her desperate feeling that her striving for union with God is bearing no fruit. Out of total dependence on Him, she cries for divine help for the fulfilment of her aspiration. In a state of deep anguish, she longs for her safe return "home" — the soul's real abode. The image of being taken across the ocean in a boat occurs in another *vaakh* where Lalla brings in the related *motif* of paying the fare to the boatman : "अथ नावुॅ तारस दिमुॅ क्या बऽ ."[10] In yet another *vaakh*, which closes with the line "कीवल तसुदुंय तोरुक नाद"[11], the concept represented by the metaphor "crossing the ocean" is linked with that of "divine call" — suggesting that God's will is the supreme factor in the seeker's spiritual accomplishment. As we read Lalla's *vaakh* making use of the boat image, directly or through suggestion, our familiarity with the *Ramayana* at once brings to our minds the episode of Kevat and Lord Rama, in which Kevat prays to the Lord to grant him a safe passage across the 'ocean of *samsara*'. Tennyson's lyric entitled 'Crossing the Bar', which expresses a longing similar to Lalla's, could also come to the reader's mind : for a safe spiritual voyage back to the soul's permanent abode in heaven. The imagery involving the concept of crossing the 'ocean of *samsara*', suggesting release from the allurements and dangers that the sensory world holds for the seeker, is specially pervasive in Indian mystical literature. Lalla has very deftly woven it into the texture of her *vaakhs* in appropriate contexts, investing the image with fresh significance in each *vaakh*.

As the reader surmises, during what probably was a phase of intense longing for God in Lalla's life, she must have passed through the agony of separation like the great *bhaktas* of all time. In this context, one is reminded of Sri Ramakrishna Parmahamsa's experience over a century ago — an experience of extreme mortification, of the kind gone through by great seekers when they feel alienated from God and pine for union, which is characterized in Christian mysticism as the "dark night of the soul". We thus hear a note of intense pain in this *vaakh* of Lalla :

लोलुॅकि व्वखुॅलुॅ वाऽलिंज पिशिम,
क्वकल चऽजिम तुॅ रूजुॅस रसुॅ।

बुजॅुम तुँ ज़ाऽजिम पानस चुॅशिम,
कवुँ ज़ानुँ तवुँ सूॅत्य मरुँ किनुँ लसुँ।।
I ground my heart in the mortar of love,
Roasted and burnt it, then ate it up;
Evil desires left me, and I remained calm,
Yet hardly do I know
If, for all this, I shall die or live!

On the one hand, we notice here that Lalla gives us an account of the determination with which she pursued the Beloved, suffering silently (aptly conveyed by the English phrase 'eat one's heart out') as the *bhaktas* do when they feel alienated from God; the more they suffer, the more intense grows their longing for the Divine. On the other hand, Lalla is not sure here of attaining her goal; she is in a state of uncertainty which is in itself a torture. Such is often the state of the true mystic, who experiences divine despair in its extreme form. This "despair" actually heralds for him "spiritual dawn" — a mystical state of joy that inevitably follows the "dark night of the soul".

In this *vaakh*, Lalla uses appropriate metaphors drawn from the butcher's trade and the culinary art : mincing and pounding of meat before it is roasted and eaten up. Lalla lived at a time when non-vegetarianism must have been in vogue in Kashmir; she gives us an accurate description of the process involved in preparing a non-vegetarian dish. Like the Metaphysical poet Donne, she does not hesitate in using images drawn from areas of experience remote from the meaning she actually wants to communicate and illuminate. Here an important phase in her spiritual life is suggested through images bordering on the gruesome. Lalla paints her situation as unbearably painful, which indicates how advanced she was in her devotion to God, matching the questing spirit of a great explorer.

In line 2 of the foregoing *vaakh*, Lalla tells us that evil thoughts left her : "क्वकल च़ऽजिम..."; in the remaining lines she conveys the great pain she had gone through in her quest for God. The ideas and images are repeated (and receive reinforcement) in the *vaakh* that follows :

मल व्वंदि ज़ोलुम जिगर मोरुम,
त्यलि लल नाव द्राम ये'लि दऽल्य त्राऽविमस तऽतिय।।
I burned the dross of my mind,
Killed my heart;
My fame as Lalla spread afar
When, in total surrender,
I spread the borders of my clothes
At His feet.

Here Lalla refers to her inward control and purification achieved through self-mortification. As her devotion gained in intensity, she mastered the discipline of self-surrender, which brings calm of mind. In the process her doors of perception were cleansed and she was now fit for "Illumination". This is confirmed by lines 3-4 of another *vaakh* of hers, which are given below :

लोलुॅकि नारुॅ सॅूत्य वाऽलिंज बुजुॅम,
शंकर लो'बुम तमिय सॅूतिय।।
I ground my heart in the mortar of love,
That's how I found Shankara.

Lalla reiterates here that she 'roasted' her heart in the fire of love, whereby she found Shankara.

In the remaining part of the present chapter, I shall discuss a sizable number of Lalla's *vaakhs* in which we have clear evidence of her accomplishment as an advanced yogini. It is on the strength of her own realization that she instructs the listener — the potential pupil or aspirant — to undertake the arduous 'journey' to the abode of the Lord, describing the 'steps' through appropriate images and metaphors when the meaning would not otherwise be accessible, and at times through simple and straightforward words when she need not be oblique or 'difficult' in her manner. Invariably, her tone is confident when she communicates the doctrine to us as a spiritual teacher. As we read or listen to her *vaakhs*, her words come home to us as much as they stir our hearts. We feel convinced that Lalla has seen the Divine close at hand, found Him within her soul and realized His presence around her. She often speaks of the Deity as dwelling within the human frame itself and, at the same time, does not forget to tell us that Siva is all-pervasive. Her spiritual doctrine is consistently theistic; as maintained earlier, it is seen to be no different, essentially, from the doctrine of Advaita Vedanta or that of the Trika, and it also parallels the monotheism of Islam. The important point to note is that Lalla's *vaakhs* characterize the Divine as attainable purely through contemplation and self-discipline, and not reachable only by the elect. The reader can see that all that Lalla has to say about *sadhana* is based on her own experience, there being nothing derivative about the wisdom her utterances embody. Lalla is a Master in her own right. Her aspiration for the Divine, revealed in the *vaakhs* we examined earlier, is intense and unmistakable indeed; at the same time, her sense of fulfilment is equally positive and convincing. It comes out triumphantly in many of her *vaakhs* which constitute, together with the *vaakhs* of the type examined hitherto as illustrative of her aspiration for the Divine, what I spoke of earlier as the poetry of direct mystical experience.

When we take into account the implications of the self-discipline emphasized in a number of Lalla's *vaakhs*, we inevitably conclude that the goal of spirituality is but attainable through the *hard* way — a fact universally acknowledged by seers and saints. Yet this is to state only half the truth. There is another aspect of spirituality — the fact of Grace, what the Indian sages characterize as *anugraha*. Lalla, the devotee, does talk about it in connection with her spiritual quest. The *bhaktas* are known to experience divine favour at the 'appointed' time, when their devotion attains the right intensity. Having found the Divine at hand, thus basking in His glory, the Masters have spoken of Him as easily reachable too if the seeker is all sincere, firmly resolved and totally dedicated. For such a seeker, the spiritual path, often described as 'difficult', turns out to be smooth and straight. In several of Lalla's *vaakhs*, we find the tone very reassuring, holding out prospects of an immediate fulfilment to the aspiring devotee.

We shall first turn to the *vaakhs* which stress self-control as the essential element of *sadhana*; in the following *vaakh*, Lalla tells us of the state of purity she had attained, in which she was indifferent to praise and blame alike :

गाल गाऽडिन्यम बोल पऽडिन्यम,
दपिन्यम तिय यस युथ रोचे।
सहज़ क्वसमव पूज़ कऽरिन्यम,
अमलाऽन्य कस क्या म्वचे।।

Let them abuse me or call me names,
Let them say what they like,
Let them worship me with flowers;
Taintless as I am, this would do them no good.

The inference that we draw from this *vaakh* is that Lalla, during her wanderings as a God-intoxicated yogini, received kindness and adoration from some people, taunts and jeers from others, while there must have been still others who did not take any notice of her. In her state of spiritual exaltation, she must have paid little attention to how she was being treated by the people she came across, ignoring alike their words of praise and of blame. Here is another *vaakh*, uttered almost in the same vein as the preceding one; Lalla speaks herein of her resolve to put up with abuses and not allow anything to disturb her mental poise :

आसा बोल पऽडिन्यम सासा,
मे मनि वासा खीद ना ह्यये।
यो'दवय शंकर बखुँच़ आसा,
मुक़ुरिस स्वासा मल क्या प्येय।।

Let abuses be heaped upon me,
I shall not feel hurt in mind
If I am a true devotee of Sankar;
How can ashes soil a mirror?

True spirituality demands firmness of character — a capacity for suffering that serves to build up the seeker's spiritual stamina, thus enabling him to approach closer to his goal. In all cultures and climes, great mystics, like Lalla, are known to have attained mastery over themselves, which won them acclaim and people's veneration. Christ-like some of them not merely bore insults and taunts patiently from hostile public but also suffered extreme persecution, even death. History bears out that those who have been crusaders for truth have in all ages ignored the hard blows of fate and social persecution alike. From whatever little we know of Lalla's life and what we particularly can glean from her *vaakhs*, we come to the conclusion that she was made of a stern stuff and faced the rough side of life with patience and courage, leaving us in no doubt that she had all the spiritual strength of a great Master. Several *vaakhs* immediately suggest the rigorous spiritual exercises she must herself have gone through to attain perfection as a yogini. In the following *vaakh*, she values *pranayama* or breath control as an important means to the control of the mind :

> पवन पूरिथ युस नियं वगे,
> तस ब्वना स्पर्शिनुँ ब्वछि तुँ त्रेश।
> तिय यस करुन अंतिः तगे,
> संसारस सुय ज़्ययि नेछ।।
> He who controls the vital air after inhaling it
> Is not troubled by hunger or thirst;
> He who can sustain this practice upto the end
> Is born to make a name in this world.[12]

Consistent with the principles and practice of Raja yoga, followed traditionally in this country, Lalla looks upon breath-control and the control of the mind as complementary disciplines. The *vaakh* that follows builds upon the theme of the earlier one in a related context :

> च़्यथ त्वरग गगन ब्रमुँवोन,
> निमिश अकि छ़डि यूज़न लछ।
> चैतन्य वगि ब्वद्धि रऽटिथ ज़ोन,
> प्रान अपान संदाऽरिथ पखच।।
> The steed of the mind roams across the sky,
> Covering a thousand leagues in a moment;
> A man of intellect and discrimination can control
> the steed
> By curbing (the movement of) the wings of *prana*
> and *apana*.

Judging from the tenor of this *vaakh*, controlling the mind is to be viewed as a vital requirement in the spiritual path; Lalla considers breath-control an integral element of the practice of mind-control. Her use of the figure of the chariot drawn by a horse, whose reins are held firmly by the charioteer, conveys succinctly all that is recommended in Patantjali's system of yoga. The figure also throws back to the teachings of the *Gita* and the *Upanishads*. Its use in the present *vaakh* suggests further that Lalla must have been brought up in a family with a literary background. The phrase "च़्यथ त्वर्ग" (steed of the mind) that occurs in this *vaakh* is one of the many similar ones we meet with in Lalla's sayings, mostly based on the concepts and terms derived originally from Sanskrit texts.

I now come to the *vaakh* which I consider to be of utmost importance to the Lal-Ded scholar who would be eager to draw vital clues to her spiritual biography and have a precise idea of her spiritual prowess — the tremendous agonizing experience she had to pass through, inwardly as also through her encounters with the external world, to perfect herself. The phases of her spiritual transformation, presented in terms of a well-knit sequence of analogies, are very clearly spelt out here :

लल बऽ द्रायस कपसि पोशि सऽच़य,
काऽडय तॅु दून्य कऽरनम यऽप़य लथ
तॅुय यऽलि खाऽरनम ज़ाऽवजि तॅुये,
वोवरि वानॅु गऽयम अलाऽजुँय लथ।
दो'ब्य यऽलि छाऽवनास बो' कनि प्यठॅुय,
सज़ तॅु साबन मऽछ़नम यऽच्युँय।
सॅुच़्य यऽलि फिरनम हनि हनि काऽच्युँय,
अदॅु ललि मे' प्राऽवुँम परमय गथ।।

Hoping to bloom like a cotton flower,
I, Lalla, set forth in this world,
But the cleaner and the carder
Kicked me hard (thus humiliating me).
Spun into fine yarn on a spinning wheel,
I was pitifully hung upon a weaver's loom.
(Turned into cloth) The washerman dashed me

Upon the washing stone
And rubbed me much with the fuller's earth and soap.
When the tailor cut me through
With a pair of scissors,
Then I, Lalla, attained the supreme state (of bliss).

This is a fine account of the hard 'journey' to the spiritual goal that a mystic of Lalla's stature is expected to undertake, whatever his or her cultural moorings. It is also a fine piece of composition, showing Lalla's command of Kashmiri as an accomplished literary artist. Here is a sequence of metaphors — an extended image drawn from different but related trades — which capture what is essentially an introvert process of Becoming, suggesting the aspirant's spiritual evolution to the state of perfection. The *vaakh* does not tell us what *exactly* happened to Lalla in psychological or spiritual terms; it gives us at best a *feeling* of the severe discipline she must have undergone to realize the Self.

Lalla attaches supreme significance to the human birth and views the body as the temple of God — a belief common to Vedanta and Kashmir Saivism, also shared by several other faiths. For any spiritual attainment, a sound physical body is a vital requirement. The human body is considered important from another point of view, too; it is seen to be a microcosm, carrying within it a miniature cosmos. Mysticism of all varieties recognizes the importance of the body; the Divine is believed to inhabit it as much as inhere in the universe without. The whole thrust of Lalla's teaching is to make the aspirant see the importance of the body in terms of its involvement in spiritual *sadhana* :

स्वमनॅु गारुन मंज़ यथ कंदे,
यथ कंदि दपान स्वरूप नाव।
लूब मूह च़लि शूब यिय कंदे,
यऽथ्य कंदि तीज़ तय सोर प्रकाश।।

Should you seek the Divine
In this very body, which is the abode
Of the Supreme self,

Greed and delusion soon dispelled,
Your body will acquire grace
And a halo of illumination.

The Hindus refer to the entry into the *Brahmcharya Ashram* as one's becoming a *dwija* (twice-born). The idea is that through spiritual initiation, one is transformed, and raised to a higher state of consciousness. The mystics influenced by Hermetics conceive of this transformation in terms of alchemical symbolism, drawing upon the belief that the 'philosopher's stone' converts baser metals into gold. In the present *vaakh*, Lalla says, in effect, that if the aspirant searches for the Divine sincerely within his own body, instead of seeking Him outside himself, he will realize the Self soon and then view the body as the temple of God. In the language of the mystics, through such an experience, the seeker attains deification. Elsewhere, stressing and valuing sustained spiritual practice in preference to the mere reading of the scriptures, Lalla maintains :

अब्यासुँकि गनिरै शास्त्र मो'ठुम,
च़ीतन आनदं न्यश्चय गोम।।
I forgot the *sastras* as I advanced in practice,
Then I attained conviction of God as Consciousness-Bliss.

Obviously, Lalla is referring here to the discipline of the body and of the mind, both comprehended in yogic practice. And the experienced conviction of the Divine that dawned on her is a realization that is attainable by the Yogi or the mystic in the body itself, which turns out for him to be the abode of the supreme Lord; Lalla identifies the Lord here as an embodiment of consciousness and bliss ("च़ीतन आनंद"). This conviction is also affirmed in other *vaakhs* in such lines as "शिवछुय अऽत्य तय कुन मो गछ़" (Siva is very much here *i.e.*, within the body; don't stray thence) and "वुछुम पंडित पनुँनि गरे" (I saw the Pandit in my own house). These experiences are brought to a sharp focus in the *vaakh* below, which tells us of Lalla's practice of breath-control, as part of her *sadhana*, that enabled her to recognize her true Self :

दमादम को'रमस दमन हाले,
प्रज़ल्योम दीफ तुँ ननेयम ज़ाथ।
अंदर्युम प्रकाश न्यबर छो'टुम,
गटि रो'टुम तुँ कऽरमस थप।।

I regularly controlled my breath in the bellows-pipe
(of my throat),
Then the flame of the Lamp shone (within me),
Revealing to me my true nature;
I seized Him in the darkness (of my soul),
Shedding inner Light out.

Lalla continues to tell us here of the rigorous physical and spiritual practice she went through with a view to attaining divine Illumination leading to Union. From several *vaakhs* discussed earlier, we could gather that the body has a crucial role in *sadhana*. In the present *vaakh*, we are given a direct account of the experience of the Divine — through the metaphor of the flame of the Lamp. Training in breath-control and simultaneous disciplining of the mind brought quick results for Lalla — Illumination, an immediate experience of being lit up with Divinity, within and without. She realized God as the indwelling Deity and as pervading "the world of sense". She could not contain herself and she burst out, disseminating her divine knowledge through her *vaakhs* — what the line "अऽन्द्रयुम प्रकाश न्यबर छो'टुम" could also be interpreted to convey.

Thus we see that Lalla realized God as the Self within and also as the universal spirit. It is her universal consciousness which underlies her deep conviction about the essential oneness of mankind. She repeats in many a *vaakh* that Siva is all-pervasive; in the *vaakh* that follows she stresses that we should not discriminate between man and man on the basis of the difference of religion (and the like) :

शिव छुय थलि थलि रोज़ान,
मोज़ान ह्योंद तुँ मुसलमान।
त्रुक अय छुक तुँ पान परज़ुँनाव,
स्वयं छय साहिबस ज़ाऽनी ज़ान।।

Siva is everywhere, abiding in all things;
Do not then discriminate between a Hindu
and a Musalman;
If you are wise, know yourself;
That itself is getting to know God.

The *vaakh* makes it clear that Lalla sees no distinction between Self-realization and God-realization. This is particularly emphasized in Kashmir Saivism, affirmed by *Advaita Vedanta* and also upheld by many Sufi mystics. Lalla's conviction, based on her realization of Siva both as her inmost Self and as the universal Self, rings forcefully in this *vaakh* too :

दीशि आयस दशि दीशुॅं तीलिथ,
चड़लिथ चो़'टुम शुन्य अदुॅं वाव।
शिवुॅय ड.यूठुम शायि शायि मीलिथ,
श्य तुॅं त्रेह त्रो'पिमस तुॅं शिवुॅय द्राव।।

I came from my Country,
Roamed the ten directions,
And wind-like I pierced the Void;
I closed the nine apertures (of the body)
And found Siva, within and every-where around.

Tracing her descent from the Country of the Soul, Lalla recounts here the realization that she had attained of the infinite vastness of the universe, and she speaks of her miraculous ability to 'ascend' to the ethereal sphere, which is far beyond the reach of ordinary mortals. Her control of the mind and the senses (implied in the phrase "श्य तुॅं त्रेह त्रो'पिमस") enabled her to realize Siva within herself; the experience endowed her with "spiritual senses". Thus transformed, she could see the world itself, including all living and non-living things, radiant with divine beauty. She realized the oneness of Man and God, of Mind and Nature; this is asserted and conveyed in a confident tone in another *vaakh* too :

तूॅरि सलि खो'ट तय तूॅरे,
ह्यमि त्रय गय ब्यन–अब्यन व्यमर्श।
चैतन्य रव बाति सब समे,
शिवमय च़राच़र ज़ग पशा।।

Intense cold transforms water into snow and ice;
As we reflect, we find water differentiated into
three forms;
When the sun of consciousness shines bright,
All different forms dissolve into One Substance;
We see the world of the living and the lifeless
As Siva Himself.

Lalla brings home to us the essential oneness of the world of multiplicity, a spiritual truth emphasized in the *Trika* (Kashmir Saivism) as much as it is in the *Upanishads*, and in the Sufi doctrine of *wahadatulwajud*. A significant feature of the above *vaakh* is that herein Lalla makes use of an analogy drawn from the field of physical science (the facts of freezing of water and melting of snow or ice) to illuminate a spiritual concept — the unity underlying all that exists, comprehended in the great Being she calls Siva.

As maintained earlier, Lalla attaches utmost importance to inward purification accompanied by self-control and introspection; accordingly, she attaches little significance to external worship. What she values highly is a balanced attitude in life and a harmonious development of the various human faculties; she stresses an integrated growth of all aspects of the individual personality. In this respect, she has the vision and calibre of a great educationist too. Thus, while insisting on physical and mental culture, she gives due place to such values as individual and social welfare, keeping in view the good of mankind in general. However, she considers meditation on the Self of supreme value. Hard practices such as fasting, remaining thirsty and subjecting the body to physical suffering in different ways are rejected by her as acts of little spiritual value. Conversely, she also rejects exaggerated attention paid to the care and maintenance of the body. In the following *vaakh*, she disapproves of the religious practices involving physical pain, while she characterizes the service of mankind as true religion :

त्रेशि ब्वछि मो क्रेशिनावुन,
यान्य छ़्ययि तान्य संदारुन दीह।

फ्रट चोन धारुन तुँ पारुन,
कर व्पकारुन स्वय छै क्रय।।
Do not afflict your body with hunger and thirst,
Take due care of it when it gets famished;
Fie on your observance of religious rites,
Do good to others; that is true worship.

We have seen earlier how much Lalla values the human body in terms of its vital role in *sadhana*. It is in the same context that she disapproves of the physical suffering that some seekers inflict on themselves in the fond hope that this will open their "doors of perception". Lalla believes that the human faculties are shaped into the instruments of spiritual knowledge only in a sound body. So she considers austerities such as fasting of little value, rather harmful to the body as a means of spiritual attainment. Nor do superficial religious rites, performed mechanically, have any use for the aspirant in her view. Having realized the Divine in man, she looks upon selfless service of mankind in general as genuine worship. Here is another *vaakh* related, in terms of content, to the foregoing *vaakh* in a significant sense :

मूडो क्रय छय नुँ धारुन तुँ पारुन,
मूडो क्रय छय नुँ रछिन्य काय।
मूडो क्रय छय नुँ दीह संदारुन,
सहज़ व्यचारुन छुय व्पदीश।।
O fool, right action does not consist in religious rites,
Or in adorning yourself; nor in providing for
bodily comforts,
Or in taking extraordinary care of the body;
Meditating on the Self (in earnest) is the doctrine for
you to follow.

One might infer from this *vaakh* that Lalla is contradicting what she maintained in the previous one. Therein she said "यान्य छ़यिय तान्य संदारुन दीह", cautioning the listener not to overtax the body but feed and maintain it properly. On the other hand, in the present *vaakh* she says "मूडो क्रय छय नुँ रछिन्य काय/मूडो क्रय छय न दीह संदारुन" conveying actually that we should not care exclusively and extraordinarily for the preservation and maintenance of the body to the neglect of spiritual culture. What is desirable in her view is that we should give due attention to meditation on the Self and not ignore it, nor should we pay an exaggerated attention to mere physical culture. Lalla is highlighting here how mindful man should be of his ultimate spiritual goal in life, which, in her view, is reachable only through single-minded devotion to the Lord. She directs the aspirant to consider this goal as the highest attainment in life. Divine contemplation, as we gather from her *vaakhs* throughout, should be the end-all and be-all of our lives. Looking at the two *vaakhs* under discussion together, we do not see any contradiction between them. In one, bodily culture is emphasised as a positive value; in the other, attainment of God, and contemplation as the chief means towards this end, are insisted upon. What Lalla evidently wants us to bear in mind is that while a sound body is an important means to taking us Godward, it does not exhaust the means. She, in effect, cautions us not to confuse the end and the means, and exhorts us to aim at the harmonious development of the body and the mind.

In several other *vaakhs* too, Lalla dwells on the theme of external worship, which we have seen she does not consider of any value in the absence of self-control accompanied by meditation on the inner Self. The burden of these *vaakhs* is her distrust of external renunciation and of hard physical penances; she instructs the aspirant to seek and recognize God within :

> असे प्वन्दे ज़्वसे ज़ामे,
> व्यथॅुय तीर्थन स्नान करे।
> वॅुहॅुर्य वऽर्यस नो'नुय आसे,
> निशि छुय तय परज़ानतन।।
>
> Laughing, sneezing, coughing, yawning,
> Taking dips in sacred waters,
> And remaining nude throughout the year
> Are of little use;
> He is close at hand, recognize Him.

The *vaakh* seems addressed to the ascetic visiting sacred places and bathing in holy waters, going about naked (as a form of penance) in the belief that all this would lead him to God. Lalla wants to disenchant the seekers who look upon external rites and penances as helpful in *sadhana*, by driving home to them the truth that God is no other than the indwelling Spirit, ever within man's reach. In matters of spirituality, penances involving physical suffering deliberately inflicted, according to Lalla, are not to be relied upon. On the contrary it is the sincerity of aspiration and the intensity of devotion, aided by contemplation and self-introspection, which really enable the seeker to recognize the Master within and without.

In the following *vaakh*, Lalla reiterates what she has said elsewhere — that we had better stay where we are and as we are. She sees no *intrinsic* significance in *sannyasa* (renouncing the world) and *grahasta* (household life) as modes of living, but lays all the emphasis on the internal state of the mind :

> कन्द्यौ गेह त्यज़ि कन्द्यौ वन्वास,
> व्यफो'ल मन रऽटिथ तॅुं वास।
> द्यन राथ गऽज़ंरिथ पनुन श्वास,
> युथुय छुक तॅुं त्युथुय आस।।
> Some renounced their homes, some the hermitages,
> All in vain, as long as the mind is not anchored in
> the Self!
> Watching (the movement of) your breath day and night,
> Stay where you are (at home or in the forest).

Lalla dwells here on the true mark of a Rajayogi, whose *sadhana* consists mainly in achieving control over the mind and consequently over the breath, or *vice versa* (the two disciplines being complementary). With this requirement fulfilled, one need not attach any value or significance to the aspirant's external state — whether he lives at home as a householder or lives in the forest as a *sannyasin* or contemplative. Talking of the wandering *sannyasin* elsewhere, Lalla observes that such an aspirant, visiting holy places in search of the Self, is actually misled in taking the distant "green" for turf. As mentioned earlier, what Lalla prizes are the intense aspiration and one-pointedness of the spiritual seeker; the outer garb of the seeker is a sheer label that hardly reveals anything of his inner condition. In another *vaakh*, Lalla exhorts the aspirant to aim at tranquillizing his mind to be able to realize God as "सर्वुंगथ प्रभु अमो'ल" (omnipresent and stainless); she considers the facts of staying at home (amidst society) and living a life of solitude in the hermitage as sheer accidents, which actually have no bearing on one's spiritual life. "The soul stays at home" says Emerson. Lalla conveys and illuminates this essential truth in her *vaakhs*.

In *vaakh* after *vaakh*, Lalla reveals her innermost esoteric experiences, giving us accounts of her direct encounters with the Lord, which confirm and are in turn validated by the concepts and doctrines recorded in the religious scriptures across different cultures. A reader familiar with mystical poetry of different hues and shades realizes soon that there is often a meeting ground between any two varieties of mysticism, despite differences of detail and despite cultural variables. Judged in the light of what constitutes the core of mysticism across cultures, Lalla's teachings and her accounts of the spiritual path surely point to the fact that she has attained perfection as a mystic. One simply marvels at her grasp of spiritual truths and the idiom in which she puts them across to us. We feel convinced that she has attained the highest point on the "ladder of contemplation", bringing her into the full view of the Lord as also very close to Him, what could be taken as Union in the language of mysticism. Thus, in several *vaakhs*, we find Lalla referring to the supreme spiritual state, which she designates as "हंसॅु गथ" (The way of the Swan). She speaks in these *vaakhs* in the confident tone of an accomplished yogini; there is a specific mention of "हंसॅु गथ" in the following *vaakh* :

> शिव शिव करान हंसॅु गथ सो'रिथ,
> रूज़िथ व्यवहाऽर्य द्यन क्योह राथ।
> लागि रो'स अद्वय युस मन कऽरिथ,
> तऽस्य न्यथ प्रसन्न स्वरग्वरॅुनाथ।।
> Consistently repeating the name of Siva,
> Performing worldly duties day and night,

One who frees one's mind from attachment and duality,
Wins for ever the favour of the Lord of Lords.

Lalla, the perfect spiritual teacher, speaks here from direct experience; her teaching does not involve any complexity but hard facts relating to *sadhana* : constant repetition of the divine Name, continuous mental repetition of '*soham sabda*' (सोहं शब्द), going hand in hand with inhaling and exhaling of vital air, which the *parmahamsas* and advanced sufi mystics are believed to practise to perfection. Lalla probably owed her knowledge of *hamsagath* directly to her spiritual preceptor, Seda Mol, or she had got to know of it, even before her formal initiation, from her elders in the family she was born into. However, Lalla's *vaakhs* devoted to the spiritual state in question reveal that she has *tasted* the thing and not merely heard of it, and she wants her fellow-beings, irrespective of what faiths they profess, to live through her experience.

That Lalla had attained God realization is frankly affirmed by her in this *vaakh* involving simple and direct statements :

शुन्युक माऽदान को'डुम पानस,
मे ललि रूज़ुॅम नुॅ ब्वद तय होश।
व्यज़ुॅय सपनिस पानय पानस,
अदुॅ कमि हिलि फो'ल ललि पम्मपोश।।

I, Lalla, accomplished my 'journey' to the field of the void,
Far beyond sense and intellect,
Then Self-knowledge dawned on me,
And I experienced sudden transformation :
The lotus bloomed for me (in mud) amidst water weeds.

What we gather from this *vaakh* is Lalla's confident assertion of her attainment as a practical yogini, her excellence in *sadhana* of the highest order. In all cultures, the goal of mysticism is looked upon as Union — direct contact with the Divine. We can rightly imagine that Lalla had set this as her goal and she pursued it single-mindedly, facing trials and tribulations, hardships of an extreme kind, until she reached it surely. The mystics are believed to pass through a very critical transitional stage before they attain perfection — referred to as the "dark night of the soul" in Christian mysticism as mentioned earlier; the aspirant "dies into life", almost literally, and metaphorically too, in this critical phase. This experience is hinted at — rather conveyed through words as best as it possibly could be — in the first two lines of the above *vaakh*. Lalla's experience of the Void suggests that mastering the little self demands a severe spiritual discipline, summoning up of tremendous daring and power of self-possession — a mortifying experience that is only followed by the annihilation of the ego or selfhood. Lalla evidently had stood the ground; she flowered spiritually and attained the supreme state of Sivahood, having cultivated "the way of the Swan" as a yogini, a Saivite or an *arifa*, by whatever title we may choose to describe her extraordinary achievement as a God-seeker.

There is a cluster of Lalla's *vaakhs*, five of them in number, translated sequentially in Jayalal Kaul's *Lal Ded*, which are linked together by the refrain "शिव छुय क्रूठ तय चे़न व्यपदीश" (Siva is hard to attain, grasp the teaching), coming at the end of each *vaakh*. These *vaakhs*, as a distinct group, serve a useful purpose in that they motivate the listener to engage in self-introspection and ponder Lalla's perceptive observations on man and the world. In turn, the 'qualified' listener shares and profits form her mystic vision of Siva.

Each *vaakh* serves as a kind of puzzle with a question in-built, which poses a challenge to the addressee's intelligence, prompting him to find the answer through self-introspection and grasp the teaching that is meant to be perceived and internalized. The gist of the *vaakhs* is that man persists in his folly in continuing to lead a purposeless life, thus falling into an endless cycle of births and rebirths. In his state of delusion, he fails to perceive the one Reality underlying phenomena; he does not realize Siva, the Substratum of this universe, nor does he perceive Sakti (who is none other than Siva in the dynamic aspect) in her diverse divine manifestations, the same feminine principle in three roles — Mother, Wife and Maya. Let us look at one particular *vaakh* from the group, which is reproduced below as an illustrative example :

> रव मतॅु थलि थलि ताऽपितन,
> ताऽपितन व्वतम दीश।
> वरुन मतॅु लूकॅु गरॅु आऽचितन,
> शिव छुय क्रूठ तय चेन व्वपदीश।।
>
> Is it conceivable that the sun will not shine alike at all places,
> Shine only on holy places?
> Is it, likewise, possible that Varuna, the God of water,
> Will not visit all homes alike?
> Siva is hard to attain, heed the doctrine.

The *vaakh* consists of indirect statements, put in the form of questions, which point to the all-pervasiveness of Siva, what Lalla has realized as a yogini. She now wants to drive this truth home to us through the indirect questioning mode of communication that she has adopted here, using analogies drawn from nature (bringing in the sun and *Varuna*), which are easy to grasp and appreciate. Lalla's manner is very appropriate to her purpose; one cannot think of a better way of putting across to the reader/listener what she wants to say. She is as unsurpassable in her style of communication as in her spiritual attainment.

Before concluding this brief study, I consider it befitting to mention a few names from the women poets and saints who provide classic examples of feminine virtue combined with spiritual genius, being as such comparable to Lal Ded. The two names that come immediately to my mind, one from the East and the other from the West, are Mira Bai and St Teresa. Mira's devotion to Lord Krishna, which flows uninterruptedly through her incomparable songs or *bhajans*, shows beyond doubt that she was wedded to the Lord in the true spirit. Sung to music, the *bhajans* are a valuable spiritual legacy the saint-poet has handed down to us. Mira often speaks of the pain of separation and also communicates to us her foretaste of the joy of divine union that she longs for. The keen listener does not, however, fail to perceive in the songs, in spite of the longing for union conveyed,

Mira's awareness of her abiding relationship with the Lord. Though they never have the teacher's tone nor are loaded with any learning or philosophical concepts, one is convinced that Mira has gone far beyond disciplines, being totally absorbed in God. She sees the world as a divine 'sport' and delights in the bond of true love that she has forged with Him; she does not recognize any other relationship than that she bears with Krishna : "मेरे तो गिरिधर गोपाल दूसरो न कोई". She calls him "गहिर गंभीरा" (profound and wise) which easily suggests that she is a *jnani* in her own right. Logical disputation and philosophical analysis have no relevance for her; leaving them far behind her, she *knows* the Lord as much as she loves Him.

St Teresa's also is a classic example of supreme devotion to the Beloved : her love of Lord Jesus Christ, which she cherished intensely throughout her cloistered life as a nun of the Spanish Church in the sixteenth century. Like Mira, she also thought of herself as the Bride of the Lord. The accounts of her spiritual experiences, of her 'encounters' with the Lord, which are conveyed in a voluptuous language involving erotic images, both touch our hearts and illuminate our minds, as do Mira's pure devotional songs. St Teresa and St John of the Cross are known to have enriched Christian mystical literature in a significant way. Mira's *bhajans* constitute a valuable part of the *Bhakti* literature in India today; they will continue to inspire and inflame the hearts of God-lovers in our country. Lal Ded, too, has passed on a rich legacy to us in the shape of the *vaakhs*, an invaluable addition, in the Kashmiri language, to the 'riches' her great predecessors, Utpala Deva and Abhinavagupta, Saivite masters, have handed down to us through their scholarly works on Self-knowledge.

## NOTES AND REFERENCES

1. Jayalal Kaul, endorsing the views of Grierson and Barnett, and of Sir Richard Temple, maintains that "Lal Ded was Saiva Yogini of Kashmir school". See his *Lal Ded*, Sahitya Akademi, New Delhi, 1973, p. 53.
2. P.N.K. Bamzai. "Lalleshwari-Forerunner of Medieval Reformers", *Koshur Samachar*, Lal Ded Number (1971), p. 16.

3. Daya Kishan Kachru. "The Light of the Valley", *Ibid.*, p. 7.
4. Quoted in B.N. Parimoo, *The Ascent of Self,* Motilal Banarsidass, Delhi, 1978; second rev. edn., 1987, p. 63.
5. I am indebted to Shri Udaynath Tiku, who was a devoted scholar of Kashmir Saivism, for his valuable comments and suggestions, which I have borne in mind in the present discussion regarding Lalla's "nudity" and her spiritual greatness.
6. S.K. Ghose. "Mysticism" in *The New Encyclopaedia Britannica* (Chicago : Encyclopaedia Britannica Inc., 1977), p. 786.
7. Quoted in Jayalal Kaul. *Lal Ded*, p. 40.
8. The text of the selected *vaakhs* of Lalla, discussed in this chapter, is generally as approved and used by the late Professor Jayalal Kaul, reproduced later in Devnagri transliteration in Nilakanth Kotru's *Lal Ded,* Utpal Publications, Srinagar/Delhi, 1989. Only here and there the text available in other studies on Lal Ded has been used. As far as the rendering of the *vaakhs* into English is concerned, I do not claim any originality in this regard. I have freely consulted the available English studies on the poet and adopted the translations I found accurate and appropriate, altering the translation (without sacrificing the sense) whenever I felt it necessary. I acknowledge my indebtedness to the authors and editors in general.
9. I am grateful to Sh. Jankinath Kaul 'Kamal', my teacher, who was a sound and seasoned Sanskrit scholar, well-versed in the Trika, for quoting to me the following slokas from *Srimad Bhagvata* in support of his view regarding Lalla's physical state, confirming mine in the essentials. Soon after the Sanskrit text, Swami Tapasyananda's English translation of the two slokas follows :

देहं चन श्वरमवस्थितमुत्थितं वा सिद्धो न पश्यति यतोऽध्यगमत् स्वरूपम।
दैवादपेतमुत दैववशादुपेतं वासो यथा परिकृतं मदिरामदान्धः ।। ३६।।

दोहोऽपिदैववशगः खलु कर्म यावत् स्वारम्भकं प्रतिसमीक्षत एव स्वासुः।
तं सप्र पञ्चमधिरूढ समाधि योगः स्वाप्रं पुनर्न भजते प्रतिबुद्धवस्तुः।। ३७।।

—एकादशस्कन्धे त्रयोदशध्याये।

Sloka 36 : Such a man of realization is not even aware of the body with the help of which he has attained that state — whatever happens to it by the power of prarabdha, whether it comes or goes, sits or works — just as a heavily drunken man knows not whether his wearing cloth is on or has fallen off.

Sloka 37 : So long as the Prarabdha-karma that led to the present embodiment lasts, the body will remain alive. But the knowing one who has attained the state of Samadhi will view the body and the world connected with it only as an awakened man views the body and experiences of his dream.

From *Srimad Bhagvata*, trans. Swami Tapasyanand (Madras : Sri Ramakrishna Muth, Madras, 1982) Vol. IV, Skandhas X-XII, p. 70.

10. For the full text of the *vaakh* see Kotru's *Lal Ded*, p. 3.
11. See the text of the full *vaakh* in Kotru's *Lal Ded*, p. 15.
12. Alternatively, the line "संसारस सुय ज़्ययि नेछ" could be translated as "will not be reborn in this world" *i.e.* will attain *mokhsha*.

# 3

# Sri Krishna and the Way of Love

IN THIS short chapter, I propose to dwell on the significance of Sri Krishna's pervasive image in our Bhakti Literature. Towards the end, I shall focus on Mira's love of Krishna as it finds expression in one of her devotional lyrics — in order to illustrate further what distinguishes the Way of Love as an approach to the Divine.

The devout, who are conversant with the Hindu scriptures, consider Sri Krishna to be an incarnation of God Vishnu, who assumed the human form as Vasudeva's son to destroy evil and establish *dharma* on earth, what he likewise did in his previous incarnation as Sri Rama. Sri Krishna is also looked upon as a World Teacher (jagadguru), whose teachings are systematically presented in the *Bhagavad Gita*, in the form of a dialogue that has attained wide recognition in the world as a great classic. Introduced as an episode in the *Mahabharata*, the *Gita* is at once a scripture of universal relevance and a piece of literature in its own right. Western scholars see it as a characteristically theistic Hindu scripture, valuing it for its richness of thought and systematic exposition of spiritual truths. Considered the most important product of the Hindu religious spirit, the *Gita* offers to the reader a fine synthesis of the "strands of pantheism, monotheism, theism and deism".[1] It is because of its great popularity that the book has been translated into numerous foreign and Indian languages.

In the *Mahabharata*, Sri Krishna is depicted as the most engaging character, who overshadows all other characters and emerges as the central hero through his wisdom and valour; his qualities as a friend of the weak and oppressed; his playful behaviour as Yasoda's darling child; and as the great favourite of the *gopis* and cowherd boys. It is no less through his human qualities than through his astounding feats that his divinity becomes manifest to those who adore him as God. His divine humanity consists in his unbounded love for all, his concern for those in distress and the valour he exhibits in performing superhuman tasks, including the destruction of tyrants like Kamsa. All through, we perceive Krishna as a supremely remarkable person, and an ideal human being invested with divine qualities — the Divine having 'descended' in a human frame.

Sri Krishna's multifaceted image, corresponding to the diverse roles he played (as depicted in the *Mahabharata*), has got deeply embedded in the collective psyche of the Hindus. That explains why it is pervasive in our Bhakti literature. It is on this account again that the devotional lyrics or *bhajans* of the popular Bhakti poets, Surdas and Mira, continue to inspire and delight men of faith. It is, however, the *Bhagavatam*, rather than the *Mahabharata* strictly, that has been the chief inspiration behind the verse that has been produced in Sanskrit, Hindi and other regional languages on the Krishna theme. Most Indian dances, including the *bharatanatyam* and the *raga*-based *bols* of our classical music are devoted to this theme.

For the learned Hindus particularly, Jayadeva's *Gita Govinda*, too, has acquired a special significance. It dwells on the theme of spiritual marriage between Radha and Krishna; the narrative employs images that seem erotic but have symbolic overtones meant to convey a spiritual meaning. There are, besides, innumerable poems composed in our regional languages which too sing praises in Krishna's glory. Many of them celebrate the love that Radha and the *gopis* cherished for Krishna : a charming lad who became their darling and played pranks on them, who thrilled and stole their hearts with the sweet notes from his flute.

History bears out that the Valley of Kashmir never, in any

significant way, came under the *direct* influence of the Bhakti movement nor has the Vaishnavite philosophy influenced the Kashmiri Hindus in any remarkable way. In spite of this, several Bhakti poets hailing from the Valley — among whom Parmanand stands pre-eminent — have composed *leelas* and *bhajans* in Kashmiri, devoted to the praise of Krishna.

As I have maintained earlier, most Hindus adore Krishna as God-incarnate, as the Master of Yoga (*Yogeswara*) and as an ideal Person, viewing him as the embodiment of the highest human virtues. Though some Hindu thinkers may see him as the best specimen of humanity rather than God, none of them, ordinarily, entertains any doubt about his historical identity. However, we have also to reckon with a different view of his personality, propagated mostly by the Western scholars and a few others from the Hindu elite, who consider Krishna a legendary figure. There are also those who characterize the whole story of the *Mahabharata* as a piece of fiction. Some see in it several strands of symbolism as we meet with in literary epics elsewhere, that can be variously interpreted. Thus Mahatma Gandhi, who highly valued the *Gita* as a scripture, sees the *Mahabharata* essentially as an allegory signifying the righteous war that goes on within ourselves between higher and lower impulses.

Even if we set aside the belief that Krishna was God-incarnate and do not pay attention to the miracles he is said to have performed, we have to concede that he is adorable as an outstanding human being : as a *jagadguru* who spoke words of wisdom to Arjuna as his charioteer on the battlefield, who was extraordinarily charming, with a winsome personality and a sportive nature; who showed through his *leela* (लीला) the utmost relevance of love in our social dealings and in matters spiritual. He not only illumined the threefold path of action, knowledge and love through his teachings in the *Gita* but institutionalized this path through his own practice. For most Hindus, he is the supreme God of Love.

Some detractors of Krishna, as he is depicted in our literature, take exception to his *prema-leela.* They fail to perceive that he was *purusottama*, a superman who educated and elevated, spiritually, his playmates : the cowherd boys of Vraja, and the *gopis*, who were drawn to him by deep love. There was nothing worldly about this love : at once human and divine, it was pure devotion of the highest intensity. Conveyed as it is through the vocabulary of sensuous love in the *Bhagavatam* and other literary works including the *Gita Govinda* and the *Sursagar*, it could be mistaken for earthly love by ordinary people. The true import of the story of Krishna and the *gopis* is to be understood in terms of the symbolism underlying the *leela* mentioned in the *Bhagavatam* and other scriptures. Herein Krishna is depicted as the God of Love, supremely beautiful; Radha and the *gopis* are shown as helplessly drawn to him as they hear the notes of his flute. For the Vaishnava devotees, who best understand the nature of the relationship between Krishna and his female adherents, there is nothing profane about it. To them the meaning of the inbuilt symbolism of the Krishna-romance is not lost. They look upon humanity 'as the Bride of God' and on Krishna 'as the only supreme male in the Universe'.[2] This ties up with the Christian concept of the human soul as the bride of Christ — a concept matched (and also contrasted) by the Sufi view of the soul as the Active Lover (*aashiq*) and the Divinity as the great Sweetheart.

It is now appropriate to come to Mira and her love of Krishna. Here we are on familiar ground, though there may be some variation in the accounts given of how she met her end (including the belief that she physically disappeared and got absorbed into the image of Krishna). One may not accept the view that she actually consumed the poison mixed with the drink sent to her by her brother-in-law. No one can, however, dispute the fact that all her life she was wedded to Krishna, whose image remained deeply impressed on her mind from her early childhood. In fact she never virtually lost hold of the physical image of Krishna until she breathed her last, practising Bhakti to the letter as prescribed in the *Bhagavatam*.

It is Mira's *bhajans* or devotional lyrics, which convey her intense love for Krishna, that have immortalized her story as his 'bride' and lent credibility to Radha's love for the historic Krishna. Mira's songs are inimitable as sober and sincere expressions of deep love that is thoroughly spiritual in character. The songs are a class by themselves and will remain our prized possession. The vocabulary of human love used in them is simple and familiar, drawn from human situations, that we come across in our day-to-day life, mostly connected with the affairs of the heart. And yet they strongly appeal to us, especially to those who are themselves devout and have got a good ear for music. Most songs pierce the heart and convince us of Mira's supreme devotion to Krishna. They unmistakably convey to us that she *knows* her lord, for sure, to be the indwelling Master and the only object of her worship — not the mere image she is fondly attached to.

To illustrate what I have said, let us turn to the song, '*Mai main to liyo hai sanvariya mole*' (translation mine) :

> Mother dear, I have bought my love
> For the price he deserved;
> Some cry 'too heavy' some 'too light',
> But I weighed to the last grain, paying in full;
> Taunting me, some say I paid more, some less,
> Surely, however, I purchased the Priceless one;
> Some call him 'thin-built', some 'stout of frame',
> I know I got what I bargained for :
> Proclaiming it by beat of drum;
> Some, jeering, call him 'dark' and some 'fair',
> I made no mistake in seeing (my eyes opened to the full)
> What he's worth;
> True to my past life's resolve,
> I'm wedded to Giridhara Nagara.

Mira knows that her detractors are not aware of the greatness of Krishna and of the intensity of her devotion to him. The metaphors used to convey the divinity of Krishna and the depth of her love for him are carefully chosen by the poet in Mira as appropriate communicative tools. 'Purchasing' the Beloved suggests what sacrifice higher love demands and 'weighing' a thing accurately in the balance tells us in clear terms that Mira knows precisely that she has staked her all for the 'Priceless' Divine. Referring to the detractors' 'jibes' painting Krishna as 'dark' or 'fair' she wants to convey that her perception of the Divine is clear, which means that she has recognized the Master she seeks. The words 'cheap' (*sogo*) and 'costly' (*mahango*) suggestively paint the pursuit of Love as something comparable to a business transaction — in which a customer should have all his wits about him : this conveys that Mira knows what the stakes involved in the 'transaction' of love are, that no 'price' is too big for union with God, the Precious one. Well set on the spiritual path, she is aware of her goal, knows fully well what true *sadhana* involves and seeks nothing short of union with the Lord.

In conclusion, I wish to emphasize that Sri Krishna's *prema-leela*, as described in the *Bhagavatam*, and in various versions of it in the works of Jayadeva, Surdas and other Indian poets, points to the fact that the Way of Love, as an approach to the Divine, is in tune with man's psychological make-up inasmuch as he is a loving creature, who hungers for his spiritual fulfilment in love — the noblest of all human emotions. This Way (of Love) at once complements the Way of Knowledge and has a decided superiority over it. Mira's love-lyrics devoted to Krishna — a class by themselves — testify to this fact.

## NOTES AND REFERENCES

1. Lin Yutang (ed.). *Wisdom of India* (Bombay : Jaico Publishing House, 1956), p. 49.
2. Sunil Kumar Chatterjee. *Jayadeva* (Calcutta : Sahitya Akademi, 1981), p. 52.

# 4

# St John of the Cross and Swami Govind Kaul : the Way of Love

THE WAY of Love, involving an intense devotion to the Divine, termed the *Bhakti Marga* in Hindu mysticism, is dominant as a theme in mysticism across cultures. *Agape* and *Eros*, sacred and profane love, often blend in mystical poetry; thus we notice this fusion in a high degree in Donne's religious poems. In our country, the theme of human love transfiguring into divine love has found its adequate treatment in the literature devoted to Krishna and the Gopis; our bhakti poets have written their finest poems on this theme. In Christian mysticism, the key concept of "spiritual marriage" is closely linked with the Way of Love; traceable to the Song of Songs, it is basic to Christian mystical theology, which considers the union of the soul with Christ (as the Bridegroom) the goal of spiritual life. The two well-known Spanish mystics of the sixteenth century, St John of the Cross and St Teresa, have given rapturous accounts of divine love in a voluptuous vein, using erotic and Christian vocabularies in the same breath. Persian Sufis have likewise made a liberal use of erotic images in their treatment of the sacred. What follows are my observations on two mystics with divergent cultural and religious backgrounds : the Spanish divine, St John of the Cross and the Kashmiri saint, Swami Govind Kaul.

St John of the Cross is an articulate mystic of a high order who writes direct from his *inner* experience; this lends both power and authenticity to his poems written in Spanish — qualities discernible to the reader even in translated versions, as the English rendering of his famous poem 'Obscure Night of the

Soul', reproduced for discussion in this chapter, will reveal. He declared his poems to be divinely inspired, a claim strengthened by the tone and compulsive quality of his verse. The poem exemplifies a fine blending of intense devotion and contemplation, an interplay of passion and intelligence that the English Metaphysical poets of the seventeenth century are credited with having accomplished in their poetry. It, however, stands to St John of the Cross's advantage that though he makes a conspicuous use of the language of paradox, his poetry is free from the artifices that meet the eye in the lyrics of the seventeenth century English Divines. The Spanish saint makes no conscious attempt at sounding 'witty'. He achieves a complexity that is rooted in his inner experience itself, and yet his poetry is not riddled with difficulties; directness and simplicity mark his style, and, at the same time, he is profound. Apart from being a gifted poet, Saint John of the Cross had the mind and erudition of a theologian, as his expositions of Christian mysticism in his prose work so remarkably reveal.

The text of St John of the Cross's poem 'Obscure Night of the Soul' as available in English translation by Arthur Symons is given below; it best reveals the poet's mystical perception and his deft use of the imagery of darkness as appropriate to the theme :

Upon an obscure night
Fevered with love in love's anxiety
(O hapless — happy plight!)
I went, none seeing me,
Forth from my house where all things be.
By night, secure from sight
And by the secret stair, disguisedly,
(O hapless — happy plight!)
By night, and privily,
Forth from my house where all things quiet be.
Blest night of wandering,
In secret, where by none might I be spied,
Nor I see anything;
Without a light or guide,

Save that which in my heart burnt in my side.
That light did lead me on,
More surely than the shining of moontide,
Where I well knew that one
Did for my coming bide;
Where He abode, might none but He abide.
O night that didst lead thus,
O night more lovely than the dawn of light,
O night that broughtest us,
Lover to lover's sight,
Lover with loved in marriage of delight!
Upon my flowery breast
Wholly for Him, and save Himself for none,
There did I give sweet rest
To my beloved one;
The fanning of the cedars breathed thereon.
When the first moving air
Blew from the tower and waved his locks aside,
His hand, with gentle care,
Did wound me in the side,
And in my body all my senses died.
All things I then forgot
My cheek on Him who for my coming came;
All ceased, and I was not,
Leaving my cares and shame
Among the lilies, and forgetting them.
(tr. Arthur Symons)

The poem makes use of the symbolism of marriage derived from the Song of Songs. It was St Thomas Aquinas who first interpreted the Song in terms of the marriage of the Church with Christ as the Bridegroom. Going a step further, St Bernard extended the analogy to the spousal relation between the soul and God. St John of the Cross's Poem 'The Obscure Night of the Soul' restricts the scope of the analogy to the union of the soul with God. The symbolism involves love-adventure as a motif, what Plotinus, in a related context, characterizes as a "flight of the alone to the Alone" : the soul's journey in quest of God. In the poem under discussion, the pursuit or quest is confined to the inner world of the aspirant, who is identifiable with the poet himself if we take the lyric to be a record of his own spiritual life. It is to be noted that in the poem, it is the Bride who is engaged in the quest; the Bridegroom graciously responds to the soul's call and the two unite in wedlock.

Interwoven with the Way of Love as the leading motif of the poem is the theme of dark contemplation. St John of the Cross builds here on the negative Christian concept of the 'Divine Dark' or 'The Cloud of Unknowing' associated with the *via negativa* traceable to neo-Platonism. The 'night' imagery acquires a complex of meaning in the Spanish saint. The title 'Obscure Night of the Soul' calls up a host of associations connected with 'contemplation', or *sadhana* as the Indian reader familiar with *Yoga* understands.

The 'night' stands for an important stage of the Mystic Way, suggesting the spiritual state of denial and deprivation, the pain and agony through which the soul must pass for its purification before it attains "illumination", which is followed by its union with the Divine. Darkness, in the context of the poem, also suggests faith; faith does not "see" with the "light" of reason, which relies on the senses alone as real. Faith relies on the Light within, the supernal Light which is "clear to perception but dark to understanding" (to use Coventry Patmore's words). In Christian mysticism, dark contemplation signifies intense meditation on the Transcendent, undertaken by the aspirant within the depths of his soul. Every step on the spiritual path, as suggested in the present poem, has to be taken with utmost care and concentration; all the powers of the mind have to be collected and focused on the goal, never to be lost sight of. Divested of all desires, the soul has to cultivate a state of self-surrender, overcome all pulls of the world of sensory experience, and seek joyful union with the Beloved. The one-pointedness of the mind, which alone can ensure the soul's total absorption in the Divine — what Christian mysticism characterizes as the soul's "nuptial union" with God — is suggested by the line "In secret, where by none might I be spied/Nor I see anything". The word 'night' acquires an extension in its meaning in combination with the sequence of related expressions like "none seeing me", "secure from sight", "disguisedly", "privily", "In secret", all suggestive of the renunciation and single-minded devotion of the spiritual seeker. Patanjali's aphorism *yogash cittavrttinrodah* (yoga means control of the modifications of the mindstuff) aptly sums up the details of the technique of meditation which the poem offers to the perceptive reader. Mounting up the "ladder of contemplation", a theme set forth elaborately in St John of the Cross's prose work titled *The Ascent of Mt. Carmel*, is hinted at here through the image of "secret stair", which signifies the steps through which the spiritual aspirant reaches his goal. The "ascent of the Self" is, in fact, a well-known mystical concept with a universal bearing; it is of crucial significance in the Hindu system of yoga, especially Kundalini Yoga.

The idiom of the poem under discussion is consistently simple and the images it employs, although loaded with suggestion, are familiar even to the lay reader. The poem reads like a moving lyric devoted to human love — the theme of painful separation and joyful union of lovers. The images of "flowery breast", "cheek", "encounter sweet" arouse erotic associations suggesting a voluptuous embrace between lovers; given the Christian context of the poem, they hint at the "mystic rapture" experienced within the soul through contact with the Divine. The "wound" inflicted with "gentle care" in the devoted lover's "side" suggests the extreme pain known to *Bhaktas*; it reminds us of the *viraha* (separation) they have to pass through for their purification, which prepares them for receiving divine grace. Total withdrawal from the sensory world must, of necessity, follow this state. The concluding stanza conveys aptly that an encounter with the Lord renders the soul utterly forgetful of the world, free from all cares and anxieties; this is the psychological condition of the accomplished yogi, a sign of the perfection he has attained in his *sadhana*.

Before I come to the other poet, Govind Kaul, a word on Kashmiri mystical poetry would be in place here. It has a richness and variety of its own, matching the remarkable fusion of cultures in the Valley. The literary tradition of mysticism in Kashmiri began in the fourteenth century with the famous woman poet and mystic, Lal Ded. Though grounded in Saivism, mysticism in Lala's *vaakhs* has striking affinities with Sufism, which spread to Kashmir through Muslim saints and mystics in her time. It is worth noting that she does not recommend external renunciation (as discussed in some detail in the foregoing chapter) nor does she consider the world of sensory experience illusory. What is perceived as the objective universe is in her parlance the *swarupa* (the Real Form); correspondingly, the physical world is looked upon as the House of God in Christian mysticism, echoing what the Sufi mystics characterize as *wahadatulwajud*. Lal Ded's influence on the mystical thought in Kashmiri literature has been strong and pervasive.

A lesser known figure among the Kashmiri poets of the 20th century, but better known as a saint, Swami Govind Kaul has not been much written upon. His devotional lyrics or *bhajans*, numbering 186, appeared in the Devnagri script in a single volume entitled *Govind Amrit* in 1975, brought out by his disciple, Somnath, with the avowed aim of spreading the Master's spiritual message. The poems are a fine addition to the growing Kashmiri literature embodying mystical devotion and thought. The discerning reader will have little difficulty in perceiving Govind Kaul's grasp of the spiritual truths that are basic to all faiths; his command of self-knowledge achieved through *sadhana* is thorough as his poems reveal. He addresses the Lord in the language and accent of the Indian Bhakti poets, at the same time echoing and drawing upon the vocabulary and concepts of Vedanta, Kashmir Saivism and Sufism. Taken together, his poems (or *leelas* as the Kashmiris would refer to them) provide valuable hints on what the Hindus understand as *yoga* and the Muslims as *irfaan*. The vocabulary of *Surat Sabda Yoga* is very noticeable in many of his poems.

From Govind Kaul's collected verse, I have chosen two poems for discussion in this chapter. I am taking up first the poem titled *mot yaavun kotye gom* ('Whither is Fled Darling

Youth'), which is reproduced below in Devnagri transliteration, followed immediately by its English translation (that I have attempted) :

मो'त यावुन को'तये गोम, ब्रोंठ ज़ोनमस नय कदर।
बे'यि यियिना दो'ह तारय, लो'कचारस वन्यतवे।।
तन दिमहा मन दिमहा, धन दिमहा सोरुय।
मेलिना मो'ल्य लोलॅु सोदा बाज़ारस वन्यतवे।।
टास ये'स्य आव तऽस्य अऽकिस आव, नतॅु सदा बूज़ सारिवॅुय।
टासॅु सॅूती क्या छु सपदान, शिकारस वन्यतवे।।
चानि दर्शनॅु सॅूती बलय, सुय मे छुम दाऽदिस दवा।
कदरि सेहत क्या छु आसान, बेमारस वन्यतवे।।
गोवेनद छुय इन्तिज़ारस, बालह यारस वन्यतवे।
प्रारान छुस इन्तिज़ारस दीदारस वन्यतवे।।

Whither is fled Darling Youth
I did not prize before?
Pray, urge him visit me
For a few days once more!
In exchange for Love,
I would barter away all —
My body, mind and wealth;
Pray, tell salesmen in the market!
The hunter hits the bird,
The remaining flock hear only the stroke;
The pain from the fatal thrust,
Pray, ask the prey to tell!
O, your *darshan* (seeing you) alone
Will cure me of illness;
What value to set on health,
Pray, ask the sick man tell!
Govind has been waiting long,
Please tell the beloved Friend!
Patiently have I been waiting,
Pray, press him grant a sight!

It is a short lyric, relatively free from the sacred terminology that often marks Govind Kaul's poems, lending them their distinctive tone. Distinguishably, it employs the vocabulary of earthly love to build up its theme of divine love, which the reader recognizes towards the end. The word 'darshan' in line 7 (of the original poem in Kashmiri), implying sight or vision, has a specific connotation in the context of the poem : theophany or divine manifestation. The intrusion of the poet's name 'Govind' in the penultimate line of the poem, a habit with him that parallels the practice of the Bhakti poets (the Indian reader is familiar with), establishes the sacred tone of the poem under discussion. In turn, the tone enables us to catch the mystical overtones as well.

The speaker's voice in the poem (excluding the last two lines) is typically feminine, expressing the pain separation brings lovers, and the soul's craving for fulfilment in love. This is a feature common to the poems of human and divine love in Kashmiri. The addressee in such poems is the Beloved, the addressor's male counterpart. Alternatively, or additionally, the persona addresses a female friend, or a plurality of such friends, urging the latter to convey her plaint or message to the Beloved. Govind Kaul's poem quite exemplifies this — the speaker addresses the plaint to a group of female friends, and later, towards the conclusion, directly addresses the Lord Himself (the masculine name of the poet in the penultimate line inevitably turns the speaker's voice into that of a male). Right at the beginning of the poem, God is nostalgically linked with 'yaavun' (youth), suggesting eternal bloom and loveliness. The diction of the poem is consistently simple and straightforward; words like 'soda' (transaction), 'shikaar' (prey), 'bemaar' (sick) and 'deedaar', (sight or meeting) relate to several areas of human experience. The analogies given serve to highlight the seeker's state of deprivation and his or her longing for reunion with the dear one. The poem gains in emotional intensity through the simple diction used in preference to the conventional. The soul's craving for communion with the Divine is effectively conveyed through familiar analogies drawn from earthly love.

The other Kashmiri poem by Govind Kaul, bearing the title *na tati moojood na tati fanaa* (There is neither existence nor non-existence) is reproduced below in part in the Devnagri script; immediately after follows my English rendering of the crucial part that I have chosen for discussion :

न तति मूजूद न तति फनाह, अमासना पथ क्या रूद।
न दो'गुना न कुन ज़ो'ना, शिन्या ततिनस गव नाबूद।।
यपार्य च़ोपार्य सुय पानह छुना, अमासना पथ क्या रूद।
बो'दि अबाव न रूद मना रिन्दॅु अथ जाये गयि रबूद।।
ज़्यव वुठ न फोरान वन्य क्या वना अमासना पथ क्या रूद।
कुनिरस चाऽनिस वुछुम न छ्यना यि मन्दछुना पथ केंह न रूद।।
साक्षी असाक्षी विलक्षना, अमासना पथ क्या रूद।
न केंह आसुना न आसुना, बासुन अबासुन न तति रूद।।
बॅु क्या वना रूद्य चॅु नॅु बॅुना, अमासना पथ क्या रूद।
पानस त तस ज़ोनुम न केंह ब्यना, पान ज़ाऽनिथ रिन्दॅु
ज़िन्दय मूद।।
गुणा तीतस कति प्वन्य तॅु गो'नाह, अमासना पथ क्या रूद।

. . .

कुनिरुक गोवे'न्दस गव सना कांऽसि सॅूत्य रूदुसनॅु म्यत्रुत विरूद।
पानॅु सान शिव ज़ोनुन पनॅु पना, अमासना पथ क्या रूद।।

There's neither existence nor non-existence,
What doth then remain in fine?
Dual nor single doth abide there,
Even the Void dissolves;
Here and everywhere,
Isn't he Himself there?
What doth then remain in fine?
Both intellect and mind
Cease to be there,
The *rindas* (unfettered mystics) are struck dumb;
Tongue-tied and lips sealed,
Powerless of speech,
What doth then remain in fine?
In your Oneness
No discontinuity I saw,
No trace was left
Of my sense of shame;
The witness, no witness,
A marvel!
What doth then remain in fine?
Neither Being nor non-Being,
Perceiving nor non-perceiving,
Nor the distinction

Of you and I;
What doth then remain in fine?
No divide I saw
Between Him and Me;
Realizing the Self,
The *rinda* died into Life;
The One beyond attributes
Knows no sin or virtue,
What doth then remain in fine?

. . .

Dumb-founded for the One,
Govind knew no friend or foe,
He saw Shiva all in himself,
What doth then remain in fine?

In this poem, we hear the voice of a mature mystic, a *sadhak* speaking on the authority of his spiritual attainment — realization of the Self. Throughout, the poet uses negative vocabulary and refers to the ultimate in terms of paradoxes and riddle-like expressions, which may confound the lay reader. The poem is 'difficult' as Eliot would characterize such a piece; precisely for this very reason the 'qualified' reader must find it enjoyable. It is not unusual to find paradoxes and negative epithets in mystical poems involving the *via negativa* theme. Eliot introduces them purposefully in the *Four Quartets*. In the present poem, Govind Kaul is aiming to convey his perception of the transcendental nature of the ultimate Reality. At the same time, he does not ignore the immanent aspect, and stresses the essential oneness of Man and God. The profusion of negative terms in the poem recalls the *neti neti* of the *Upanishads* and also echoes the language of Sufi mysticism. Concepts like 'fanaa' (annihilation) derived from Sufism, and 'shinya' (*sunya* or void) assimilated from the nihilism of the Buddhists, drawn upon by the poet, indicate his acquaintance with various mystical traditions. The word 'rind' occurs in the poem twice; we owe it to Persian mysticism. As mentioned in the previous chapter, it refers to the true lover, a liberated soul, who is not tied to dogmas — qualities which speak of the mystic's accomplishment and excellence in divine love. With its rich associations, the word has been absorbed into the Kashmiri language. Govind Kaul has purposefully introduced it into his poem as appropriate to its lofty theme. On the whole, the poem demonstrates how the mystic poet deviates from normal language use and employs negations to give us a hint of the spiritual realm that lies beyond language.

The above study has shown that the behaviour of the human psyche towards the Unseen, approached as Love, falls into the same pattern whatever the devotee's cultural and religious background. Man's encounter with the Divine may present a variety of detail as we move across cultures, but the various accounts given are one in essence.

# 5

# Coventry Patmore's Psyche Odes

AS MAINTAINED earlier, there is a close connection between the activities of the poet, contemplating the mystery and meaning of life, and the articulate mystic, who invariably depends on the poetic medium to give to the world authentic intimations of the Divine. This is supported by the many examples of mystic poets we come across in the East and the West, in almost all cultures. One such mystic poet was "that unduly neglected poet Coventry Patmore"[1] who represented the growth of a "new religious poetry, Catholic and mystical in motive...owing a spiritual allegiance to the religious poetry of the seventeenth century".[2] The mysticism his poems express is Christian in inspiration : it is markedly erotic in character, making a consistent use of the nuptial analogy in relation to the Divine. In this chapter, I shall discuss, at some length, what religious mysticism of the erotic type involves and then examine Patmore's treatment of the nuptial theme in the Psyche Odes as illustrative of this type.

Mystics of all times have generally emphasized the imageless character of Reality. Among the Christian mystics of the Middle Ages, Dionysius the Areopagite (who wrote between 475 and 525 A.D.) deserves special mention in this regard. As a mystical thinker, he faithfully followed Plotinus and introduced the seemingly contradictory concept of the "divine dark" into Christian mystical theology. The concept was somewhat perplexing to the Christians since it put unusual emphasis on the attributeless character of Reality.

Religious mysticism expressed poetically displays universal characteristics, beyond the terms and accents it may owe to a particular creed or dogma. It has been seen that devout mystics, whatever their cultural background, have generally depended on the language of human love when faced with the difficulty of communication. The types of love-relationship that human beings know of and mostly value are those between man and woman, between parent and child, between master and servant, between friend and friend. Mystics of the communicative type have been found using one (or more) of these relationships in their attempts to convey their experience of divine love, the precise nature of which cannot be adequately described but only hinted at. Actually, "poetry concerned with mysticism does not present us with mystical experience as it is but is constantly rebodying it and bringing it back into the realms of nature."[3]

An important feature of mystical literature in general is that it celebrates divine love in terms of images drawn from earthly love. The concept of "spiritual marriage" (mentioned in the foregoing chapter) is, significantly, central to Christian mystical theology. St John of the Cross and St Teresa represent Christian mysticism in its most authentic and characteristic from.[4] Consistent with this tradition, the nuptial analogy is a persistent motif in English mystical verse, making use of the erotic images one meets with in secular verse. Mysticism of the erotic type is rather conspicuous in Lady Julian of Norwich, Richard Crashaw and Coventry Patmore.

It may be pointed out here that the marriage analogy was actually intended to convey just a hint of the "mystic rapture" that is inexpressible in ordinary language. The intention does not seem to have been to glorify the love between man and woman as much as to suggest the supreme significance of divine love. As a singer of wedded love, Coventry Patmore follows both St Thomas Aquinas and St Bernard in celebrating the love between husband and wife as the precursor of divine love; this is specially true of Patmore's odes included under *The Unknown Eros*. However, the influence of St John of the Cross and St Teresa is more directly seen in these poems. Both the Spanish mystics have expressed their love for Christ (visualized as the

'Bridegroom') in a heightened language using highly erotic imagery. Patmore's mysticism, especially in the Psyche Odes, is expressed in similar terms. St John of the Corss's poem 'Obscure Night of the Soul', discussed in the previous chapter, illustrates best his use of the spousal analogy.

Caroline Spurgeon says of Patmore that "he was so entirely a mystic that it seems the first and the last and the only thing to say about him".[5] She categorizes him as a Love-mystic concerned with the unity that underlies the relationship between God and the soul. His first poetic success, *The Angel in the House*, published in 1854, brought him immediately into the limelight as a singer of wedded love, a theme dear to the Victorians. The Victorians, however, praised the poem for its superficial qualities; they failed to discern and appreciate the transcendental element subsumed under the domestic story. Patmore stressed, to begin with, the realism of words and also aimed at preciseness of description. In his later poems, *The Unknown Eros* odes, he developed the theme of wedded love into an elaborate symbolism embodying rare mystical concepts, a thing the Victorians could not appreciate. Here he made a conscious use of imagery and symbolism as the appropriate tools of a mystical poet aiming at an apprehension of the Unseen. In his well-known essay 'Love and Poetry,' he maintains that "parables and symbols are the only possible means of expressing realities which are clear to perception but dark to understanding".[6] Writing in the same vein elsewhere, he observes about the Prophets and mystics : "some light of their meaning forces itself through the, in most cases, purposely obscure cloud of their words and imagery; but when, by chance, a glimpse of the disc itself is caught, it is surprisingly strong, bright, and intelligible".[7] Patmore's preoccupation with the marriage theme, especially in the odes, has to be understood in terms of the underlying symbolism conveying the esoteric relation between the soul and God.

In his exposition of the doctrines of Christian theology,

St Thomas Aquinas (using Aristotelian ideas and logic) dwells, among other things, on the unity of body and soul and stresses the need of keeping the impulses of love under the control of reason. Following him, Patmore rejects the body-soul dichotomy and sees the true significance of the Incarnation in the Word becoming Flesh. He distinguishes love from passion, holding that the former, being governed by the law, has "form" while the latter, not so governed, is "formless". Giving supreme importance to love, he follows the medieval Christians in upholding the union of sense and spirit. In his view, "what love does in transfiguring life that religion does in transfiguring love".[8] The Christian humanist in him sees the body as the "Temple of God" and that, in a nutshell, explains his belief in the sacramental value of love and of the natural world that we experience through the senses. He conceives of "spiritual marriage" as an act of conjunction between *unequals*, between God as the condescending male and the soul as the favoured female :

> In the infinite distance between God and man, theologians find the secret of the infinite felicity of divine love; and the incomparable happiness of love between the sexes is similarly founded on their inequality. There is a mystic craving in the great to become the love-captive of the small while the small has a corresponding thirst for the enslavement of the great.[9]

This view of love provides a valuable clue to the symbolic meaning of the Psyche Odes which will now be examined at some length.

Patmore, as Edmund Gosse maintains, believed that "the Pagan myths, even when they seem gross and earthly, contain the pure elements of living Christian doctrine in symbol".[10] In the three Psyche Odes, he contrives to employ figures from Greek mythology, Eros and Psyche, to establish the nuptial analogy. He relinquishes the Nature symbolism he had exploited in some of the odes of *The Unknown Eros* BK I (to elaborate the nuptial theme and bring out its transcendental significance). Instead, he makes an audacious use of the sexual analogy, presented in terms of the pains and raptures experienced by Psyche, who, according to the myth, is secretly visited by Eros at night. The imagery used in the 'Psyche' poems follows closely the form and pattern of the sexual imagery we are familiar with in St John of the Cross and St Teresa. Both the saints, as mentioned earlier, describe their experience of divine love in a language reminiscent of the *Song of Songs*. The ecstatic experience of the deepest intimacy with God known to the mystics (when they attain the highest reach of contemplation) is suggested in the Psyche Odes through the images of physical contact between the two figures of the Greek myth. Love between God and the soul, conceived as a spousal relation, is a daring symbol that has got assimilated to the language of mysticism. In the ode 'Eros and Psyche,' Psyche's reply to Eros, when the latter is about to depart, is couched in a language that recalls the 'dark night' images (we owe to St John of the Cross) :

> Thou leav'st me now, like to the moon at dawn,
> A little, vacuous world alone in air.
> I will not care !
> When dark comes back my dark shall be withdrawn !

Elsewhere in the same ode, as we shall see, we find several images, overtly sexual but functioning as symbols, which illumine rare mystical concepts. R.C. Zaehnar, commenting on the appropriateness of the sexual relation symbolizing the spiritual (showing the human soul in the feminine role) observes : "The sexual image...is particularly apt since the man both penetrates the woman, is both within and without her, just as God who dwells at the deepest point of the soul also envelops it and covers it with His infinite Love."[11] Psyche's words spoken to Eros suggest the same mystical union :

> Kiss me again, thy Wife and Virgin too!
> O Love, that, like a rose,
> Deckest my breast with beautiful repose,
> Kiss me again, and clasp me round the heart,
> Till filled with thee am I
> As the cocoon is filled with the butterfly!

The 'naked' sexuality of the Psyche Odes shocked even some of the Catholic admirers of the poet such as Aubrey de Vere and Cardinal Newman. Newman openly disapproved of them for "mixing up amorousness with religion". G.M. Hopkins, although he was struck by the "novelty and beauty" of the poems, reserved his judgement on them on the same account. Patmore was convinced that his poems had either not been rightly understood or had not evoked a favourable response. He wrote to his younger contemporary and co-religionist, Francis Thompson :

> I am too concrete and intelligible, I fear greatly lest what I have written may not do more harm than good by exposing divine realities to profane apprehension.[12]

On the whole, the response to these poems has been mixed, but perceptive readers have not failed to see their merit and appreciate the significance of the symbolism they embody. It is on account of their symbolic meaning that Shane Leslie finds "the Psyche series...unique in English poetry".[13] Edmund Gosse is of the view that in these odes "Patmore's genius may be said to have culminated".[14] The reader does not find it difficult to trace the concepts symbolically represented in these poems to St Thomas Aquinas and St Bernard with whose writings the poet was very familiar. The other inspiration can likewise be traced to the writings of the Spanish mystics mentioned earlier.[15] Psyche, as conceived by Patmore, is as much the Virgin as the individual soul; she is the Spouse of God. She is shown as overwhelmed by the love Eros bestows on her as an act of Grace. This can be explained, in Patmore's own words quoted earlier, as the "mystic craving in the great to become the love-captive of the small". The following lines in 'Eros and Psyche' pointedly express the same view :

> 'Tis but in such captivity
> The unbounded Heav'ns know what they be!

St John of the Cross speaks of God's love for the soul in similar terms.

In many of *The Unknown Eros* odes, Patmore speaks in the first person. In his earlier poems, *The Angel in the House* and *The Victories of Love*, he, however, uses the impersonal mode of narration, which is again followed in the 'Psyche' poems cast into the form of a dialogue — between Eros and Psyche in 'Eros and Psyche' and 'Psyche's discontent,' and between Psyche and her mother, Pythoness, in '*De Natura Deorum*'. In 'Eros and Psyche', the soul's immediate response to the sudden promptings of divine love, that is mysterious in its influence, is suggested in the account given by Psyche, in these introductory lines, of how she felt drawn towards Eros :

> Love, I heard tell of thee so oft!
> Yea; thrice my face and bosom flush'd with heat
> Of sudden wings,
> Through delicatest ether feathering soft
> Their solitary beat.

The poem begins with a significant image of the 'Bird' and the 'net'. Love as a 'game' or 'hunt' is a familiar theme in mystical literature and the 'Bird' is also a symbol for the Beloved in Sufi mysticism, carrying associations of the paradisal state. Psyche says :

> Long did I muse what service or what charms
> Might lure thee, blissful Bird, into mine arms;
> And nets I made,
> But not of the fit strings.
> At last, of endless failure much afraid,
> To-night I would do nothing but lie still,
> And promise, went thou once within my window-sill,
> Thine unknown will,
> In nets' default,
> Finch-like me seem'd thou might'st be ta'en with salt;
> And here — and how thou mad'st me start —
> Thou art.'

Psyche's stratagems to catch the 'Bird' prove futile and she realizes that she must 'lie still' : the soul has to cultivate the state of receptivity and learn to submit to the will of the Lord before she can attain full communion with Him. St John of the Cross's experience confirms this view. The passive receptivity of Psyche is rewarded; Eros appears and addresses her in these lines :

Ah, Psyche, guess'd you nought
I craved to be caught?
Wanton, it was not you,
But I that did so passionately sue;
And for your beauty, not unscath'd, I fought
With Hades, ere I own'd in you a thought!

The image of bird-catching is repeated here. Psyche's craving for union with Eros and its fulfilment are pointers to the spiritual states of pain and ecstasy experienced by the mystic. Of the erotic images used in the poem, that of the rose in "O Love, that, like a rose/Deckest my breast with beautiful repose", is specially significant. Readers familiar with Sufi poetry will at once associate it with the image of the rose garden, symbolizing consummation of the mystical experience. This image has also been absorbed into the European tradition; we find it, for example, in Dante's *Paradiso* and in St John of the Cross.

God's gift of love to Psyche is "This flame...pure." The 'flame' signifies the pain and penance the mortal must undergo to achieve 'deification'. The purgative value of 'fire' as a symbol is specially stressed in the mysticism of love related to the Hindu tradition. St Bernard too speaks of the "consuming fire of God", Eros demands this penance of Psyche :

My Darling, know
Your spotless fairness is not matched in snow,
But in the integrity of fire.

He desires her to make a total surrender of her ego; that alone would make her a worthy recipient of divine love :

Whate'er you are, Sweet, I require.
A sorry God were he
That fewer claim'd than all Love's mighty
kingdoms three!

The fire symbol is again used in the lines spoken by Psyche :

'O, too much joy; O, touch of airy fire;
O, turmoil of content; O, unperturb'd desire,
From founts of spirit impell'd through brain and blood!'

According to the original legend, Psyche's mind is crossed by doubts about the divinity of Eros. Patmore faithfully incorporates this detail in his poetic treatment of the legend (though he deviates from the original in several other details).[16]

'How know I that my love is what he seems!
Give me a sign
That, in the pitchy night,
Comes to my pillow an immortal Spouse,
And not a fiend, hiding with happy boughs
Of palm and asphodel
The pits of hell !'

Eros' reply to Psyche regarding the 'sign' is very reassuring :

''Tis this;
I make the childless to keep joyful house.
Below your bosom, mortal Mistress mine,
Immortal by my kiss,
Leaps what sweet pain?
A fiend, my Psyche, comes with barren bliss,
A God's embraces never are in vain.'

In Eros' reply is emphasized the certainty of spiritual fulfilment following the soul's blissful contact with the Divine, sharply contrasted with 'barren bliss' that a fiend may 'bestow' on its victim.

The allegorical meaning of the story dealt with in the 'Psyche' poems acquires amplification in the episode of the Gipsy Maid and the King that Patmore has so thoughtfully introduced into 'Eros and Psyche'. Psyche is at a loss to understand why Eros, a god, confers love on a mortal, an insignificant thing such as she :

'Much marvel I
That thou, the greatest of the Powers above,
Me visitest with such exceeding love,
What thing is this?
A God to make me, nothing, needful to his bliss,
And humbly wait my favour of a kiss!
Yea, all thy legions of liege deity
To look into this mystery desire.'

Eros likens his graceful disposition towards Psyche to that of the King, in the legend, towards the Gipsy Maid :

Should a high king, leaving his arduous throne,
Sue from her hedge a little Gipsy Maid,
For far-off royal ancestry bewray'd
By some wild beauties, to herself unknown;

. . .

Feeling her nothingness her giddiest boast,
As being the charm for which he loved her most?

In terms of the analogy implicit in the legend of the King and the Gipsy Maid, Eros advises Psyche not to 'quake' at her elevation but behave like a goddess and thereby rise to his expectation. He makes his point through another analogy — the Gipsy Maid is compared to a 'reed' through which the King desires to produce 'love-tunes'. The suggested meaning is that Psyche should take pride in being Eros' bride and overcome the feeling of her baseness. The individual soul, symbolized by Psyche, is comparable to a hollow reed, which is elevated, through Grace, into a musical instrument producing divine harmonies, although in itself insignificant. One can also look upon the hollow 'reed' as representing the soul freed from all traces of the ego and as such fit for contact with the Divine : 'baseness' undergoes an alchemical transformation into 'royalty'.

'*De Natura Deorum*' handles the theme of pain and ecstasy in its detail, its implications having a psychological validity. Such statements as "...pain is/The exceedingly keen edge of bliss" illuminate the psychological aspects of the mystical states of exaltation and deprivation. The poem abounds with details which may strike the reader as being obviously connected with sex, such as the reference to Psyche's wounds, but have to be construed as pointers to experiences both mystical and psychological in significance. It also makes an extensive use of the 'dark night' motif, showing the pervasive influence of St John of the Cross and St Teresa :

'Yea, this I know, but never can believe!
O, hateful light! when shall mine own eyes mark

My beauty, which this victory did achieve?'
'When thou, like Gods and owls, canst see by dark.'

The conversation between Eros and Psyche continues in 'Psyche's Discontent'. We see Psyche on terms of intimacy with her Lord. Though advanced in her love of Eros, which has now taken complete possession of her, she cannot yet stand its burden and seeks temporary relief from it. In the language of mysticism, she is to undergo the ordeals of the pre-unitive stage; she expostulates with Eros :

'Enough, enough, ambroisal plumed Boy!
My bosom is aweary of thy breath.
Thou kissest joy
To death.
Have pity of my clay-conceived birth
And maiden's simple mood,
Which longs for ether and infinitude,
And thou benign God, cravest littleness and earth!

. . .

Me, to quite other custom life-inured,
Ah, loose from thy caress.
'Tis not to be endured!
Undo thine arms and let me see the sky
By this infatuating flame obscured.
O, I should feel thee nearer to my heart
If thou and I
Shone each to each resplendently apart,
Like stars which one the other trembling spy,
Distinct and lucid in extremes of air,
O, hear me pray — ?

The erotic images used in the first two poems of the 'Psyche' sequence are repeated in 'Psyche's Discontent'. Mystical states continue to be suggested by the images of physical union — the 'embrace' and the 'kiss'. Love is the 'infatuating flame' which obscures the 'senses', the 'Uncreate light' or 'Divine Dark' passing human understanding. Psyche says to Eros :

Thou com'st like bolt from the blue, invisibly,
With premonition none nor any sign,
And at a gasp, no choice nor fault of mine,

Possess'd I am with thee
Ev'n as a sponge is by a surge of the sea!

The analogy of the sponge "possessed...by a surge of the sea," traceable to the account of the mystical experience given by St Teresa, parallels those of physical union mentioned earlier. Sexual in suggestion, it also signifies the state of mystical union between the soul and God.

In the Psyche Odes discussed in this chapter (and in several other *Unknown Eros Odes*), Patmore is evidently aiming to convey experiences of a highly esoteric nature related to that plane of contemplation which transcends speech. The reader may find it rather difficult to perceive the meaning underlying the sexual symbolism used in the poems. It is equally likely that he may find this poetry "fleshly". One needs to be familiar with Christian mystical theology to grasp the significance of the overtly sexual language used. Familiarity with this tradition gives us a context in which to interpret the poems in terms of Patmore's known mystical concerns. Whether Patmore personally had experienced mystical contact with God is perhaps ultimately unknowable. J.M. Cohen passes an adverse judgement on the 'Psyche' poems when he draws our attention to "Patmore's weakness to speak of things a little beyond his perceptions, things he knew of but could not taste".[17] But it can be seen that the poems exemplify mystical symbolism that has a universal validity; they can be properly understood and appreciated in the light of the *Song of Songs* on which they are ultimately modelled.

## NOTES AND REFERENCES

1. Edith C. Batho and Bonamy Dobree. *The Victorians and After* : 1830-1914 (1938; third rev. ed., London : The Crescent Press, 1962), p. 66.
2. B. Ifor Evans. *English Poetry in the Later Nineteenth Century* (London : Methuen, 1933), p. 13.
3. Mark Schorer. *William Blake : The Politics of Vision* (New York : Vintage Books, 1954), p. 85.
4. Striking parallels to this kind of mysticism are available in the poetry of several Persian Sufis and the poetry in India devoted to the love between Radha and Krishna, exemplified by Jaya Dev's *Gita Govinda*.

5. Caroline Spurgeon. *Mysticism in English Literature* (1913; London : Kennikat Press, 1970), p. 47.
6. Coventry Patmore. *Principle in Art, Religio Poetae and other Essays* (London : Duckworth & Co., 1913), p. 336.
7. *Ibid.*, p. 74.
8. *Ibid.*, p. 338.
9. *Ibid.*, p. 347.
10. Edmund Gosse. *Coventry Patmore* (London : Hodder Stroughton, 1904), p. 238.
11. R.C. Zaehnar. *Mysticism : Sacred and Profane* (London : O.U.P., 1973), pp. 151-52.
12. Quoted in Shane Leslie, *Studies in Sublime Failure* (London : Earnest Benn Ltd., 1932), p. 156.
13. *Ibid.*, p. 155.
14. Edmund Gosse. *Coventry Patmore*, p. 237.
15. Edmund Gosse informs us that Patmore was acquainted with the poems of St John of the Cross in a French prose translation and that "Santa Teresa's *Road to Perfection* had exercised upon him a profound impression." See his *Coventry Patmore*, pp. 241-42.
16. Robert Bridges also wrote a long poem entitled 'Eros and Psyche' which was published several years after Patmore's 'Psyche' poems appeared. In Bridges' poem, Psyche's sisters, who are jealous of her lot in being loved by a god, plant a suspicion in her mind about Eros' divinity. Thus duped, ignoring Eros' earlier warnings, she uses a lighted candle to discover if her lover was a monster and not a god. Seeing Eros' radiant beauty, Psyche was convinced of his divinity, but, in the process, she provoked her lover's wrath.

    Bridges' poem easily lends itself to an allegorical interpretation : Psyche has to undergo very severe and prolonged penance before she is permanently united with Eros through wedlock and thereby elevated to the position of a goddess.

    In Patmore's poems, the story acquires a consistent mystical meaning through the use of a sustained sexual analogy. The allegorical interpretation is, comparatively, plain enough : the soul has several reversals before it can claim perfection through Grace. The mystical meaning comprehends this interpretation too.
17. J.M. Cohen. "Prophet without Responsibility : A Study in Coventry Patmore's Poetry," *Essays in Criticism*, I (1951), p. 292.

# 6

# The Poetry of Shams Faqir : Some Observations

THIS CHAPTER focuses on religious mysticism as we come across it in Shams Faqir, noted Sufi poet of Kashmir. We notice a pervasive mystical element in his lyrics (composed in Kashmiri) that is Sufi in content and inspiration, compatible with Islam and, at the same time, comparable in significant ways with other varieties of mysticism.

From the biographies of the renowned mystics of the world, supported by what has come down to us in the form of their sayings and writings, we gather that while some of them remained mostly absorbed in contemplation, the majority also practised love and piety as the benefactors of mankind in general. Unlike religious zealots, tied to this or that creed, they quietly pursued their own ways (as lone adventurers) though they continued to stay within their traditions. Only a small minority of them dissociated themselves from orthodox creeds, asserted their freedom and even professed heretical views.

As consistently maintained earlier, mysticism shares universal characteristics across cultures despite the variety it comprehends. That explains why the religious mystic is tolerant and accommodating as far as his attitude to other faiths is concerned. We, in India, are proud of being the inheritors of a rich culture, presenting a fine synthesis of diverse strands. The Hindu ethos itself has been largely responsible for this synthesis, conducive as it has been to free inquiry into the nature of Reality or Truth, and consequently to the flowering of the mystical sensibility.

The country has built up a rich mystical tradition going back to the Vedic times, which later absorbed the influence of the Sufi mystics, who in turn were themselves influenced by the cross-cultural interaction on the Indian soil. Having had a steady growth over centuries, our mystical literature involves a wide range of approaches to Reality. This is consistent with our cultural diversity. Of these approaches, as mentioned earlier, *Karma*, *Bhakti* and *Jnana* are specially characteristic of Hindu mysticism corresponding to what is respectively termed practical, devotional and philosophical mysticism by Christian scholars.

Another feature, discussed at some length in the preceding chapters related to the Way of Love, that is specially common to Christian and Hindu mysticism, is the theme of love between God and the soul conceived as a spousal relation. In fact, across cultures, human love has been a dominant *motif* in poetry of all hues including the mystical. Most mystics have looked upon earthly love as being basic to spirituality, having in it the potential of transfiguring into divine love. This theme has been dealt with in a variety of ways in mystical literature throughout the world.

Islam, as a world religion, lays utmost emphasis on the oneness of God. Thus thoroughly monotheistic, it has also stressed God's transcendence and man's creature-hood. This is something that does not seem compatible with mysticism — a dimension of religion that stands for an intimate relationship with the Divine. In actual fact, however, Islamic worship does not ignore the immanental aspect of God, including man's innate divinity. Those who uphold the Sufi path assert that in the *Koran* itself there are several passages which affirm God's immanence and quite suggest the possibility of a close communion between the Maker and man.[1] It is on this account that they justify the doctrine of *Irfaan* or *Marifat* (spiritual *gnosis*) as also the practice of *Mahabba* (the Way of Love).

As the spiritual offspring of Islam, Sufism had its fine flowering on the Persian soil. The Sufi orders that grew up in Persia and other Islamic countries evolved approaches that were mutually coherent and also consistent with the essential spirit of Islam. Eschewing 'high and dry intellectualism,'[2] the Sufis, like the Christian saints, practised poverty and penance, preaching their doctrine through love and gentle persuasion. Although Islam does not encourage monasticism or renunciation of household life, many Sufis spent their lives as wandering *faqirs*. The Sufi way had its impact not only on the Muslims themselves but it impressed the devout in other communities as well, leading to a healthy interaction and mutual accommodation, a thing borne out by what happened significantly in India. The receptiveness of the indigenous culture, specially characteristic of the Hindu ethos, and the liberal attitude of the Sufis have both contributed, in no small measure, to the composite culture that continues to be our rich legacy.

Islamic mysticism in its literary form, largely Sufi in content and inspiration, found its adequate development in classical Persian poetry. The Persian poets showed remarkable ability in using the language of human love to convey mystical concepts related to the Divine. The terminology of erotic love particularly, used in relevant contexts, enabled them to give a hint of the 'rapture' (*wajd*) the mystic experiences within the deeps of his soul. The Persian lyric, called the *ghazal*, evolved as an appropriate form in their hands for unfolding experiences profound and esoteric in nature, rooted in their mystical craving for union with God. Maulana Rumi, the supreme exponent of the Sufi Way, and other poets like Attaar, Sadi, Hafiz and Jami, wrote excellent poetry using highly suggestive images charged with significance, which gave superb expression to the theme of divine love. The profane and the sacred are seen to intermingle in Sufi poetry as they, for example, do in the metaphysical lyrics of John Donne. Written seemingly in a voluptuous vein, they evoke and suggest what touches our inmost Being.

With the advent of Islam in India, Persian studies gained popularity among the literary sections of society, that included the Hindus and the Muslims alike. This led to an interchange of concepts from Vedanta and Sufism between the two communities. The Bhakti movement in India provided an additional stimulus to this process of interchange. The mystical poems of Shams Faqir, the Sufi poet of note from the Valley of Kashmir, exemplify this cultural synthesis in a remarkable way.

Mystical poetry in Kashmiri (spoken by the natives of the Valley) has a richness and variety of its own, traceable to the mingling of several cultural streams. Its growth began in the fourteenth century with the famous woman poet and saint, Lal Ded. It was in her time that Sufism first came to Kashmir through Muslim saints and mystics.

The great Muslim saint, Sheikh Noor-ud-Din Wali, of Chrari Sherif (Kashmir), revered by all communities in the Valley and popularly called Nunda Rishi, is believed to have been blessed and directly influenced by Lal Ded. This is confirmed by the reverential tribute he paid her in one of his *shruks* (*slokas*).[3] Religious in thought and aphoristic in form, his *shruks* have impressed and influenced both the communities, Hindus and Muslims, in Kashmir as the *vaakhs* of Lal Ded have done. Accordingly, in the mystical poetry that was produced mostly in the 18th, 19th and 20th centuries (after a long gap, following the two saints), we notice an interfusion of parallel literary motifs and images drawn from diverse cultural sources. This intermingling is specially noticeable in the poems of Shams Faqir (A.D. 1843-1901). It is also to be seen in varying degrees in the poems of a number of other Kashmiri poets.

No authentic biography of Shams Faqir, giving full details about his life including what his literary antecedents were, has been complied so far. What has, therefore, to be depended upon most in this context is the text of ninety-six of his poems included in the anthology of Sufi poems in Kashmiri brought out by the J&K Academy of Art, Culture and Languages, Srinagar.[4] The perceptive reader can gather many facts and draw useful inferences from them about the life and literary background of the poet.

As we gather from the scanty biographical information available, through his upbringing at home and later under the influence of several seasoned teachers, Shams Faqir was drawn towards divine contemplation during his early formative years. He got connected with the Qadri Sufi order and thereafter, around the age of twenty-five, he went to Amritsar in pursuit of spiritual knowledge. Here he came into contact with an accomplished Master, under whom he got fully conversant with the Sufi doctrine and practice. On his return to Kashmir, he got married and had four children. Yet he remained well set on the spiritual path and lived throughout in the true spirit of a Sufi saint.

An intensive reading of Shams Faqir's poems reveals a lot to us about his religious background and the literary sources that must have inspired him. This in turn enables us to appreciate better his communicative skill as a mystical poet, precisely the tools he used to articulate his perceptions and experiences. As we get familiar with the linguistic tools and the kind of imagery he employs, we conveniently judge for ourselves the main sources of his inspiration.

Thus the poem '*Naat*', the first in the group of his poems available, indicates immediately that Shams Faqir is a devout Muslim, well acquainted with the teachings of Islam based on the *Koran* and also with the life of Prophet Mohammad. The poem '*Merajnama*' that follows '*Naat*' recounts the story of the Prophet's spiritual journey to the abode of God. In a number of other poems there is unmistakable evidence of the poet's awareness of the Mystic Way — of the steps and stages leading to Union that the Sufi Masters are believed to have gone through.

To the discerning reader, Shams Faqir's description of the Sufi path must appear suggestively similar to the accounts of the spiritual 'adventure' given in other varieties of religious mysticism (including Hindu and Christian mysticism). In several poems, he makes use of the *via-negativa* and *via-affirmativa* approaches in his accounts of the Divine. Each of these approaches to Reality involves a characteristic language use, which the poet accomplishes so well; sometimes we find the two approaches deftly interwoven in the same poem. In quite a few poems, we come across direct allusions to the Persian mystic, Mansur-ul-Hallaj, and the doctrine of *An-ul-Haq* (I am Truth) that he boldly preached.

The Sufi concepts of *fanaa* (annihilation), *baqaa* (continuity), the terms *zikir* (remembrance of God) and *fikir* (contemplation), the symbolism of the 'diver' in search of 'pearls', the images of *zulf* (seductive curl) and *khaal* (the mole on the cheek of the Beloved) are seen to recur in many a poem. The imagery of *jaam* (wine cup) and *mai-khana* (wine house) associated closely with *makhmur* (the 'intoxicated' mystic) is also recurrent in Shams Faqir, linking him with his distant predecessors, the Persian Sufi poets, in the background. It is they, in fact, who were the first to make innovative and creative use of language in starting the vogue of this imagery. At places, Shams Faqir speaks of his experience of the inward music of the soul, of the 'vibrant string within' that reminds us of *anahata* (unstrung sound) mentioned in Surat-Sabda Yoga.

A striking feature of Shams Faqir's poems is the diction : using largely the Kashmiri idiom current in his time, he also employs words from Persian, Arabic and Sankrit. He can bend language to his needs, blending harmoniously words from diverse sources together — an achievement creative in a high degree. In some poems particularly, we notice that he makes a consistent use of terms (and related concepts) derived from the Hindu Sastras (including both Vedanta and Saiva texts) with remarkable ease and facility.

As examples we may mention terms like *zagrat* (wakefulness), *sopan* (dream), *sushapt* (deep sleep), *turya* (superconsciousness), terms relating to the four elements including *pavan* (air) and *akasa* (ether), words like *soham* (He am I), *sunya* (void), *rav* (the sun), *shiv* (Siva), *anand* (bliss), *om, raaza honz* (King of swans). He handles the vocabulary and the related concepts so well that the poems acquire a distinctive Hindu tone. Of such poems the one that specially comes to my mind is titled 'Pad' (the first piece of the sequence). The interfusion of two cultures is indeed very conspicuous in the Sufi poet.

Several lyrics of Shams Faqir centre round the theme of the mystic's quest for the primal cause of this universe. As an illustration, the lyric titled *'Aagur Kami Manz Drav'* repeatedly poses the question, 'what is the fountainhead of the stream?', which serves as its refrain. Here is my translation of some significant lines of the poem (attempted to convey the essential meaning) :

च़ो'नुॅवुॅन्य बवनन पवनुक पाऽनी,
शब रोज़ छुसनुॅ ठहराव।
आव कति गव कोर ओस यक्साऽनी,
आगुर कमि निश द्राव।।
Day and night does *Pavan* flow
Through the four *Bhavans* non-step;
Whence did it come
And whither did it go?
It was even (all of one hue),
Whence did the stream come forth?

. . .

यसुन्दुॅय वव्लुरतय तसुंदुॅय पाऽनी,
कत्रुॅ मंजुॅ दऽर्याव द्राव।
वातखय सो'रवनन गोडुॅ गछ़ फाऽनी,
आगुर कमि निश द्राव।।
IIc who owns the sea
Is the Lord of water,
The river issued from the drop;
To get to the meaning,
Sacrifice yourself first;

. . .

शम्सुॅ अछ़ दरुॅ किन्य सपदरव ज्ञानी,
दिलु कुय बर मुच्राव।
आफताबुॅक्य पाऽठय फेर अस्माऽनी,
आगुर कमि निश द्राव।।

O Shams, to attain *gnosis*,
Throw open your heart's door;
Sun-like, roam the sky through
(to fathom the Secret);
What is the fountainhead?[5]

We can see that the poem poses vital and thought-provoking questions regarding the First Cause. It instructs the seeker to pursue the spiritual journey inwardly to realize the Self. This would naturally call for annihilation of the little self. The answer to the imponderable question regarding the source of the cosmos is provided through the intertwined images of the 'drop' and the 'river'. They parallel the images of the *bindu* and the *sindu* given in Hindu mystical literature, conveying what Swami Ram Tirtha equally aptly suggests through the phrase 'Infinite in the Finite'. In the concluding lines, that lay stress on cleansing the heart as a means to inward transformation, the tone of the poem changes as the poet addresses his own self. Without sounding didactic, the changed tone stimulates self-introspection in the reader/listener.

The Persian Sufi poets have often used the word *rinda* in their lyrics. With its rich associations, it has been absorbed into Kashmiri mystical poetry and has by now got into common usage among the Kashmiris. It occurs frequently in Shams Faqir's verse too. One poem titled '*Rinda Sara Ho Sapdi Kunu Ye*' is specifically addressed to the *rinda*. This is how the poet instructs the aspiring gnostic :

जि़न्दुँ पानय गछ़ि मरुनये,
रिंदुँ सरुँ हो सपदी कुनये।
O *rinda,* in order to realize the One,
Learn to die while still alive.

Emphasis is laid in the poem on self-conquest as being the stepping stone to advancement in spirituality. Whether we call the aspirant a yogi or an *aarif,* his *sadhana* has to consist in 'cleansing of the doors of perception' which involves a disciplining of the mind and the senses. He has to be discriminative and mentally alert throughout. Shams Faqir is explicit about this quality required of the true aspirant :

ओ'न लाऽगिथ वो'न गछ़ि ह्युनये,
नेरि ब्यो'न ज़ग तय प्रो'नये।
हथ दल दिथ नेरि म्वलवुनुँये,
रिंदुॅ सरुॅ हो सपदी कुनये।।

Seemingly blind, look keenly for
What you seek, O *rinda*!
Sifting the pure grain
From the impure,
Winnowing the grains a hundred times
Will reveal the Precious One to you.

The poet draws our attention to the strenuousness and pains involved in the spiritual effort, in these lines :

अनि गटि गछ़न कनि फुटरॅनये
अछ़्दाह मंजुॅ लाल रवालुनये।
ज़ाल चा'गिं रथ माज़ रव्यू पनुनये,
रिंदॅ सरुॅ हो सपदी कुनये।।

Break the stones at the dead of night,
To take away the Gem guarded
By the cobra;
Feed the burning lamp
With your blood,
Eat up your own flesh;
Thus will you, O *rinda*, realize the One.

Special stress is laid in the closing lines on belief and divine grace :

पच़नुॅ ब्रोठुंय गछ़ि पचुनये,
शम्स फकीरुन ती वचुनये।
गछ़ि साह्यब तोरय परुनये,
रिंदुॅ सरु हो सपदी कुनये।।

Believe before you verify,
That's Shams Faqir's gospel;
When you get the 'Word'
As a God-sent gift,
O *rinda*, you'll realize the One.

In one particular poem titled '*Walo Mashoka Deedar Haav*', the poet employs 'dark imagery' throughout, from the beginning to the end, and mentions 'black light' specifically in these lines :

> सियाऽही मंज़ छु आबि हयात,
> सियाह नूरस दपान नूरि ज़ात।
> सियाऽही मंज़ छु गाशुक बसाव,
> वलो माशोकुँ दीदार हाव।।
> The Elixir of life is hidden in the dark,
> The light divine is dark, too;
> Light itself is grounded in darkness,
> Pray, meet me Beloved!

This poem reminds us of the images of 'darkness' that are so recurrent in St John of the Cross, especially in his poem titled 'Dark Night of the Soul'. There is a close parallel between the Christian concept of 'divine dark' and what Shams Faqir conveys through his images. Similarly, the names of Hindu divinities such as Krishna, Shyama, Kalaratri, Megshyama, suggest "the night for the great release into the oneness of Self"[6] which is dark only to the senses, not to the spirit.

The 'human form divine', in its feminine aspect, is celebrated conspicuously in the poetry of the Persian Sufis. Parallel motifs and images are seen to occur in both Hindu and Christian mysticism. This form functions as a *wisdom figure*, which is, in fact, a recurrent image in literature. It is also identifiable as the 'theophanic figure through whom the manifestation of God takes place'.[7]

Shams Faqir too follows this Sufistic tradition as a poet. In several poems, he introduces a lady as embodying 'Beauty' and 'Truth', but the images of woman that he employs do not suggest 'flesh'. In one such poem titled 'Rov', the feminine form, described as 'ashqa sondar', recalls the Greek goddess Aphrodite. Her physical graces are rendered in fine detail — red lips, charming teeth, incomparable mouth (*dahaan*), seductive locks (resembling coiled snakes) and the like. All these images are charged with mystical significance in the Sufi tradition.

Another such poem of deep import, addressed to a woman hailed as the 'esteemed lady', is titled '*Manareniye Paan*

*Badlaav*'. It makes an elaborate use of the symbolism that we come across in Christian mystical writings — depicting the soul as the spouse of God. In the poem under discussion, the 'honoured lady' is cautioned not to be remiss in 'throwing the precious stone away'. She is advised to undergo 'alchemical' transformation to deserve the rare gift and the elevation that she seeks as her goal — which is nothing short of Union with the Beloved.

In conclusion, I should like to reiterate that as a Muslim poet writing in Kashmiri, Shams Faqir is outstanding in his grasp and assimilation of many mystical concepts and images that occur in the sacred Hindu texts. He owes this assimilation not only to his contact with the coexisting Hindu culture of his time but also to his own receptiveness and openness of mind. After Sheikh Nur-ud-Din Rishi of Chrari Sherif, it is he who paid glowing tributes to Lal Ded in a poem wholly devoted to her, titled 'ज़ान मिलुॅनाव भगुॅवानस सूॅत्य'. The poem shows how high he held her in his esteem, how familiar he was with her story and how thoroughly acquainted he must have been with her *vaakhs*. His poems deserve to be read with care, being a great source of delight and spiritual instruction.

## NOTES AND REFERENCES

1. See A.J. Arberry. *Sufism* (London : George Allen & Unwin, Ltd., 1950; rpt. 1956), pp. 17, 27.
2. See Cyprian Price, O.P. *The Persian Sufis* (London : George Allen & Unwin Ltd., 1964), p. 28.
3. Quoted in B.N. Parimoo, *The Ascent of Self* (Delhi : Motilal Banarsidass, 2nd rev. edn., 1987), p. 6 (footnote no. 2).
4. See Motilal Saqi, *Kashmiri Sufi Shairi* (Srinagar : J & K Academy of Art, Culture and Languages, 1985), vol. 1, pp. 311-439.
5. Onwards also, I have quoted a few more passages from Shams Faqir's verse (rendered into English by me for illustrative support).
6. Jankinath Kaul 'Kamal', tr. & annotator, *Indrakshi stotram* (Srinagar, Kashmir; Sri Rama Krishna Ashram, 1955), p. 38.
7. E.B. Greenwood. 'Poetry and Paradise : A study in thematics', *Essays in Criticism* (1967), p. 19.

# 7

# Zinda Kaul's *Smaran* — Part I : A Critical Reading of the Poems

AFFECTIONATELY AND reverentially called Masterji, Zinda Kaul made his mark as a Kashmiri poet with the publication of his volume of verse titled *Smaran* ('The Rosary as a Token of Love' and other Kashmiri Poems) consisting of Parts I & II.[1] In this volume, he broke new ground in providing his own translation of the poems in flawless English prose. In a significant way, the translation enhanced the value of the work for the scholarly and for the educated readers in general conversant with English. The poems are thematically related, being mostly devotional in character. They have a novelty about them that reveals Zinda Kaul's originality as a poet. Deep concerns of the human heart are brought out in them in a straightforward and befitting manner : divine love is shown as no different from human love except in its purity and intensity.

We notice a degree of novelty, and of technical accomplishment too, in the poet's creative use of language. He sounds original in terms of his intellectual strenuousness and also in his apt choice of words — giving the readers a feeling reminiscent of the English Metaphysical poets of the 17th century. Masterji's individual talent, revealed in his creative command of Kashmiri, is matched by his conformity to the native tradition of devotional and mystical verse that he inherited from his predecessors — especially from the great Parmanand, who was his most favourite religious poet in the background and a constant source of inspiration as well. Another celebrated Kashmiri poet, Krishan Joo Razdan too, though not a potent influence on Zinda Kaul, cannot be overlooked as his predecessor — in whose hands the traditional Kashmiri *leela* gained in excellence, that consisted in lyrical intensity marked by flowing rhythms and felicitous phrasing.

As a creative writer, Masterji's success in providing his own authentic and competent English renditions of the pieces in *Smaran* is his signal achievement — in which no Kashmiri poet (to the best of my knowledge) has surpassed him so far. Above all, his originality and skill in producing fine lyrics, his wide learning and his intellectual ability that is of a high order, are all evenly balanced in the *Smaran*. It is this many-sided accomplishment that accounts for Zinda Kaul's distinctiveness as a 20th century Kashmiri poet.

The volume *Smaran* was well-received by readers and some of the poems it contains became very popular when sung to the accompaniment of music by vocalists on festive occasions and at marriage ceremonies. It was this very book that earned the author an award (carrying some cash besides the citation) conferred on him by the Sahitya Akademi in the year 1956. The recognition came to him rather late in life, when he was 62 years old. And he was the first Kashmiri poet to be the recipient of such an award.[2] Having begun by composing verse in Urdu, Persian and Hindi much earlier (he wrote as many as 70 poems in Urdu), Zinda Kaul probably realized that in spite of his proficiency in these languages, he couldn't easily achieve distinction as a poet in one of them at the national level. Then he devoted himself wholeheartedly to the study of Kashmiri poetry — he delved deep into the compositions of major poets starting from Lal Ded's *vaakhs* alongside Nunda Rishi's *shrukhs,* produced during 14-15th century, down to the noted Kashmiri writer of devotional lyrics, Parmanand (d. 1885) and his (Parmanand's) illustrious successor in devotional verse, Krishan Joo Razdan.

However, of all the poets that attracted Zinda Kaul's attention and impressed him, he was most fascinated by Parmanand. He studied the whole corpus of his works and read, for long, his poems in depth. This involvement proved very fruitful for him inasmuch as he took up the challenging task of translating Parmanand into English. In consequence, English translations of Parmanand's three series of poems, *Radha Soyamvar, Sudhama Charitra* and *Sheva Lagna,* accomplished by Masterji, were brought out as low-priced publications, that were found very useful especially by the English-knowing readers.

It can be surmised, and is probable too, that Zinda Kaul's familiarity with the poetic compositions of Parmanand, in particular, followed by his engagement with the literary translations of the three series of poems mentioned, served to strengthen the translator's resolve to compose Kashmiri poetry himself in all earnestness. He must have found composing poems in his native tongue delightful as he soon emerged as an outstanding Kashmiri poet : his poetic genius really flowered in his native language. Of that genius, he had already shown the first sparks in his non-Kashmiri poems too. The strenuous and disciplined effort that the translations demanded from Masterji must have released fresh creative energy in him. Under this new upsurge, he tapped his extraordinary potential for producing excellent pieces of Kashmiri verse and the resultant output was the *Smaran* — consisting of the poems in Kashmiri and their superb English translations, almost inimitable as authentic prose renditions in a foreign language (as English was seen in Kashmir when the book was published).

As pointed out earlier, Zinda Kaul, as a Kashmiri poet and as a translator, stands apart from most 20th century Kashmiri poets in several ways — in terms of the evidence of his learning in his poems and his innovativeness. He is a conscious craftsman, whose similes and metaphors are always apt, looking, at times, as if carefully forged. He freely draws upon the images and concepts he has assimilated from his reading; he is an allusive writer and employs a diction that is invariably simple and straightforward, including words drawn from Hindi and Sanskrit that have not yet become common idiom — used perhaps in preference to the more alien Persian words — and also some

Kashmiri words, which though not in common use now, are chosen for their appropriateness and their native origin.

Though self-effacing and unostentatious by nature, Zinda Kaul made his mark as a man of parts right from his boyhood, especially in the literary field. Born at Srinagar in 1884, his teachers at school were deeply impressed by his remarkable ability in learning languages. Proficient in Urdu and Hindi as only a teenager, he also did not take long in learning Persian and could use it competently for literary expression. Likewise, he showed an early promise in his command of English, and could use it very competently. Having matriculated in 1902 with distinction, he got a clerical job in the Accountant General's office at Srinagar on the basis of his excellent performance in the qualifying test. Finding the job not to his taste, he soon relinquished it. Then he got in touch with Mr. Moore, an Englishman, who was the Principal of the first college in Srinagar. He provided Zinda Kaul a teacher's job and was particularly pleased with his translations — a promise in the poet more than fulfilled later through his English translations of his own Kashmiri poems and those of Parmanand. It was during the period Zinda Kaul held a teaching job that he passed his Intermediate examination in 1908 and his B.A. in 1915 with English, Persian and History as his elective subjects. Since teaching was what he liked most as his profession, he sought to improve his academic qualifications -- joined the B.T. (Bachelor of Teaching) course in a college at Lahore. He couldn't complete the course in view of several compulsions; he returned home and resumed teaching until 1922, when he joined the Dept. of Archaeology, Srinagar, as a Surveyor. I should like to touch briefly on two points : (i) the main facets of Zinda Kaul's personality and (ii) how adequately (or inadequately) the poet has been written upon; is he still potential, and what aspects of his work have remained untouched so far or need to be investigated further?

Masterji was revered by his admirers not merely as an outstanding teacher and scholar or as a distinguished poet, but as a *saint* too. He was a householder, pure and simple, and didn't have in his bearing or dress, any conspicuous marks of a Kashmiri household saint either. Yet he was looked upon as a *saint* because of his qualities of character — his humility and human warmth. Above all, it was as a teacher that he was adored most; his image as a saint-scholar has sustained itself and not faded in the minds of those who loved and revered him. He attained his stature as a philosopher and sage through his erudition and, conspicuously, through the devotional lyrics he wrote, which is quite in tune with his composite image as Masterji — saint, scholar, poet, teacher, writer all fused into one.

In spite of Zinda Kaul's excellence as a Kashmiri poet, he has not been adequately written upon. Conceding that the corpus of his Kashmiri poems is not large, he deserves more attention than he has been given, taking into account the richness and depth of his verse. The only monograph-length study on him titled *Zinda Kaul*, authored by Dr. A.N. Raina, was brought out by the Sahitya Akademi, New Delhi in 1974. Though useful in several ways as an introductory book, it is in the main a biographical and historical work, not focused on the poems, their literary interpretation and evaluation. A full-length *critical* study on the poet has not been brought out so far. A few stray articles on him in the *Shiraza* (the journal of the J&K Academy of Art, Culture and Languages), some discussion on his verse in Prof. Jayalal Kaul's *Kashmiri Lyrics* and in a special issue of the *Koshur Samachar* followed by Prof. B.L. Kaul's well-written published article on the poet make up the available material on him besides Dr. Raina's book. Zinda Kaul's translations, of his own verse in the *Smaran* and of *Parmanand,* by themselves constitute an essential part of his total output as a writer that requires to be examined carefully and evaluated. Considering what has been published on the author so far, which is obviously inadequate, he is still potential.

**Textual Study**

Poetry by its very nature, and by all accepted standards, is a form of art marked by "condensed" expression. There are always gaps in a poetic text here and there, and things are often suggested rather than explicitly stated in it. Zinda Kaul's verse too is no exception and conforms to the poetic pattern universally followed. A responsive reader of poems enjoys them all the more because of their suggestive power. If a piece of verse conveys all that the poet wants to say without posing any difficulty to the reader, it may fail to interest or inspire him. It could be considered "inferior" unless it is deceptively simple and communicates much more than "meets the eye". Though Zinda Kaul's poems look largely simple, they do pose a "challenge" to the reader's understanding. An appropriate response to such a challenge brings its own reward in terms of the reader's intelligent grasp of the meaning of the poetic text — his satisfaction, and the resultant enjoyment of the text in question.

Since Zinda Kaul has chosen to translate his poems into English, the translations could rob the original pieces of some initial charm for the native speakers of Kashmiri. However, the English-knowing reader, whose mother-tongue is Kashmiri, appreciates the poems better after he has gone through the translations. Each translation piece in the *Smaran*, given in lucid English prose, helps the reader to fill in the "gaps" in the text thus clarifying any possible obscurities that could bedevil his understanding. At places, additional details are also furnished within parentheses in the translations, that serve to illuminate the meaning fully. This feature of the book might make the task of the critical reader of the Kashmiri poems somewhat difficult inasmuch as the author's own translation is bound to influence and sometimes inhibit the reader's response. The intelligent and enlightened reader will, however, turn such a difficulty too to his advantage; it is very likely that he may be enabled to communicate in terms of his well-thought out critical response, something very original about the poems, the poet's manner and craft etc. and may thus facilitate their sound interpretation and evaluation.

Let me begin with the first poem of the *Smaran* (Section I), thoughtfully chosen by the poet as the introductory piece. Titled

'लोलुँ दयस प्रार्थना' (Hymn to Love), it is a key-poem that reveals what the main theme of the volume as a whole is.

God of Love is addressed as the Beloved and the word 'लोलो' (lolo), derived from the Kashmiri word (lole), meaning 'love', carries musical associations, linking the poem to the native tradition of lyric poetry in the Valley. In fact 'लोल' (lole) is a pervasive word in Kashmiri mystical verse including the verse of Sufi saint-poets. As Zinda Kaul himself wants to convey through his translation of stanza 2 (each stanza of the poem being a quatrain with the rhyme-pattern abbc except the first, in which the pattern is abcd), the senses themselves serve as the means of *gnosis* (spiritual knowledge). They transmit to the perceiving mind "sensations sweet" from "the mighty world of eye and ear".[3] Obviously, as it soon becomes clear to the reader, God of love addressed by the poet is none other than the indwelling Self of every individual human being. It is as a lover of beauty — of colour and form, and of melody — that the poet invokes 'lole', God as love, conceiving him as a deity that dwells within. The quatrain is reproduced below along with Zinda Kaul's translation (I have, however, reshaped the translation pieces into free-verse form).[4] At the end of the piece, the gist of the original quatrain has been conveyed by the poet through this line :

*All powers of mind are meant to help love grow.*

बो' चाने वेरि सो'मुँरावय,
अऽछयव किन्य रंगुँ रूपुक रस।
कनव किन्य शब्दुँ साजुक मस,
अऽनिथ रवास्यन बरय लोलो।।

I'll gather for thy sake
Essence of form and colour through my eyes,
And through my ears
The vintage of sound and song
To fill thy cups.

Herein the thinker and the aesthete in Zinda Kaul have collaborated to drive home to us the truth contained in the italicized line reproduced earlier.

The next stanza focuses on *viraha* — separation from the beloved, stressing how it is unbearable for the lover. The beloved plays pranks on the 'persona' (identifiable with the poet if we consider the poem autobiographical) from the heavens afar, remains inaccessible, as the hidden hero in the tales of adventure :

मेंʼ कुन वुछ्य वुछ्य असान छुख,
दूरि रूज़िथ आसमानन मज़ं।
गुपिथ छुख दासतानन मज़ं,
यि दूर्यर नो ज़रय लोलो।।

Thou smilest at me
From distant heights,
Hidest in stories of heroism;
This distance I cannot bear!

In the fourth stanza, we hear distinctly the voice of an intellectual, who is capable of self-introspection and has the outlook of an emancipated thinker. Keen to rise above prejudices based on narrow dogmas, he does not approve of an isolationist attitude of withdrawal into a shell, shunning the main-stream :

फिज़ा त्राऽविथ मेʼ रवऽनिमुॅत्य ज़िस्य,
ज़ऽमीनस तल तुॅ पूरॅन्य छिम।
स्यठाह देवार लूरॅन्य छिम,
चे़ʼ रोʼस्तुय कया करय लोलो।।

Forsaking the open air,
I have dug pits that I must fill,
And have raised round me many walls
That I have to pull down;
How can I do all this without thy aid?

The choice of words such as 'फिजा' (implying open air), 'ज़िस्य' (pits), 'देवार' (walls), 'लूरॅन्य' (to dismantle) is very appropriate to what is meant to be communicated. The words serve as figures of speech, here precisely as metaphors expressing implied comparisons.

The verse that follows, stanza 7, employs a conceit — tears being compared to pearls. Though a worn out figure, the word gets enlivened as an image in the poetic context. Life is conceived by the poet as a thing comparable to cultivating "a piece of land" — the expression functions as a metaphor. An individual involved in such an activity is shown as reaping 'pearls' in the shape of tears. Then Love's sandals described as "adorned with pearls" clinches the conceit used. It can be maintained, therefore, that in a manner reminiscent of the English Metaphysical poets of the 17th century, Zinda Kaul also, at times, delights in making a point through comparisons that seem far-fetched ordinarily, but appropriate in the poetry of love — divine or human :

> ज़ऽमीनस ज़न्मुॅकिस वऽव्यमुॅत्य,
> अशिक्य दुर्दानुॅ कंह बऽविमुॅत्य।
> अऽछिन मज़ं छिम रऽछित थऽविमुॅत्य,
> तिमय ख्रावे जरय लोलो।।
> My life is like a piece of land
> In which I have sown tears and reaped pearls,
> As you come, I'll adorn thy sandals
> With the pearls reaped.
> (Implying that he will weep at Love's feet)

In the next stanza, the poet expresses his eagerness to drink at the very source, which conveys suggestively that he wants to attain *gnosis* (spiritual knowledge) through direct contact with God rather than from various streams, standing for diverse creeds. In the final stanza of the poem he is explicit in seeking union with God, whom he addresses as the "remover of darkness" (गटि हुॅदिं गाशरय लोलो). The overall tone of the two stanzas at the end of the poem suggests the poet's deep aspiration for an encounter with God that the mystics experience and talk about.

The next poem titled 'योर आमुत गिंदने' sounds both doctrinal and philosophical. The title, translated literally, would read 'He has come here to amuse himself'; this has become 'He manifests himself for Amusement' in Zinda Kaul's rendition. The reader familiar with the Vedanta philosophy and the doctrines of Kashmir Saivism will make no mistake about the religio-philosophical theme of the poem. The verse is saturated with the essence of the wisdom contained in our scriptures, conveyed here poetically and presented as a narrative. The theme centres round the concept of man's spiritual origin, his innate divinity, and that of God's descent to the earthly plane as a kind of divine sport, as the expression 'योगॅु माया' (Yoga Maya) implies. The main Saivite doctrine, as set forth in the *Prativigya* philosophy of Utpal Dev, holds that the great Atman assumes embodiment on this earth and remains involved in divine "play", temporarily forgetful, as the Jiva, of his state of Sivahood. Known as the doctrine of Recognition, it maintains that the infinite or the ever-free Siva, forgetting his spiritual state of exaltation through human embodiment, fancies himself to be a limited individual. However, he can reverse the process through thoughtful reflection and self-introspection leading to Self-recognition. Here is the first stanza of the poem :

राजॅु पनॅुने देशॅु द्रामुत,
योर आमुत गिंदने।
नच़नस ज़न मोर आमुत्त,
योर आमुत गिन्दने।।

The King has of his own will
Left the Country of the Soul,
And descended to this planet
To amuse himself,
As the peacock delights in dance.

The simile of the 'peacock' given here suggests the refined tastes that amuse the King on this earth : artistic pursuits like song, dance and the game of love (प्रेम लीला). In such a frame of mind (as the King's or the peacock's) life acquires a significance of its own — becomes a celebration as the great Indian poet Tagore would conceive of it. Krishna's sports as a divine child too, in which the *gopis* and cowherd boys of *Gokul* got inextricably and inevitably involved, had a special meaning and significance when viewed in this light. The celebration in question should, however, not be mistaken for luxurious indulgence, consisting in one's preoccupation with something illusory — rooted in the *senses* and as such ephemeral. The King's sojourn to the earthly sphere is marked by a seriousness of purpose, as we gather from stanza No. 2 :

मटि ह्यो'तमुत छुस सफर,
त्राऽविथ गर्युक आराम प्रंग।
तथ बरस दिथ तोर आमुत,
योर आमुत गिंदने।।

Leaving his seat of bliss, he has accepted
The discomforts of his earthly sojourn,
Locking up his house of bliss and comfort
For a while.

This verse brings into sharp focus the contrast between the two states of the Divine : (i) the everlasting, transcendental state of bliss and tranquillity, and (ii) the earthly sojourn that the great Atman undertakes for a while to amuse himself. Zinda Kaul views this "descent" as the Atman's involvement with Maya, an engagement of far-reaching significance, a trial of his spiritual prowess aimed at vanquishing Maya. This becomes very clear in the next stanza :

पानुँ दिथ मायायि बल तथ पानुँ द्रामुत ज़ानुँने,
आज़मावनि ज़ोर आमुत। योर आमुत गिंदने।।

Having himself given great power to Maya,
He has come to overpower it
And show his prowess.

Stanzas 5 and 6 touch upon the theme of divine manifestation : the One becoming the Many, underlying the principle of Unity and Diversity. From this very principle stem the pairs of opposites such as "spirit and matter", "life and death", "light and darkness" and so on (quoted from Zinda Kaul's translation). One is reminded here of Shelleyean lines "Life, like a dome of many-coloured glass/stains the white radiance of eternity" and the corresponding scientific phenomenon of the dispersion of white light into the seven colours of the spectrum :

रंगे रो'स्त आऽसिथ खो'तुम मा रंग लाऽगिथ पुछय,
छो'त क्रुहुन तय होर आमुत। योर आमुत गिंदने।।

He did not have fun when he was 'without colour',
So to paint his picture

He assumed colours —
White, black and their combinations,
For his amusement.

ठानॅं रो'स्तुॅय बानॅं पलज़्या, बानॅं रो'स्तुॅय ठानॅं क्या?
कुन बऽनिथ, यिम ज़ोर आमुत। योर आमुत गिंदने।।

A utensil without the lid is not much use
Nor a lid by itself serves any purpose,
Hence the One has manifested in pairs.

Stanzas 6 and 7 bring out further implications of divine "descent". God, seen as the Transcendent, has two specific attributes : (i) He has his abode beyond the limits of time and space and (ii) He is in a state of perfect Rest and Peace. In assuming the human form as the Jiva, he has taken upon himself 'bondage' in sharp contrast to 'swatantraya' (absolute freedom) that is native to him. In this aspect — that marks the transition from the state of Being to Becoming — he is no more *still* but constantly on the move. And he plays multiple roles, as stanzas 8 and 9 suggest :

मुश्क अबंर बाऽगरान, कुनि सुय चऺदुंन तुॅ ही,
कुनि स्वय अरखोर आमुत। योर आमुत गिंदने।।

Giving clouds of fragrance
He is sandalwood and jasmine in some places,
Elsewhere he is nettle and *arkhor*
Whose touch causes pain or disease.

That God assumes diverse human forms is made explicit in the 11th (final) stanza of the poem :

कुनि सुय टऽगोर आमुत, शंकराचार्य तुॅ बुध,
कुनि असि ह्यू चोर आमुत। योर आमुत गिंदने।।

There he is a Buddha, a Shankara, or a Tagore,
Here a simpleton like myself.

The third poem of the series in Part I of the *Smaran*, titled "अज वाति" (He will arrive today), is a piece apart, charged with intense devotional feeling. It employs, throughout, images of human love that serve to bring out the deep implications of man's love of the Divine. It is relevant to mention here that human love is often used as a leading *motif* in mystical poetry across cultures. As is generally seen, the mystic, when faced with the difficulty of communication (inevitably posed by the "unutterable"), uses the terminology of earthly love to suggest man's experience of the Divine based on the various types of love-relationship that we are familiar with as human beings. A devotional mystic may, by natural inclination or deliberate choice, cultivate an attitude of mind based on any of these relationships as a means of his spiritual fulfilment — union with the Divine. In the terminology of Hindu mysticism, these relationships are spoken of as the various *bhavas* — called *Madhuri* (erotic), *Dasa* (servant-master), *Mitra* (friendship), *Vatsalya* (parent child), etc.[5]

In the present poem 'अज़ वाति', Zinda Kaul has used the father-figure to designate God — the *Paramatman*, sought by the devoted 'son' as the Beloved. What the 'son' proposes to do to honour and entertain the 'divine guest' serves to convey the depth and intensity of the love-relationship between the two.

We come across a number of significant expressions in the poem that strike the reader as very aptly chosen : to unfold the theme in its depth through fine touches and also to highlight the intensity of divine love. The father-son relationship built into this religious love-lyric illustrates one of the four *bhavas* mentioned earlier.

Let us now look at these lines of the second stanza of the poem :

> लछ़ ज़न डुविथ संताप पाप,
> अतं:करन गर नावसय।
> I'll cleanse my mind's house,
> Sweeping away sin and sorrow
> As one removes dust.

The second line of the verse has two phrases as its components : 'अतं:करन' (meaning the internal instrument including the mind and the senses) and 'गर नावसय', (I'll cleanse the house). The line as a whole suggests the persona's resolve to attain self-purification : purging the mind of all unholy thoughts and filling it, instead, with unalloyed love of the Divine. The compound word 'अतं:करन' is of Sanskrit origin, that has been absorbed into

Kashmiri by learned Kashmiri Hindus (like Zinda Kaul). The phrase that follows it *i.e.* 'गर नावसय' is closely related to the Kashmiri word गरनावय (dropping the letter स), commonly used by the Kashmiri Hindus in particular when they clean their houses just before they observe festivals like Shivratri or celebrate marriages.

When the poet talks of cleansing the 'internal instrument' in the verse under discussion, he wants to emphasize that the purification of our innerselves consists in purging and overhauling our *psyche* thoroughly, considered a prerequisite for self-illumination, that is often accompanied by a *darshana* (vision) of one's chosen deity. Mysticism of different shades, including Christian, Hindu and Islamic mysticism (or Sufism), as mentioned earlier, speaks of the spiritual path to the divine as marked by certain stages or steps, which the aspirant has got to traverse before he attains the goal. The description of the Mystic way, however, varies in detail from one form of mysticism to another.

In stanzas 3, 4 and 5 of the poem, the important images used are — those (i) of a nice seat of rest or honour (suggested by the word 'प्रगं' in Kashmiri), (ii) of cups of fruit-juice served to a guest, (iii) of the feet being washed by the holy water of 'tears' and the sweat wiped by a fine handkerchief, all meant to convey the warmest hospitality that the devotee wishes to offer to the beloved 'Father', the divine guest. Stanza 8 deserves special mention :

> बावुक गन्यर लोलुक सन्यर,
> वाऽलिंज मुच़रिश थावसय।
> I'll lay open my heart
> To show him the depth and intensity
> Of my love and reverence.

The words 'गन्यर' and 'सन्यर' serve to convey the highest love and regard in which the loved Father is held by the persona; they rhyme perfectly in Kashmiri. The internal rhyme linking the two words in the line intensifies their impact through the sound-effect.

The last two stanzas, 12 and 13, are packed with meaning, that can be grasped better if we bear in mind Zinda Kaul's intimate knowledge of the finer details of yoga practice connected with *Pranayama* (breath control) and the *Kundalini*, as taught in our *shastras* (including both *Vedanta* and Saiva texts). Let us look at the two verses mentioned :

> गटॅुं पऽछ्‌य च़ऽदंर ज़न नामरूप,
> अख अख कला व्यगलावसय।।
> I'll give up all attachment to name and form
> As the moon in the dark fortnight loses digit after digit.
> सुर्यस अदंर लय प्रावि जून,
> सार्यय बनन त्यच़ मावसय।।
> The moon will get absorbed in the sun
> And all days of the month will become *Amavasi*.

In these two verses, the poet focuses on what is involved in the individual soul's union with the Divine. From the Vedantic standpoint, so long as the aspirant continues to be under the spell of the multiplicity of outward objects, he is caught up in the prison-house of 'name and form'. Attachment to 'names' and 'forms' has to be given up before one can comprehend and realize *Brahman* (the ultimate Reality). The waning of the moon during the dark fortnight until it loses the last digit suggests total annihilation of the ego (as Zinda Kaul explains in the translation). In the final verse, the meaning gets amplified through the image of the moon getting absorbed into the sun, the moon standing for the ego (or the *Jiva*) and the sun for the universal Self. Those who are conversant with the practices connected with breath-control and the Kundalini yoga can better appreciate what the two verses point to in terms of *sadhana*. Having *Amavasi* on every day of the month (see the last line of the concluding verse) suggests a state of transcendence, of perpetual absorption in the Divine. This transcendence is described as the 'Divine Dark' in Christian mysticism. It is appropriate to quote the following verse from Utpal Dev's *Shivastotravali* in this regard :

यत्र सोऽस्तमयमेति विवस्वां
श्चन्द्रम : प्रभृतिभि : सह सर्वैः।
कापि स विजयेत शिवरात्रिः
स्वप्रभा–प्रसर–भास्वरूपा।।

That blessed state in which the sun, moon and all other lesser luminaries (including the stars) are obscured by the effulgence of the luminous self, that ineffable and marvellous experience of Shiva-ratri (Shiva's night) — may the glory of this unique night ever prevail.[6] (translation mine)

One can surmise that Zinda Kaul must have been aware of this *sloka* and the related slokas in the *Bhagavad Gita* (15/16) and the *Svetasvataropanisad* (6/14) when he composed the present poem. His description of *Amavasi* as a sustained phenomenon ties up with the account of the *Shiva-ratri* given by Utpaldeva — as the state of the soul's abiding union with Siva, termed *Parasamvit* or Supreme Consciousness.

The fourth poem of the *Smaran* (Section I) bearing the title 'गुरु भक्ति' is a poem of devotion to the Guru, expressive of the seeker's aspiration to persevere in serving and adoring him. The seeker would not merely revere him as his teacher but love him as his *Ishtadev* (chosen deity) for his beauty and grace, his wisdom and benevolence. The diction of the poem indicates the poet's *penchant* for Hindi and Sanskrit words used in appropriate contexts (when precise Kashmiri equivalents are perhaps not available) that function as content-words in a significant way. At a few places, the poet has used words of Hindi origin in a novel way :

आमुँच मनस रुँच़ वासना,
ईश्वर सफल करिनासना।

A pious longing has arisen in my mind,
May the Lord fulfil it!

Here the words 'वासना' and 'सफल', which are Sanskrit in origin and freely used in Hindi, have been incorporated in the verse as Kashmiri words though their usage is restricted to the speech of Kashmiri Hindus. Of course, they are intelligible to the other Kashmiris too. The point to be made is that such usage is deliberate on the part of Zinda Kaul as a conscious craftsman. The words come naturally to the poet and perform their communicative function well. Two other words, 'एकांत' and 'उपराम' (with their original pronunciation and spelling intact in the verse) seem conspicuous as 'adoptions' from Sanskrit/Hindi in the second verse here :

> एकांतकिस गऽहीलिस अंदर,
> उपरामकिस शिहिलिस अंदर,
> पंपोश पादन द्वन मलान,
> पनुँनिस ग्वरस बो आसुँहा।
> In the density of solitude
> And the cool shade of retirement,
> May I be pressing the lotus-feet of my Guru.

The foot of the revered guru or of the beloved *Ishtadev*, likened to the lotus, is an image that has a high frequency of occurrence in Hindu devotional verse, and Zinda Kaul is here just following a time-honoured convention. However, what he says in the next verse (stanza 3) and the weightage he gives to the expression of pure love, in preference to the prescribed ways of worship, lend a special significance to these lines :

> पूज़ायि विध केंह ज़ानुँमा,
> लोलस निषद केंह मानुँ मा,
> छ्यपि चूरि कुनि म्यूठा दिवान,
> लो'त तथ ख्वरस बो आसहा।
> I don't know the prescribed way of worship,
> Nor do I see any flaw in love;
> I wish that stealthily and quietly sometime
> I planted a kiss on those holy feet!

Further onwards, stanzas 6 and 7 tell us of the devotee's craving to hear the *updesh* (teaching) direct from the lips of the Guru and then to fall at his feet — an act of surrender visualized by him as the means of his deliverance. Imagining himself as the darling child of the Master, the devotee expects to be fondled by him while he himself would have got merged into the ocean of bliss (through the divine touch); here are the relevant lines from the concluding stanza 8 :

> वुज़ तात वऽन्य वऽन्य गारिहम,
> कर पदम् ह्रदयस सारिहम,
> ज़ल बिंदु ज़न मीलिथ गो'मुत,
> सुख–सागरस बो आसहा।
> May he say "wake up, my dear"
> And feel my heart with his lotus-hand,
> While I have merged like a drop
> Into the sea of bliss.

What we infer from this concluding verse is the poet's belief in the soul's final absorption into the Universal Soul and his conviction that love, accompanied by dedicated service to the Beloved, is the sole means for the seeker to attain union with the Lord. The other thing noteworthy about this four-line stanza is the diction. There is at least one Hindi word in each line : 'तात' (dear) in line 1, compound word 'कर–पदम्' (lotus-hand) and 'ह्रदय' (heart) in line 2, compound word 'जल–बिंदु (drop of water) in line 3, and another compound word 'सुख–सागर' (ocean of bliss) in line 4. The frequent occurrence of such vocabulary items from chaste Hindi in Zinda Kaul's Kashmiri verse is a feature that is very striking.

The poem that follows, titled 'प्रेमुक निशानुँ' (Token of Love) is among the finest in the entire volume *Smaran*. It is also important from the point of view of (i) its being another key-poem, besides the introductory piece 'लोलुँ दयस प्रार्थना', (Hymn to Love) and (ii) the popularity it has gained because of its great appeal as a devotional lyric with an exalted theme and an inbuilt argumentative structure. The poem continues to be sung as a devotional piece set to music on festive occasions. It is the very first word 'स्मरण' (Smaran) of this poem that Zinda Kaul has chosen as the title of his book.

The narrator or persona in the poem (projected as a female, indicated by the gender used) bewails the loss of a rosary she had received as a token of love from the beloved Master. Considering the choice of the gender used, the present lyric can be seen as comparable to the mystical poems of the 16th century Spanish poet, St John of the Cross. Christian mysticism views the relation between the soul and God as a spousal one, in which the latter is identified with Christ in relation to whom all individual souls are considered feminine. This ties up with the form of Hindu mysticism based on *madhuri bhava* (erotic love) : that, for example, bound the *gopis* (cowherd women) to Sri Krishna as a boy, as depicted in the *Bhagavad Purana*.

Before the narrator overcomes the feeling of depression, mention is made in the poem, indirectly, of the Hindu belief in reincarnation and the related belief in the accumulated virtue or sin that one earns through a chain of lives. Obviously, the unworthiness of the narrator in having lost the choicest gift (in the shape of the rosary) is attributed to the fact of such a virtue not having been earned by the concerned. However, after some melancholy verses, we notice a shift in the mood of the poem and the tone changes, melancholy giving rise to optimism. The Divine is shown to be very considerate and benevolent in the end. There is, in fact, an argumentative evolution in the poem, a logical development going hand in hand with the sequence of thoughts in the narrator's mind, marked by reasoning and self-introspection. On the whole, we sense a depth in the content, a richness of thought and feeling matched by the use of words and phrases appropriate to the exalted theme.

The poem opens dramatically, striking the keynote :

स्मरन पनॅुन्य दिच़ाऽनम,
प्रेमुक निशानॅु वे'सिये!
रऽछ़रुन तो'गुमनॅु रोवुम,
ओसुम न बानॅु वे'सिये!

He gave me his rosary
As a token of his love,
I proved unworthy of the gift
I couldn't keep it with care,
And so lost it, what a pity!

The verse that follows offers a comment on the loss suffered — an explanation involving the Hindu belief in past *karmas* (actions) :

पथ कालि छुम नुँ दितुमुत,
हावुन थो'वुम अथस प्यठ।
राह कस छु को'र मे' पानस,
नो'क्सान पानुँ वे'सिये।

In my past lives, I haven't
Given away any rich gifts —
Such as gold and pearls given in charity;
How can I retrieve the lost beads
In my present blindness, my past life
Having been devoid of any virtue earned.

The next verse elaborates how the loss of the rosary, an invaluable gift, came about : the persona, instead of keeping it as a precious possession, exposed it to public view, made an exhibition of what should have been 'entrenched' well within and thus secured from harm :

मानवज़ि अऽस्य ह्यमव पथ,
छोर्या तसुंद मो'हब्बत?
पै वदं यि आदनुक छा,
शुर्य दोस्तानुँ वे'सिये?

Supposing we withdraw,
Will his love let that happen?
Is the eternal love between Him and us
Fragile as passing friendships between children?

In the poet's view, God's bounties are spread all-around us and his kindness knows no bounds. He is ever gracious to his devotees whatever their failings :

दिल फ़ुटिमत्यन छु तोशन,
यऽच़ गऽरिमत्यन छु रोषन!
गछ़ वऽरिमत्यन सो'दामन,
पृछ़ गाऽयिबानुँ वे'सिये!

He is kind and considerate to the repentant,
Though he pretends to be displeased with the clever sort,
Go and confirm this aside from
Devotees like Sudama, whom he favoured!

As we mentioned earlier, the persona, or the poet's mouth-piece in the poem, is a female devotee speaking of her experience to her female friend (conveyed by the form of address 'वे'सिये'). In the concluding stanza of the poem, we hear an optimistic and reassuring note — say, the voice of the poet Zinda Kaul himself — based on an experienced conviction, the conviction of a seasoned thinker and scholar (as the allusion to 'Sudama' earlier and the other to 'Surdas' in this verse testify to) :

अंऽद्य पऽख्य ततीछु आसन,
बो'धुँ ब्रोर सूर दासन!
बोज़ान छु माय लाऽगिथ,
लोलुक तरानुँ वे'सिये!
The Omniscient Child divine,
Stays quietly around watching closely
His devotees like the blind Surdas;
Unobtrusively, he listens to the song of loving devotion.

The poem 'नातयाऽरी' (Unprepared), the sixth one in the sequence contained in Part I, is *distinct* from the previous ones in several ways, though essentially allied in theme. It makes a departure in respect of its stanzaic structure, tone and style. It has a touch of the dramatic lyric, of the "interior monologue" too, involving mental analysis and self-examination. It has also a narrative element in the shape of the reported speech of the "lover" (दिलदार). The length of the verses varies — stanzas 1, 2 and 3 have 5 lines each; there are 9 lines in stanza 4, 7 in stanza 5, 11 in stanza 6, and 8 in the 7th (which is the concluding stanza). Although the verses have, more or less, a consistent rhyme-pattern, they sound like prose and seem less lyrical on that account. If the poet had dispensed with the rhyme, the verse would have easily approximated to the free-verse form. The conversational tone — the "dialogue" bordering on the "monologue" — anticipates the free-verse form that Zinda Kaul's successors (strictly speaking some of the noted modern Kashmiri poets) have experimented with and accomplished too. The narrator's voice continues to be that of a female in the present poem too. We hear her mention the fine qualities of her "आदनुक

यार" (eternal lover) in the first verse; he is depicted as extremely loving and considerate, a sincere friend who has been steadfast to her since the blissful days of her childhood. The loving Master is quoted in the second stanza :

तऽम्य दो'पुम केंह यथ देशस अंदर,
यथ मकानस रोज़ म्याऽनी वथ वुछान,
दूरिरस मज़ं वारि फो'लनय लोलुॅ पोष,
आऽस्यज़ि हमसायन हकन तिम बाऽगरन,
तार चोन अदुॅ ज़ानुॅ बो तय कार म्योन।।

Sending me here, he said, "Live for a while
As an occupant of this house
In this land, ever seeking me;
Away from me, flowers of love
Will bloom in your little garden;
Distribute them among your neighbours;
And I'll take care of your welfare —
That's my business.

The lines are allegorical and should not be taken literally. What is meant to be conveyed through the allegory is that the soul, as the "occupant" of the physical body, is actually on a sojourn here to do God's bidding : never to forget the great Master and ever to seek him. Living in separation from the Lord (in physical terms only) and ever remembering Him will produce positive results for the soul. It will serve to cultivate the "little garden" that represents the human heart here, and "flowers of love" will bloom in it. Distributing these flowers among the neighbours, which in terms of the allegory means sharing love and joys of living with them, would elevate the individual soul (charged with a mission) as this sharing would entitle it to become a recipient of divine grace.

In the third stanza, God's instruction becomes further explicit. He is the source of all forms of human love; in loving our fellow-men, we indirectly love God. The first line of the stanza makes this clear through an analogy : "यथ कुलिस सग दिख ज़ऽमीनस वाति" (whichever tree you water the moisture will be absorbed by the earth). The truth that the poet wants to drive home is that it is through the practice of love alone that man can attain his salvation.

Stanza 4 also serves to communicate to the readers fuller implications of the divine mission man is charged with. The poet makes use of Nature symbolism here. One is reminded of the famous 19th century English poet, William Wordsworth, who looked upon nature as a universal teacher. Perhaps having this great poet as well in his mind, Zinda Kaul wants to convey how various natural objects, fauna and flora, different sights and sounds serve to educate us provided we are receptive to their influence. Likewise, we also learn from wise men such as the saints and sages who have controlled their minds. It is in fact through our interaction with Nature and men around, especially the enlightened ones, that we get wiser about God and his ways.

Stanza 5 paints a beautiful natural scene witnessed by the narrator or persona at early dawn — the late-risen moon in the sky, and the air filled with the sweet fragrance of flowers, the song of the nightingale, the music of the brook. The enchanting scene made the narrator infer that the eternal lover had come uninvited, a mistake of judgement realised soon. This is what the concluding lines of the stanza have to say :

> त्युथ समा साऽपुंन मे' दो'प सुय यूर्य आव,
> सालॅुं रो'स्तुय आव बालय यार म्योन।
> The scene became so beautiful that I thought
> My eternal lover has come
> Without my invitation.

Zinda Kaul explicates in the translation of the stanza what is only faintly suggested but not said explicitly in the verse :

> But how did he come without my invitation?
> God is ever ready to come to us,
> But will not come to us uninvited.

(see p. 35 of the *Smaran*)

The next verse (no. 6) presents a vivid picture of the persona's state of unpreparedness. On introspection, she realises that she has not done as she was instructed to do : she has neither distributed the flowers of love among her neighbours, which have, therefore, got withered, being thus not fit to be offered to the Master in devotion. The verse contains an image of the *pujaghar* (meditation-room) painted as very dusty and unclean, turned into a store-room packed with household goods. The picture serves as a poetic image of the psychological state of the aspirant. Let us see how the poet has conveyed what "ails" the unprepared devotee's psyche. The image suggests to the reader that in order to perceive the Divine, the devotee has to undergo *sadhana* to achieve purging of the senses and the spirit. The last 4 lines of the concluding verse throw light on the state of awareness of the 'unprepared' devotee — that God will wait for the opportune moment to come and then shower grace on the seeker :

युथ समा आऽरवुर नन्यव रवत ओस ब्यारव,
पानॅु को'त यियिहेम ज़ाऽनिथ नातयार
शर्म रछिवुन म्योन, पर्दयदार म्योन,
प्रार वुन मे आदनुक दिलदार म्योन।

It became evident that this was another 'epistle' —
Saying that He couldn't come,
Knowing that I wasn't prepared yet,
As my eternal lover
He'll wait for me ever —
Not expose me or put me to shame!

On examining some of the poems contained in the *Smaran* critics might feel tempted to categorize Zinda Kaul as a philosophical poet rather than a religious or devotional poet. This is because there is evidence in his Kashmiri poems of ideas rooted in *Vedanta* and *Kashmir Shaivism*. A literary critic might even characterise these poems as didactic : meant to convey moral or spiritual truths to the readers. If this view of his poetry is emphasized, that will naturally detract from its literary value. The image of the poet as a mere 'teacher' is likely to affect his (Zinda Kaul's) standing as a creative artist. John Keats has remarked about didactic poetry that it fails to 'delight' : "We hate poetry that has a palpable design on us". This, of course, I contend, is not applicable to Zinda Kaul's *Smaran* as a whole;

most of the poems included in it thrill us as much as they educate and elevate us. Yet they are not patently religious. They employ mystical symbolism to convey deep religious truths and experiences that are not ordinarily communicable. In fact, Zinda Kaul achieves literary communication through appropriate imagery and symbolism as also through the art of story-telling in verse — the narrative element has often an underlying or inbuilt symbolism.

Thus the 7th poem of the *Smaran* contained in Section I, titled 'जोगिराय' (The great Yogi) is narrative in the main, involving subtle spiritual symbolism. The poet makes a strategic use of the narrative art-form to convey to the readers how he views spirituality and what he considers indispensable for one to advance in the spiritual path. In the poem, the narrator continues to be a female — a woman advanced in age, who leaves her home, belatedly though, and roams about in search of a Master who would initiate her into yoga. Reaching the Manasbal lake, she takes a dip into the holy water and then encounters the yogi, his lustrous body smeared with ashes. The remaining story is unfolded in stanzas of varying length — containing lines numbering 2, 4, 7, 8, 10 and 12. The verse-pattern is, on the whole, similar to that of the previous poem (No. 6). The present poem sounds mystical in terms of its suggestive imagery and the overtones, conveying much more than the words state :

तस बालॅु पानय इषृदेव,
यऽच़ लोलॅु प्ररव–ट्योमुत बुना
रूज़ित दमा आलव गर्युक,
बूज़ित वुफित गोमुत बुना
तऽम्य वोलमुत अमृत अऽमिस
व्यसरित वऽसित प्योमुत बुना,
मूर्छ़ायि पतॅु प्रथ शायि तस,
छ़ारान वेह ख्योमुत बुना।
During his boyhood itself
His Ishta-deva, who he loved immensely,
Had appeared before him, stayed awhile
And then flown back,

Hearing a call from his home above;
Sorrow-struck, the yogi had let fall from his hand
The nectar brought down for him by the Deva;
Fainting down and then recovering himself
He had fruitlessly searched for the divinity everywhere
And felt like poisoning himself!

Consequently, as we gather from stanza 3, the yogi had become disconsolate and got totally indifferent to the world. Inwardly, tormented by the feeling of separation from the Divine, he would shed tears profusely. All his thoughts were fixed on the Beloved — described as his "cruel love" in stanza 4 :

स्मरन रुमॅु रुमॅु मारुॅ मो'त,
सुय द्यान दो'र गोमुत सऽनिथ,
युस रूप तथ द्यानस अंदर,
सुय रऽछ तॅु सुय सीनस रवऽनिथ,
सुय बाव ह्रदयस आवरिथ,
पूरिथ, बऽरिथ, व्याऽपिथ, घनिथ,
नरिपान निथ त्ऽत्य आलवान,
तमि दीपकुय पाऽपुंर बऽनिथ
मोक्षिक तॅु वैकोंठॅुच नॅु जाय।

Remembering every moment his cruel love,
His picture engraved deep within his mind
And etched for good within his heart —
All filled with affection for the Beloved,
Having become a 'moth' of that 'lamp'
Ever hovering around it,
There was no room in the yogi's heart
For thoughts of heaven or salvation.

The narrator (depicted as a female) could not stand the sight of the yogi, of the condition he was in — of his abstracted air, being all absorbed in the thoughts of love. The encounter (with the yogi) made her realise what true love is like — what a rare experience it is, the risks it involves and the sacrifice it demands (all conveyed in stanza 6). The narration is continued in the next stanza (No. 7) :

मदंछित गो'मुत अंदर बो'डित,
वदॅु वॅुन्य पे'यस जूगिस परन,

दो'पमस दया द्रे'ष्टी करुम,
थऽचिमुॅच़ छसय आमुॅच़ शरन,
सेवायि हुॅज़ं आज्ञा दितम,
रूज़िथ यऽती छलुॅहय च़रन,
वुछनय मे' कुन क्याहताम असर,
को'रुनम अऽछिन जोदूगरन,
मल–कल छ़ऽटित अऽदंर्युम न्यबर,
दागव बऽरिथ डयूठुम फ्यरन,
तवुॅ रो'स्त कवुॅ ह्यकुॅहा वुछिथ,
पानय पनुन अतः करन।

Abashed, weeping and drenched in perspiration,
I fell at the yogi's feet and said,
"O pray, look kindly at me,
All tired, I've come to seek refuge in you,
Grant that I may serve you here,
Stay with you and wash your holy feet."
Without looking at me — I somehow felt —
He cast a spell on my eyes, the wizard as he was!
All my impurity came to the fore,
I found my outer garment full of stains;
How else could I have perceived
The impurity of my mind?

Realising the need of cleansing herself — going through the process of "purgation" such as observances in the form of dips in holy waters accompanied by penances in the shape of repentance, prayer etc., the persona ran to the nearby brooklet and washed her soiled clothes (suggesting self-purification). Having washed some of the stains, she returned, but was dismayed to find the yogi gone. Since then, in her state of agony, she has been weeping, feeling sometimes an irresistible urge that compels her to go again to *Manasbal* where she first met the great yogi (narrated in stanzas 8, 9 and 10). There she calls the yogi from the hill :

जोग्यो सो'दंर नावस लगय,
बडि लो'लुॅकिस बावस लगय,
दर्शुन दितम अच़तम बरय,
पादन प्यमय पूज़ा करय,

अऽश्य मो'त्तुॅ तथ ख्रावे जरय,
पंपोश पादन तल मरय,
ग्वरूॅ म्यानि हा योगेश्वरय।

Oh Yogi, I am enthralled by your beautiful name
And the greatness of your love.
Pray, come to my house and let me see you,
I'll fall at your feet and worship you,
Adorn your sandals with my tears as pearls,
Die at your lotus-like feet.
Oh you great yogi, my Guru!

The next poem titled 'सन्याऽस्य' (Sannyasi) merits attention as a devotional piece conforming to several conventions of the Kashmiri love-lyrics. As a *leela,* however, it looks somewhat 'modern' too inasmuch as it is distinguishable from the religious lyrics of the great Parmananda or his illustrious successor Krishna Joo Razdan. The *leelas* of the latter two are usually addressed to a single deity or divinity — Lord Rama, Krishna or Shiva, whose virtues, exploits and glories covered by the term *leela* (also meaning a divine sport) are based on the classical epics like the *Mahabharata* or *Ramayana* and the *Puranas* like the *Bhagavatam* etc. In the present poem, we come across expressions like 'लोलुॅ अफसानय' (tales of love), 'तीरि मिजगानय' (arrows from eyeleashes), 'नाजुक बदन' (having a tender body) that frequently occur in the poems of Mehjoor, celebrated Kashmiri poet (a contemporary of Zinda Kaul), who writes of refined love from an earthly rather than a religious or mystical angle. Images and terminology of earthly love, however, often occur alongside or may be seen blended with sacred images or symbols as used in the mystical poetry of diverse shades including the verse of Kashmiri Sufi poets. The language of human love related to the Divine acquires a sacred tone when handled by accomplished Sufi poets like Shams Faqir or the more modern Rasul Mir; the tone serves to suggest the Unseen or the Unutterable. The expression 'म्यानि जानानय', meaning 'my beloved', is consistently used in the concluding line of each stanza of the present poem as the refrain. Many Kashmiri love-lyrics as also mystical poems are invariably addressed to the

'जानान' (signifying not only the beloved as the object of love but also the Master). They employ the images of erotic love and some have in them a blend of sacred and profane images (as we specially notice in the poems of John Donne, well-known English Metaphysical poet of the 17th century). Zinda Kaul's poem 'सऽन्याऽस्य' (sannyasin) can thus be seen as a devotional lyric that at once conforms to the traditional form of the *leela* and deviates from it in bringing in an element of variety and novelty, as the analysis of the relevant stanzas attempted hereinafter will reveal :

> सऽन्याऽस्य बे पर्वायि मस्तानय,
> पाऽर्य हो लगय म्यानि जाननय
> O God-intoxicated, care-free Sannyasin,
> I admire you dearly, my beloved.

This is the introductory stanza — a couplet. The diction here is a blend of words from two distinct sources — the word 'सऽन्याऽस्य' (a sannyasin), rooted in Sanskrit, has been assimilated into Kashmiri, the other two words 'मस्तानय' (intoxicated mystic) and 'जानानय' (Beloved) are Persian in origin. This kind of interfusion of languages is a common phenomenon that is the direct result of cultural fusion. It happens when literatures associated with two different languages come into contact with each other through the social interaction of communities with diverse backgrounds. We notice such intermingling of words (of diverse origins) conspicuously in Kashmiri lyric poetry, produced during the 20th and the preceding 19th century.

In stanza 4, Lord Krishna is the chosen deity addressed :

> मोहन चे'ति छिया मन मोहन?
> चानि खो'तुं स्वदंरा ति वोपद्याव कांह ?
> चे'ति छुम ना सु विलज़ार बोज़ानय?
> आर यीतनय म्यानि जानानय।
> O Mohan (the charmer), is your heart too captivated?
> Is there any one born more beautiful than you?
> Doesn't he too listen to your woes?
> O my beloved, let your heart soften towards me!

Here we virtually see no difference between the poetry of earthly love and that of divine love. Onwards, in stanza 5, the Beloved is painted as a *sannyasin*, whose body is smeared with ashes — used often as the image of Lord Shiva :

अऽद्रिंमि रागॅु अगनॅु दून्य प्रज़लानय,
लूकॅु त्याग छुय न्यब्रॅु मो'लमुत सूर,
ओ'ब्रॅु तऽलय यि वुज़मल छे' द्रेठं यिवानय,
सूरॅु गोसानि म्यानि जानानय
Fire of love is ablaze within you,
And as a mark of detachment from the world
You've smeared your lustrous body with ashes,
Suggesting comparison
With a flash of lightning seen through a cloud,
O you ash-covered *gosain* (sadhu), my beloved.

In stanza 7, the beloved is depicted as himself a votary of the 'deva' (deity), which ties up with the closing line of the previous stanza no. 6 (that reads : 'पूज़ हो करय म्यानि जानानय') (I would worship you, o my beloved), confirming that the relation between the seeker and the loved one is based on love in its sacred or higher form. Verse 7 is reproduced here :

गरि गरि स्वरहरव चॅु देव सुंद द्यानय,
तोति क्याज़ि रटहक ग्‌वफ तय बाल?
मन म्योन कऽरिज़िहे खलवत–खानय,
चूरि हो थवथ म्यानि जानानय।
You would constantly meditate on the Divine,
Still why need you dwell in caves and haunt mountains?
You could retire into the 'cave' of my heart instead,
I wish I kept you there concealed from view.

These lines describe a love-relationship that looks intensely human as much as it speaks of the higher form of love, conceived as an act of pure 'worship'.

In stanza 12, the beloved is described as Shankara-like in form, with a tuft of hair in his head made into a serpentine knot :

शानन प्यठ केश छिय परेशानय,
तालि प्यठ गऽडिंत जटॅु सर्पाकार,

कालुॅ बोबुंर गन ज़न छु नाऽपानय
अबंर मोयुॅ म्यानि जानानय।
Locks of hair hang loose on your shoulders,
On the head the tuft forms a serpentine coil;
Your hair shines like a swarm of black bumble-bees,
O my fragrant-haired beloved.

In Kashmiri Sufi poetry, the image of a woman, as the 'universal sweetheart', is used sometimes to suggest the Divine. Among the marks of a woman's beauty, the seductiveness of her locks of hair is focused upon in such poetry, the locks being compared to snakes — that can 'sting', which signifies the erotic. Likewise, the black mole on the beloved (conceived as a woman) is another image that we meet with in Sufi mystical poetry. In Christian mysticism too, as mentioned particularly in an earlier chapter, special significance is attached to the concept of 'Divine Dark'. In fact, black Beauty is associated with the ultimate Reality in its transcendental aspect in mystical literature across cultures. In stanza 12 (reproduced above), Zinda Kaul's use of the image of loose hair and of the lock of hair tied into a serpentine knot as also the shining hair prompting comparison with the swarm of black bees provide unmistakable clues to his learning, especially to his familiarity with the literary sources of the images he employs.

In the concluding stanza (No. 17), the beloved is compared to a physician who alone can cure the seeker, who is love-sick, of his sickness :

यिम च्राऽन्य खतुॅ खाल याद पावानय,
दूर्यरुक दोद तान्य मऽशरान छस,
बलि दोद यऽलि वैद असि वातानय,
दाऽदिस वात म्यानि जानानय।
Remembering these features of yours,
I, for a while, forget the pain of your separation;
I can only be cured of my pain
When the physician arrives,
O my beloved physician, diagnose aright my ailment !

The image of the Beloved as the physician who alone can cure the patient afflicted with love is often used in love poetry in most cultures. The mention of the physician in the stanza here reminds us of the image used in an appropriate context by the celebrated Bhakti poet, Mira, in her poem 'हे री मैं तो प्रेम देवानी'

> दर्द की मारी बन बन डोलूं,
> वैद्य मिल्यो नहीं कोय।
> मीरा के प्रभू पीर मिटेगी,
> वैद्य सांवरिया होय।।
>
> I roamed about, in pain, through many a forest,
> But didn't come across any physician,
> My pain will cease, O my beloved Lord,
> When you act as my physician.

The poems 'शीना वालुन' (The Snow-fall) and 'सोंत' (Spring), ninth and tenth in the sequence, are very special pieces, excellent in almost all respects. They could be set beside some of the most beautiful of Mehjoor's Nature poems inasmuch as both the poems capture the scenic beauty of Kashmir in fine detail. Yet the "local colour" will not restrict the appeal of the poems to those who are fond of the Valley as Kashmiris or have enjoyed its natural beauty as visitors. Zinda Kaul's feeling for Nature, his accurate portrayal of its various aspects and his appropriate language use, that serve to convey the enchantment of the land — the cumulative effect of colour, scent and music — remind the reader of such poets as Wordsworth and Keats, of Tagore and Mehjoor, who must have been Zinda Kaul's favourites. Yet he remains distinctive and retains his individual touch in spite of what has impressed or influenced him through his reading. His descriptions are interwoven with his major thematic concerns — especially his love of God and the high place he gives to love as the means of man's deliverance. It is essentially as a singer of divine love and as a teacher dedicated to spiritual values that Zinda Kaul has earned his reputation as a noted Kashmiri poet.

The poem 'शीना वालुन' (The Snowfall) reveals Zinda Kaul's sensitive response to Nature — a perception that is at once aesthetic in a high degree and mystical in essence. There are six verses in all devoted to the description of the natural phenomenon of snowfall; they provide enough evidence of the poet's mythopoeic ability to read into the phenomenon in question a deeply religious or mystical significance. The scene is painted in all its detail with a fine Keatsian touch as it were. The pictorial quality of the first verse is note-worthy :

शीना वालुन त जूनुँगाशुव फर्शा त्रावुन,
सन्यर तुँ वो'गन्यर फम्ब–तूदन तल व्यपरावुन,
खर्वुन तुँ मलकुत कूत सो'दंर बासनावुन,
अकी जामुक नाल दो'ल पाथुल हावुन।

It has snowed heavily — the ground is covered
With a white sheet of moonlight, it seems,
And unevenness is hidden under heaps of 'cotton',
The snow makes bright what is ugly or dirty,
The high and the low are made to look
As the top and bottom of the same garment.

This verse conveys a profound perception — of the all-pervasiveness of God — through the image of widespread snow, "a white sheet of moonlight", that levels things and thus resolves differences.

How the snowfall, quietly, brings about a transformation, reducing difference to naught and establishing homogeneity, thus pointing to the divine unity that underlies all phenomena, is made explicit in the next verse :

अनुग्रह वर्षन हावि यिथुँ देव दर्शुन कुनुय,
दो'युत गाऽलित एकरस थवि पथ कुन कुनुय,
वुजुन शेंगुन ज़्यो'न मरुन, युन तुँ गछुन कुनुय,
अदंर तुँ न्यबर प्रेममय पर तुँ पनुन कुनुय।

As divine grace reveals the all-pervasive Lord,
Removing duality and unfolding Unity,
Showing that waking and sleeping, birth and death,
Coming and going, within and without, stranger and kinsman,
All such contrasts are resolved in love,
Unity prevails, just as the snowfall levels differences.

The closing verse projects the seeker as one who pines for union with the divine Master and for whom the pain of separation is unbearable :

वसवुन यि चऽद्रंम म्योन च़्यतस पाव्यस नाये ?
या शामुँ सुबहुक सोज़ि दिल म्योन बाव्यसनाये,
यरव बस्तुँ थऽर नऽस्तुँ म्योन तस्वीर हाव्यसनाये,
कुनि पाऽठय कांछ़ा माय स्नेह वुज़नाब्यसनाये।

I wish the setting moon
Prompted him to remember me,
Or, the candle fading away at morn told him
Of the love I cherish for him in my heart,
Or else, will the frozen bush
Make him visualize my plight?
Would that some one, somehow, awakened in him
Love and affection for me!

The images of the setting moon, the candle exhausted by the morning and the frozen bush, drawn from Nature, are exploited by the poet for their suggestive quality. Cumulatively they perform a symbolic function : highlight the intensity of the seeker's yearning for fulfilment in love (directed towards the Divine).

On going through the poem 'सोंत' (Spring) I feel tempted to place Zinda Kaul alongside his contemporary — the celebrated poet Mehjoor. The latter sings invariably of love and the beautiful objects of nature together, linking them as correlated entities. Though Zinda Kaul does likewise, especially in his Nature poems, there is an important difference between the attitudes of the two poets to love. Mehjoor depicts human love as the most desirable passion and as something immensely valuable in its relevance to life and man's psychological needs, generally shorn of any metaphysical or philosophical underpinnings. He does not show any explicit interest in the religious or philosophical dimension of love. For Zinda Kaul, as a poet, on the other hand, religion and metaphysics have, professedly, an essential bearing on love.

Another poet who comes to my mind on reading the poem in question is again the great English poet Wordsworth. His whole outlook on life was shaped by the high regard in which he held Nature. In his view, Nature exercises a decisive influence on human beings in forming their character. It chastens man morally and has a healing touch — the power to assuage our anguished feelings and soothe our souls. In the poem under discussion, we come across some verses which employ motifs of this kind. Here is a specimen (stanza 2) :

आरुॅ बऽठ्य मस्त फो'लमुत बेदजारो,
नीजर तम्युक दियि नेत्रन नूर,
जिगरुक ताव कासवुन सु शेहजारो।
Along the bank of the brook,
The willow grove has a luxuriant foliage :
Their green is refreshing to the eye
And their cool shade will cure heated liver;
Come forward, friend, to enjoy the delight of summer.

In Stanza 4, we come across a fine picture — that of a cascade :

आरवान्युक बलवीर शाहसवारो,
पल प्यठय सुॅह ज़न मारान छ़ाल,
दुॅह त्रावान ग्रज़वुन आबशारो,
सोंत छावनि बालयारो नेर।
The gushing water of the brook
Leaps over a rock like a tiger,
The water-fall on the other side
Roars and fumes;
Come forth to enjoy the spring, o friend.

That Zinda Kaul's use of natural description in his poems of love involves sacred images and carries religious overstones is evident from stanza 5 of the poem :

अज़ं मज़ं नच़वुन बादि कौ बहारो,
नारुद ज़ाऩ स्वर्गॅु प्यठ आमुत!
प्रथ जायि युन तऽम्यसुदं ख्वशगवारो,
सोंत छावनि बालुयारो नेर।
The spring-breeze dancing
In the midst of all,
Reminds one of Narada's descent from heaven,
Who is welcome everywhere;
Come forth, O friend, to enjoy spring.

In stanza 11, there is evidence of Zinda Kaul's mythopoeic faculty in his use of a conceit :

पोषि बऽरगन आसि गोमुत खारो
सबज़स प्यठ वथरावान पान
असि प्यठुॅय पकिनाज़ि ख्वशरफतारो,
सोंत छावनि नबबहारो नेर।

Driven by jealousy, flower petals
Will lay themselves flat on the green grass;
"Would that the fine-gaited beloved
Walked over us rather than on the green",
So would they desire;
Come forth, Oh friend, to enjoy the spring!!

Obviously the poet's mythopoeic faculty is at work in weaving the threads of a story, as it were, drawn from a natural phenomenon : the fall of wind-dispersed petals which are conceived as lying flat on the turf so that they would take delight in being trampled upon by the beloved Guest, who is invited to come.

In stanza 13, the poet brings in "celestial singers" that can be linked with Narada, mentioned in stanza 5 — the highest divine singer, who functions as a messenger between gods (as mentioned in our epics and *puranas*) :

गन्धर्व यिन वायन सेतारो!
गायन वुज़नावि विगिन्यन सोज़!
मजुॅ रऽस्यत्यन ति साज़ वज़नावे तारो,
सोंत छावनि बालयारो नेर।

Celestial singers will come and play their *sitars*,
Their singing will awaken the souls of musical fairies,
The instrumental music will touch
The inner chords of even those
Who have no ear for music;
Come forth to enjoy spring, my friend.

In stanza 14, the poet dwells on the transitoriness of life — the short-livedness of youth and spring. He offers it as a plea, on behalf of the seeker, to induce the Beloved to come forward (and not shy away!), the season being propitious for lovers to meet.

The same logic is developed further in the concluding stanza (No. 15) into a persuasive argument :

> नेर फेर छाव गुलशन तुँ कोंहसारो,
> दयिगत वुछवुय छि दय सुँजं पूज़!
> सो'य पूज़ न्यथ करान बीना दारो,
> सोतं छावनि बालयारो नेर।
>
> Come out, move around and enjoy gardens and hillsides,
> Enjoying God's wonderful works as true worship :
> What the wise always perform;
> So, come forth to enjoy spring, O dear friend.

After the two Nature poems 'शीना वालुन' (The Snowfall) and 'सोंत' (Spring), there are three lyrics 'यीछा जान' (Is this right?), 'मिलाप' (Meeting) and 'वनन मंज़ लाल' (Gems in wilderness) in Section I of the *Smaran*. The first two lyrics are very closely related thematically. 'यीछा जान' (Is this right?) is a very short lyric, consisting of just three stanzas. It is a plaint from the 'persona', the female aspirant, addressed to the beloved conceived as the Divine. She expresses her grouse to him — that he frustrated her after making a benevolent gesture of love, withdrew immediately the gift he had offered her; took her hand, kindled hope in her and then abandoned her, thus breaking her heart. This is the gist of the three verses. The third stanza is reproduced here :

> मनवारि म्यानि आशुँ पोश रुवनाऽविथ,
> सग दित वारुँ फो'लनाऽविथ,
> पानय को'रथस फान मस्ताना।
> यी छा जान?
>
> Of your own accord, you planted
> Flowers of hope in my heart's garden,
> Watered them with care and made them bloom;
> Then you uprooted them yourself,
> Is this right, my inebriated love?

In the next poem 'मिलाप' (Meeting), which is much longer and contains 13 verses, the Beloved is addressed as 'जोगिराय' (Sovereign Yogi) and the 'persona' seeker is, as usual, a female. The first three verses convey a plaint addressed to the Beloved as the whole of the preceding poem does. The 'persona' pleads that she has been hood-winked in love. Initially, the Beloved, she says, revealed himself to her, raised hopes in her and then soon deserted her. The tone of the poem changes in stanza 4, with the 'persona' sounding conciliatory; it (tone) becomes reassuring and optimistic in later stanzas. Stanza 4 bears out the tonal change :

यव किन्य व्यसो'म छे' कोमल ह्रदयस कठोर वाऽनी
ग्रावन दिमव यऽती छ्यन बस म्यानि जोगिरायो।

Since it is unbecoming of me to speak harshly
To a soft-hearted person (like you),
Let us stop complaining here and now,
O my sovereign yogi.

The speaker in the next verse (No. 6) blesses the Beloved mother-like, wishing him long life :

भगवान सोन बूज़िन असि चाऽन्य आश रूज़िन,
हथ वाऽसिं माजि माऽलिस लस म्यानि जोगिरायो।

May God grant that we
Continue to pin our hopes on you (for favours),
That you live a hundred years
To the joy of your parents.

The beloved is further blessed in verse 7 :

न्यथ इषृदेव सऽद्यंन पंपोष पादन तल,
बोबुंर बऽनिथ चवान गछ़ रस म्यानि जोगि रायो।

May you ever drink nectar
Like a bumble bee,
From the lotus-feet of your chosen Deity!

In the following verse (No. 9), the devotional character of the poem is made explicit by the poet. His major concern with the pursuit of the Divine through love (as the only means) finds adequate expression here :

दयि सुंद प्रसाद सतज़न भक्तन छि बाऽगरावान,
प्रेमुक चवान तुॅ चावान मस म्यानि जोगिरायो।

Holy men share God's *prasad* with the devotees
They drink the holy wine of love
And make others too drink it.

The 12th verse is significant :

यव किन्य चुँ परमुँ त्याऽगी लो'ग छुख नुँ राज़द्वारन,
यथ फुटि मुँतिस मनस मज़ं बस म्याऽनि जोगिरायो।
As you're a man of great renunciation
And do not seek palaces,
Pray, dwell in my broken heart,
O my sovereign yogi.

The last poem of Section I, titled 'वनन मंज़ लाल' (Gems in Wilderness) is a significant piece providing a fitting close to the sequence. We find in it a reaffirmation of the poet's belief in the divinity of love. He ascribes the utmost value to human love as a means of attaining union with the Divine. It is the human heart that is valued as man's priceless possession. Its cultivation as the temple of love is emphasized and considered the best form of *sadhana*. Zinda Kaul's own voice and his cherished views on spirituality find adequate articulation in the repeated emphasis laid on God's immanence in the poem under discussion and the preceding ones — Love is seen as man's indwelling Self.

The poem is narrative in form. The poet, as the narrator, speaks of the experiences of the "love-sick" heart as having been transported by some mysterious wind into the "garden of love". This is what we gather from verses 1-2. The narrative is continued in a long sequence of 20 more verses. Verse 3 reads :

मस्त गव युथ कांह वुडर तापस पऽकित,
त्रावि ने'न्दुॅर बोनि शेहजारस अंदर।
There it (the heart) felt intoxicated with bliss
As one having trudged in the scorching sun
May fall asleep in the shade of a chinar.

It felt as if returning parched from the plains of India, it had plunged into the ice-cold water of the Sind valley in Laar (Kashmir). Stanzas 5 and 6 are very suggestive :

तोशिवुॅन्य या होशुॅ आमऽच़ गोपिया,
रोशि च़ामच़ रासकिस आरस अंदर।
As a gopi (shepherd girl/woman) may have found
her way

Unobserved into the rasa-ring (a ring formed by dancers),
And experienced consciousness-bliss.

अंदर गडंस मज़ं वुछिन आज़ाऽदिया,
न्यबर गऽडिंत ओस मो'क जारस अन्दर।

Inside (the ring), it found real freedom in bondage,
And outside, bondage was pervasive
Though things were seemingly free.

The two verses sum up Zinda Kaul's philosophy of life. Based on the principles of *Vedanta*, the philosophy conforms to the teachings of the *Bhagavatam*, glorifying Krishna's way of love. Precisely speaking, Zinda Kaul advocates a philosophy that synthesises the ways of love and knowledge, constituting the core of Krishna's teaching in the *Gita*. In line with this philosophy, the accomplished yogi looks upon God as his indwelling Self and as the soul of the Universe. Likewise, he sees both human and divine love as rooted in the Self. For Zinda Kaul, again, there is no dichotomy or antithesis between 'Form' and the 'Formless' as verse 9 bears out :

बूज़मुत तऽम्य ओस दय ड़यूठुन मनुष,
युस निराकारुँय छु आकारस अंदर।

It (the heart) had heard of God
Whom it saw, in fact, as only Man —
The very formless manifest as form.

It is relevant here to refer to the Persian mystic, Mansur-ul-Hallaj, who had to pay the price of his own life for daring to say 'अन–अल–हक' (I am Truth). The widely read scholar that Zinda Kaul was, he was aware of the common message of Vedanta and Sufism : that all men are potentially divine and that God is reachable through love. This is emphasized in verse 11 :

षय बऽनित डयूठुन रगन मंज़ दोरवुन,
बाग बनुँ नुक शोक प्रत खारस अंदर।

It saw, coursing through the fibres of every thorn,
The aspiration to become the Garden itself.

The close relationship that subsists between the Divine and the human heart is beautifully described in verse 13 :

दिल छु लोल बेबहा इनसान सुदं,
दय छु लोलुक शोलुँ दिलदारस अंदर।
The human heart is a priceless ruby,
And God is the glow of love in the noble-hearted.

Stanzas 14-16 emphasize that the loving heart has one essential characteristic, it is a close kin of pain and suffering. One who loves truly has to go through the penance of pain to achieve illumination, that leads to union with the Divine. Fine images illustrative of spirituality are presented in stanzas 17 and 18 :

लाल ज़ज़रित ताज़ुँ गोमुत लोल दाग,
संग असवद रवस्तुँ देवारस अंदर।
The black scar of love has become the fresher
Within the tulip that has got withered;
The scar looks like the sacred black stone
Of Mecca set in a dilapidated wall.

गोलमुत फाकव तुँ फुकरव सूँत्य पान,
नुन्दुँ ऋष ज़न तप करान गारस अंदर।
Having got emaciated through fasts and self-denials,
She was reminded of Nunda-rishi,
Practising *tapas* (penance) in a cave.

The references to the 'black stone' sacred to the Muslims, and to Nunda Rishi, who inspired the Rishi-cult in Kashmir among the Muslims and won esteem as a younger contemporary of Lal Ded through his *shrukhs*, are appropriate in the present poem devoted to a spiritual theme. Together with the earlier allusion to Mansur-ul-Hallaj, the references give us an idea of Zinda Kaul's breadth of outlook and his catholicity as a mystical poet.

Verses 20-22 continue to highlight (i) the value of human love as the means of man's union with the Divine, and (ii) the significance of pain as a concomitant of the experience of love, that is vital to the achievement of self-purification. The concluding stanza throws light on the title of the poem :

यिम वनन मज़ं लाल डेशन ज़ाऽन्य वाऽल्य,
मेलुँ वुँन्य तिम मा छि बाज़रस अंदर।

Such diamonds as are seen in forests
By those who can spot them,
Are not available in common markets.

Here Zinda Kaul is drawing our attention to the fact that advanced mystics, the *rindas*, are a rare phenomenon; they form a microscopic minority and are not to be found in places commonly frequented. And they are accessible to the select few who have a discerning eye. Such mystics are, in fact, the very men who have cultivated the human heart.

## NOTES AND REFERENCES

1. Kashmiri verse is tranliterated into Devnagri (the Govt. approved script having been used for transliteration in a separate edition of the book).
2. For this and other biographical details concerning Zinda Kaul, I have drawn upon Dr. A.N. Raina's book titled *Zinda Kaul* brought out by the Sahitya Akademi, New Delhi in 1974.
3. The quotes used here are from Wordsworth's well-known poem 'Tintern Abey'.
4. Henceforth too Zinda Kaul's translations will be given as rendered into free-verse form by me (retaining mostly his language with minimal alterations).
5. See A.N. Dhar. *Mysticism in Literature*, Atlantic Publishers and Distributors, Delhi, 1985, pp. 55-56.
6. Translated (by the present writer) from the Hindi paraphrase of the Sanskrit verse provided in the *Shivastotravali* of Utpaladeva, edited with Hindi commentary by Rajnaka Laxmana, Chowkhamba Sanskrit Series Office, Varanasi-1, 1964. Also see N.K. Kotru's *Sivastotravali of Utpaladeva*, Motilal Banarsidass, Delhi, 1985, p. 63.

# 8

# Swami Govind Kaul and Shams Faqir : Affinities as Mystical Poets

IN PART I of this chapter, I shall attempt to present an overview of some samples of the lyric verse of the saint-poet Swami Govind Kaul and noted Sufi poet Shams Faqir. The aim herein is to properly introduce the two poets through my English translation of their select textual pieces, followed by my brief comments and observations on them. The idea is to indicate what broadly their thematic concerns are and how, as mystical poets, they communicate their perceptions of the Divine and how they suggest their profound experiences through image and symbol. Finally, in part II, I shall take up two select lyrics of each poet that I have translated into English for the specific requirements of this chapter. I shall analyse the poems in order to show how appropriately Govind Kaul has used some concepts and images of the Sufis and likewise how effectively Shams Faqir has employed the vocabulary of our *shastras* while handling parallel concepts. The basic idea of the chapter is, in fact, to illustrate the intermingling of diverse cultural streams in Kashmiri mystical poetry — related to the Indian Vedanta/Bhakti and Sufism.

## PART I

Well-known in the Valley of Kashmir as a saint-poet, Swami Govind Kaul has made a special impact in recent years on the displaced Kashmiri Pandits through his posthumously published poems. His devotional songs have also reached *bhaktas* (devotees) beyond his close followers through the audio-cassette in which the songs are recorded in the voice of the famous

Kashmiri singer, Arti Tiku. That is, in fact, how I myself first came to know of the saint-poet. What is remarkable about his poetic compositions is the richness of their content; his spiritual knowledge is well matched by his expressive power as a poet. A fairly large number of his poems are unobtrusively didactic and lyrical at the same time — they serve to convey an *updesh* (spiritual instruction) to the aspirant in a delightful way. Govind Kaul impresses us with his informal learning as also with his intimate knowledge of the Mystic Way, based on his own experience or *sadhana*. How do we explain his impressive knowledge, especially his grasp of the *shastras* (our scriptural texts) including the *Upanishads*, and his awareness of the native Shaivite and Shakhta doctrines?

On the basis of what little biographical information about the Swami is available from the preface to his book of poems titled *Govind Amrit* (1975), it could be maintained that he had virtually no formal education and the only language that he spoke was his mother-tongue, Kashmiri. It is, therefore, quite amazing to note the wide range of concepts and terms, related to yoga and *irfaan* (connected with Sufi Mysticism) alike, that we come across in appropriate contexts in his poems. His understanding of some of the crucial concepts related to the Mystic Way is thorough, revealed specially in his ability to achieve a synthesis of the corresponding images and concepts drawn from two or more cultural streams.

Before the diffusion of learning took place in this country and elsewhere through the written word, in the form of hand-written manuscripts, followed later by the printed word, some of the illiterate in various communities managed to have access to knowledge, that became mainly possible because of what was then handed down by word of mouth and acquired through aural culture. That should explain the startling "learning" of such master-minds among great saints as Sri Ramakrishna Parmahams though his own innate wisdom was his main qualification as a world teacher. However, in the case of Swami Govind Kaul, the saint-poet we are immediately concerned with, the poetic gift is as remarkable as his "learning" acquired through cultural assimilation.

One significant biographical fact about Swami Govind Kaul is that he was a nephew (sister's son) of the celebrated Kashmiri poet, Krishan Joo Razdan, known to be unrivalled as the master of devotional lyrics, most of which are superb in quality. The nephew's lyrical gift too found expression in his devotional poems — *bhajans* and *leelas*. This gift can be attributed both to the genetic factor and to the influence the elder poet might have had on Govind Kaul as a youngster during the latter's formative years. In one of his poems, the younger poet acknowledges his debt to his "maternal uncle, the saint". Judging by the quality of the poems published under the title *Govind Amrit* it can be maintained that most of them are pieces of accomplished verse. Lyrical and at once packed with thought, they present a variety in respect of both content and form. As their titles indicate, they constitute a number of sequences addressed variously to (i) the Divine Mother, (ii) Lord Shiva, (iii) Lord Krishna, (iv) the Gurus, (v) saints, etc. Likewise a sequence of poems is devoted to the theme of 'लोल' or love in its human and divine form — the poems sing of the pain of separation and of the joy of union. Several poems, here and there, dwell on the theme of Self-hood — consisting in an assertion of man's innate divinity culminating in Self/God-realization. A number of poems scattered through the volume can be grouped together as the poems of meditation. We gather from these poems vital clues to Swami Govind Kaul's spiritual affiliation to the founder of the Radha Swami cult — Guru Dayal, who was known earlier as Shiv Bharat Lal Varman, noted author of many books. Swami Govind Kaul was among the disciples of Guru Dayal, and had been initiated by him into *Surat Sabda Yoga*.

We come across the terminology of the Radha Swami cult in a large number of Govind Kaul's poems. We also notice in his poems a fusion of images, symbols and metaphors that have a direct or indirect bearing on *Kundalini* yoga, some of them being specially associated with Persian Sufism and the related theme of the Mystic Way including the concept of *irfaan* or spiritual *gnosis*.

From among the poems addressed to the Divine Mother, let us turn briefly to the one titled 'निर्मल ब्वद कर में'सरस्वती' (Oh Saraswati, make my intellect pure). Here are some lines from the poem (followed immediately by my translation; the remaining verses of the poet Govind Kaul as also the verses of Shams Faqir provided in this chapter are likewise followed immediately by the translations attempted by me) :

> निर्मल ब्वद कर में सरस्वती, माऽर्यमऽती हय तम्बॅुलोवुस,
> दीशि कालुॅ रो'स्त छुय निर्वासॅुय, क्याज़ि को'र्थस बो' उदासॅुय,
> वादुॅ थविथ प्रारस बो' तऽती, मार्यमऽती हय तम्बॅुलोवुस।
> Make my intellect pure, O goddess Saraswati,
> The ardent lover has made me restless;
> Abiding beyond the realm of time and space,
> He has frustrated me (why, I would like to know?)
> I wish he promised to meet me at an appointed place,
> I would await his arrival there!

The poet invokes the aid of Saraswati, goddess of knowledge, being aware that he must attain self-purification in order to be able to realize the Self, perceived both as the indwelling and all-pervading spirit. Govind Kaul conceives of the ultimate Reality as transcendental in character — as the Reality beyond time, space and causation. Essentially, the universal Self has no name and form; being the nameless One, it has no lineage and belongs to no clan. It is the "One without the second". Here are the relevant lines that convey, in essence, how the Self is to be perceived :

> क्याज़ि छांडान न्यबर चॅुहिये, मनसॅुय मज़ं पानस छुय,
> मन साऽरवी यस लाग हीय फो'ती, माऽर्यमऽती हय तम्बॅुलोवुस।
> Why are you looking for the jasmines outside?
> The plant is rooted in your mind,
> That bears witness to the Lord
> You should adore with basketfuls of jasmines;
> That very ardent lover has deprived me of rest.

The next cluster of lyrics is devoted to the praise of Lord Shiva, who is addressed by other names too — Mahadeva, Sada Shiva, Param Shiva, Hara, etc. Reproduced below are a few lines from the poem titled 'बर्यम लोल कर्यम नुॅ तारि' (He will offer me love in full and not let me down) :

लोलुॅ ही फो'ज्य हृदयिचि दारि, तथ कलुॅ दारि सदाशिव,
लो'लुॅ पोश सुय तस कित्य च़ारि, मे' तिहो तारि सदाशिव।
सुय तस होरि युस तस दारि, चे'ति हो छ़ारि सदाशिव,
ग्वरुॅ शब्दस रवस सवारि, प्यठ ताकुॅ दारि सदाशिव।

Jasmines, expressive of love, have bloomed
Around my heart's casement,
Lord Shiva will let his head be adorned with them;
I'll look for select flowers to adorn Him,
Who will deliver me,
And every one else by turns,
Across *sansar* (temporal existence);
The Lord will seek you too
And you will repay what you owe Him;
Mounted on the Guru's word
Soar to the window where Shiva is seated.

In many a poem, Govind Kaul sings in praise of the Guru and saints, dwelling on what sainthood involves and how important divine grace is for the spiritual seeker — that descends on him through a human being who is usually a saint, an accomplished Guru. Often, the divine qualities associated with the various incarnations of God — call him Shiva or Kesva — are also described as the attributes of a saint seen in the role of a Guru or Godman.

In the poem 'सत चित आनंद अखंड अगादुॅय' (existence-consciousness-bliss, indivisible, infinite), saints are thus described :

गरे दय लो'बुख तिमय गऽयि सादुॅय,
दमुॅ दमुॅ दमुॅनुॅय सूॅत्यन दम सह।
ब्रम च़ऽलिथ पथ छु सूहम दम सह,
रवसुॅ वसुॅ दम करान यी समादुॅय।

They're the saints
Who found God (in themselves),

Restraining their breath every moment,
Overcame the illusion (of duality),
Inhaling and exhaling — breath moving up and down,
Conversed with God (the indwelling Self)
Followed by *samadhi* (union with God).

In the poem that follows, titled 'सतचित आनंद निर्मल' (existence-consciousness-bliss pure), Govind Kaul, asserting man's innate divinity, says that God is One indivisible realised as 'Shivoham' (I am Shiva) :

सत चित आनंद निर्मल, सुय कीवल शिवोहम,
सोरुय ज़ान पनुन पान, पानस ब्यन के'हं मो ज़ान।

He who is consciousness-bliss-existence
Absolute and Pure,
Is the indwelling Self, the one Reality
Perceived as "I am Shiva,"
Know your own Self as all-in-all,
There's none other than you.

This theme of realizing the Self as the ultimate Reality is reiterated by the poet in numerous lyrics, and the saints, in particular, are credited with its attainment. Here are some relevant quotations from the poems that dwell on the significance of sainthood and the role of saints in promoting spiritual knowledge/awareness :

संत छिग बे परागाग, तिमन छ़ाग दिलस नो,

The saints are care-free,
Their hearts are taintless (Poem No. 32, *Govind Amrit*)

सतंव ज़ोगुय व्यच़ोरुय, यि छु सोरुय गोवेंद,
मुच़रोवहम पानुँ तोरुय, यि छु सोरुय गोवेंद।

The saints came to know through contemplation
All that we behold is Govinda (Divine),
It's they who threw open to me
The door of the spiritual realm,
Making me realize that all is Govinda Himself.
(Poem No. 33, *Govind Amrit*)

संतो वऽन्य द्यू पनुँनिस पानस, पनुँनिस पानस तील्यज़े,
पनुँनिस पानस श्री भगवानस, पनुँनिस पानस तील्यज़े।

Oh you saint, look within yourself,
Leave nothing unexplored to know your self —
That is none other than the Divine.

On the basis of his own spiritual experience (*sadhana*) as a spiritual seeker, and the knowledge of his own saintly life as he lived it, Govind Kaul has recognized the true value of sainthood and the intrinsic worth of a true saint. He has realized the great value of self-inquest that alone serves the seeker as the master-key with which to unlock the doors of divine perception. So his advice to the aspiring saint is to "look within" and unravel the divine mystery for himself.

Let us now look at a few of Govind Kaul's poems to know specifically what they offer us on the technique of meditation. I quote first these lines from the poem 'ग्वरुँ द्यान कर त्रे'य बंद बंद' (Meditate on the Guru, close the three doors) :

ग्वरुँ द्यान कर त्रे'य बंद बंद कन थव वज़न छुय नाद,
पांछ़ नाव सुमरनुँय कऽरिथ ब्रूँमदि कुन दृष्टी दऽरिथ ब्यदं,
सो'रिथ गुरू च़रनार ब्यदं, कन थाव वज़न छुय नादुँ ब्यद्,
ज्योति हुन्दुय नज़ारु वुछ फो'लिथ सहसरार वुछ।
ओंकार वुछ ओंकार ब्यदं, कन थाव वज़न छुय नादुँ ब्यदं
वुछुन अऽछव किन्य सु दय, आकाशिसुँय मंज़ गंड मुदय,
उदय बने गऽयि रौ तुँ च़ंद, कन थाव वज़न छुय नादुँ ब्यदं।।

Meditate on the Guru, close the three doors,
Hear the creative sound, emanating from the point of Light,
Chant the five names, fixing your gaze
On the midpoint between the eyebrows,
Contemplate on the Guru's lotus-feet
And hear the divine sound;
Enjoy the beauty of the Flame, the crown-chakra all illuminated,
Perceive the Omkar along with the still point
And hear the musical *nada-bindu* (creative sound and light),
The sun and the moon will come into your view,
Listen to the creative sound
Emanating from the still point (of light).

These lines make it abundantly clear that Govind Kaul has had a first-hand experience of inward illumination. He adopts the vocabulary of the Radha-Swami cult to shed light on the various preparatory steps that the seeker has to negotiate in order to have a direct encounter with the Divine. It is actually what is called the technique of Surat Sabda Yoga that the poet advocates as a spiritual teacher. He directs the aspirant to turn his or her inward gaze on the *ajnya* chakra (the central point in the forehead immediately above the eyebrows) where illumination is experienced. When the practitioner of yoga concentrates on this point, the "inner space" is lit up and, at the same time, "sound of silence" or "unstruck music" is heard by him. With his inward gaze turned upward to the illumined "sky within", he feels ecstatic and attains an awareness of the Divine. In this yogic state, the seeker experiences pure consciousness-bliss.

For a more explicit and detailed account of the technique of meditation, let us turn to Govind Kaul's poem 'भवुँ दुख कासि दियि तार' (He will cure us of our mundane pains). The technique conforms to the steps prescribed in our scriptures such as the *Gita* (specifically in the 6th chapter titled 'yoga of meditation'). Here is the core of the poem :

बेह ईकांतुँ जाये, सूत्य प्रेमुँ तुँ माये,
बऽडरिथ श्रधाये, स्वर सुय नाव जुवो।
बऽन्यियिज़ि न्यर वासन, दाऽर्यिज़ि स्यद्ध आसन,
रवाऽर्यिज़ि ह्यसुँ श्वासन, त्राव लो'त वाव ज़ुँवो।
ह्योर कुनुय नज़र कर, लोलुँ सूँत्य मनुँय बर,
नेरिय पानय शर, बर मुच़राव जुवो।
श्यद कर च्यत आकाश, चमकान ज्योति प्रकाश,
ज़न लछ सिरियि शाबाश, छुय मन पाव जुवो।
अछ़ वुछन अंदर गाश, अऽन्द्रिम सिर मकर फाश,
पापन बनी नाश, ग्वरुँ आश थाव जुवो।
अछ़ बर दारि त्रोपराव, यियि वुछरव तिय व्यपराव,
सू सू चुँ' श्रो'पराव, हमसू त्राव जुवो।
तत शब्दस नुँ छे'नुँय, शब्दस थव कनुँय,
तूर्य कुन गडं मनुँय, कर मो ग्राव जुवो।

सत ग्वर तति यिये आलव हा चे़'ति दिये,
पानस सॅूत्य निये, युस छ़ांज़ाव जुवो।
Sit at a solitary spot
With intense love, faith and devotion,
Chant the divine name :
Adopting *Sidhasana* posture,
Rise above desires,
And inhale with care,
Letting the air out slowly,
Filling the mind with love,
Turn your gaze upward,
You will attain what you seek —
Open the door, discern the pure *aakash* (ethereal space)
And the luminous flame
Bright as thousand suns,
Bravo, curb your mind;
Mark the interior light,
Keeping what you perceive as a secret;
Depend on the Guru, you'll be purged of your sins,
Look within, sealing all doors and windows,
And don't give out what you see;
Listen to and assimilate the music
Of the continuous 'सू' (He)
And let go the sound 'हं' (I);
Listen to the inward melody,
Your mind fully attuned to it,
And do not have any grouse, whatsoever,
The Sadguru you seek will meet you there,
He will take you under his care.

From the above piece, we can easily infer that Govind Kaul must have been an adept in the art of meditation, well-versed in *Raja Yoga* — performing the various steps with perfect care and with all the alertness of mind. The yogic posture recommended in the poem as *sidhasana* and the choice of a tranquil spot, away from noise and various distractions, are the essential requirements for one to achieve stability in meditation. Writing from his own experience of inward illumination — which must have been the fruit of his sustained *sadhana* — Govind Kaul's account of the spiritual path sounds authentic. As a follower of the Radha Swami cult, he is imaginably recounting in verse his first-hand experience of *Surat Sabda Yoga* as maintained earlier : silent chanting of the mystic word 'soham' accompanying the inflow and outflow of air through the nostrils and the resultant inward vision, the gaze directed upward toward the "inner space" flooded with effulgence.

We will now look briefly at two poems of Govind Kaul's on divine love which are highly lyrical, charged with religious feeling and, at the same time, Sufistic in vein. They have a lot in common, in terms of tone and imagery, with Mehjoor's poems of human love which one wouldn't ordinarily categorize as religious lyrics. Here are some verses from Govind Kaul's poem 'कन थाव्यम ज़ारुँ पारस' (He will listen to my prayer) :

कन थाव्यम ज़ारुँ पारस, वनतय यारस लो,
बुल्बुल छुस इतिंज़ारस गुल्ज़ारस लो,
छुय मुबारख नव बहारस वनतय यारस लो।
यियि कर दियि करारस बेकरारस लो,
वैद्य प्रॅछिना बेमारस, वनतय यारस लो।
फुलय लऽज्य गुल्ज़ारस बुति प्रारस लो,
सब्जी फेरि शेहजारस, बुति प्रारस लो।
लोलुॅकि फम्वारस, आबशारस लो,
सर वदंयो बऽ सरदारस वनतय यारस लो।
साऽरी छ़िय इतिंज़ारस, दीदारस लो,
अऽस्यति छा कुनि शुमारस, वनतय यारस लो।
नचुॅ अचुॅसुॅय मंज़ आरस ताजदाररा लो,
लोलुॅ पोशी बुति चारस, वनतय यारस लो।
लोलुँ तीर आव शिकारस, सर बऽ दारस लो,

Pray, tell my friend to listen to my request,
A nightingale, I am longing for the garden;
Hail the spring season, when will the Beloved come
And give me peace, restless as I am?
Being his patient, will he not
See me as the physician?
The garden is now in bloom, I'll wait for my love!
Tell my friend that verdure will appear

Where there is shade;
Love will gush forth as a fountain,
(let him come)
I'll offer my head for my Master (Chieftain),
All are waiting anxiously for him!
Although I am of no consequence,
I'll dance and join the ring
As the crowned one comes;
I too shall offer him select flowers of love,
And bow to him as the victim of his love's arrow!

The vocabulary and tone of the poem suggest that it is a love-lyric comparable to those of the famous Kashmiri poet, Mehjoor. However, in the following lines of the poem, we notice the occurrence of sacred words 'सतज़न' (the true), 'शिवजी गगांदरस' (Lord Shiva from whose hair flows the *Ganges*) and 'अवतारस' (incarnation) :

सतज़न बीठ्य शेहजारस, वनतय यारस लो,
शिवजी गगांदरस, अवतारस लो।
The true *bhaktas* (devotees) sat in the shade,
Pray, convey my word to Lord Shiva, the incarnate God,
From whose hair flows the (perennial) *Ganges*.

These words naturally provide a religious touch to the lyric; they alter the tone into the sacred, distinguishable from that of a poem concerned with sensuous love.

The next poem from the *Govind Amrit* that we shall discuss is titled 'तम्बुॅलाऽविथ चो़'लुम यार' (My friend tempted me and left me). The poem can pass as much for a love lyric, pure and simple, as for a mystical poem dealing with divine love, reminding us of the sacred lyrics of the Sufis. Let us consider these lines, in which the speaker is a 'female' addressing another female sympathetic to the former's woes :

तम्बुॅलाऽविथ चो़'लुम यार, बे आर हय वे'सिये,
वन्य नय छुम करार, बे आर हय वे'सिये!
छावव सब्ज़ सब्जार, करसन यियि बहार,
बुलबुल वुछि गुल्ज़ार, बेखार हय वे'सिये।
बोज़ान कोनुं छुम ज़ार, आमुतुय छुम मे' चार,

गोमुत छुस बेमार, बेकार हय वेसिये।
तन मन को'र निसार, तस पथुँय लो'कुँचार,
दज़ुँवुन नार समसार, युथ कांह नय बाऽज़ीगार,
अशिच छम चलन दार, फम्वार हय वे'सिये।
अंदर अऽच़िथ ओ'मकार, स्वर ज़ुवुँ बारम्बार,
कनदार बोज़ स्वय तार, सेतार हय वे'सिये।
लोलस ह्युव न मज़ुँदार कांह चीज़ करतुँ वे'चार,
गोविन्दुँ यियि गुफ़्तार, असरार हय वे'सिये।।

O friend, the Beloved tempted me,
And then the pitiless one left me alone,
Depriving me of my cheer!
When will he come again
As welcome spring,
When we'll enjoy verdure all-around?
The nightingale will be delighted
To see the garden in bloom, with no thorns around;
Helplessly sick, I don't know what to do,
Why doesn't he listen to my wailing?
I seek only the beloved Friend,
Having sacrificed my all for him —
Body, mind and youth!
This world is unbearable as fire —
Most deceitful as the tricky juggler,
Tears course down my eyes fountain-like
(Distressed as I am),
O my self, go within,
Contemplating the syllable Om constantly,
Listen to the tune of the *sitar*
(inner melody of the soul);
The truth is that there's nothing
Sweet as love;
This is the secret doctrine
That Govinda has to convey.

The poem employs some significant images depicting the relationship between the individual soul and God as essentially no different from a human relationship based on love. What, however, distinguishes divine love from human love is the former's high intensity and its abiding quality. Divine love is free from the taint of worldliness, looking beyond earthly love to the soul's union with God. The spiritual seeker looks for the Beloved in the depth of his own soul or psyche and hears the melody of the indwelling Master. The poem in question, on the whole, sings of a love that is mystical in character, not ordinarily communicable. However, it can be suggested poetically through appropriate literary figures — images and symbols involving analogies.

There are quite a few poems in the *Govind Amrit* that are devoted to the theme of Self-hood, involving inquiries into the nature of the indwelling Self. For a class of seekers, self-knowledge is of supreme value and importance. They consider it as the sole means of man's emancipation. For them, God-realization is possible only through the conquest of the little self by the higher Self. Here is an illustrative piece from the *Govind Amrit* :

प्रथ प्रभातन न्यथ व्यच़ोरुम, सत व्यच़ोरुम सू तुॅं सू
ओ'मुय ओ'म दम ह्यथ व्यच़ोरुम, सत व्यच़ोरुम सू तुॅं सू।
चुॅय ओसुख तुॅं चुॅय आसख चुॅय दो'हय सनातन,
ब्रोंठ कुन चुॅय पथ व्यच़ोरुम, सत व्यच़ोरुम सू तुॅं सू।
ने'ति श्वद्ध असंग छुख ने'ति म्वख्त, सत चित आनंद प्रकाश,
परि पूरण नब वत व्यच़ोरुम, सत व्यच़ोरुम सू सुॅं सू।
चान्यन पादन सतंन साधन, आदन बाजन लगयो,
सोरुये भगवत व्यच़ोरुम, सत व्यच़ोरुम सू तुॅं सू।
दीवन ति द्वर्लब छु मनुशि शऽरीर, युथ दीह प्राऽविथ,
यि दम मे' गऽनीमत व्यच़ोरुम, सत व्यच़ोरुम सू तुॅं सू।
गोवे'न्दुॅय छु वीदव ग्यो'व युस, उपनीशदव तुॅं पुरानव,
सु कुस तुॅं बुॅं कुस न्यथ व्यच़ोरुम, सत व्यच़ोरुम सू तुॅं सू।
सत संगुॅय अमृत व्यच़ोरुम, सत व्यच़ोरुम सू तुॅं सू।।

I meditated regularly on Him every morning
As the embodiment of Truth,
Holding my breath, I concentrated on the syllable Om,
And thought constantly of you as eternally abiding —
In the past, present and future;
You're ever pure, unattached and free,
Truth-consciousness-Bliss in one, Self-luminous,

I conceived of you as the whole — the sky above;
I perceived all as divine and as the Truth,
I wish to make an offering of myself
To your feet, to the saints and to my childhood friend;
Knowing that the human birth is a rare gift,
Difficult even for the *devas* to attain,
I thought how amazing it is
That in spite of this, man doesn't seek the divine,
So valuing the present moment, I meditated on Him;
The Vedas, Upanishads and Puranas —
All sang of Govinda himself as the Divine,
I constantly thought of "He and I" as referring only
to Him,
And realized that associating with the holy
Serves as the divine nectar
That confers immortality on the seeker.

In a nutshell, on the basis of the samples of Govind Kaul's verse examined in this chapter so far and taking into account his approaches to the Divine as a saint-poet, it can be maintained about him that he is a devotional poet and, at the same time, he is capable of metaphysical speculation; he is also well-versed in the art and technique of meditation. Above all, however, he is a follower of the path of Self-knowledge. His utmost concern is the attainment of self-realization. And this calls for harnessing of all mental powers — devotional intensity matched by self-introspection and self-analysis — to apprehend the Unseen. He identifies the Transcendent as well as the Immanent with Govinda — his own name signifying the indwelling Self that he conceives as no different from the ultimate Reality.

We now turn to Shams Faqir, in whose case too no authentic biography is available. As mentioned in the earlier chapter on the poet, it is said about him that through his early upbringing at home and later under the influence of some seasoned teachers, he was drawn to the Qadri Sufi order. Having got married as a young man of 25 years, he led the life of a householder; yet he lived throughout in the true spirit of a Sufi saint. There are 96 of his poems included in the anthology titled *Kashmiri Sufi Shairi* brought out in 1985 by the J&K Academy of Art, Culture and Languages, Srinagar, edited by Motilal Saqi. These poems bear testimony to Shams Faqir's creative genius as a mystical poet. Rich in content as the poems are, a perceptive reader can draw useful inferences from them about the poet's religious and literary background.

Let us consider Shams Faqir's poem titled 'मनकबत' (Arabic word meaning 'praise') that is addressed to Prophet Mohammad. It provides some significant clues to the poet's faith and his religious background. Here are some crucial lines from the poem mentioned :

पतॅु लारय बडि सरदारो, बालॅु यारो लोल हो आम,
सर बऽ वंदय नऽबी ताजदारो, बालॅुयारो लोल हो आम।
यनॅु आदम गव इज़हारो चॊरि चीज़य आऽडॅुरनॅु आम,
तति शेतान गव गिरिफ्तारो, बालॅु यारो लोल हो आम।
दो'पुरव रूहस अछ़तॅु अंदरो मतॅु कऽऱ्यतोम छुस बऽ खोचान,
वादॅु द्युतनस कडथ दूबारो, बालॅु यारो लोल हो आम।
ताम रूहस लो'गुय करारो फिक्री सॅूत्य ज़िक्रि अल्लाह,
पो'रुन हू हू कर्यन कथॅु तारो, बालॅु यारो लोल हो आम।
सारि नॅुय थेा'द रो'सूल मो'ख्तारो, तस शूबान सॅूत्य चॊर यार,
सथ छिय ज़ऽमीन नव आस्मानो, नवन फलकन नव छि
डीड बाऽनी,
मति शमसो करतॅु इज़्हारो, बालॅु यारो लोल हो' आम।।

Oh my beloved Friend, my Master,
I'll pursue you in earnest,
Since I yearn for you,
I'll offer you the sacrifice of my head —
You who wear the crown as Prophet;
Man came into being out of the four elements,
While the Devil felt helpless and desperate;
As the soul was asked to enter the 'tabernacle',
It hesitated first, feeling afraid,
And was promised it'd be freed before long;
Reassured thus, it steadied itself
Repeating God's name
Accompanied by contemplation;
It spoke the words 'hoo hoo' (referring to God)
Followed by some utterances;

Mohammad, who is supreme,
Has four friends as his associates;

. . .

There're seven earths and nine skies
Guarded by nine gatekeepers;
O ardent Shams, reveal these mysteries.

It is to be noted that Shams Faqir is writing here about divine mysteries as a devout Muslim. The mystics aspire for a direct experience of the divine. And the present poet too shares this aspiration. He is evidently a religious mystic known to have belonged to the Qadiri order of the Sufis. From the above verse, we gather that he is conversant with Islamic theology : unmistakably evident from his account of how God "breathed" a soul into the human tenement. In the same breath he expresses his belief in the efficacy of contemplative prayer as mystics of all hues and shades do. They lay stress, as he does, on the twin-means of 'fikir' (thoughtful reflection) and 'zikir' (repetition of the divine Name) that reinforce each other. Sufism as a form of religious mysticism draws inspiration from the personal virtues of Prophet Mohammad himself : his purity, simplicity, poverty and penance. On this basic edifice, it has built up the doctrines of 'irfaan'/'marifat' (spiritual '*gnosis*' or full perception of Truth) and 'Mahabba' (the way of love) — the two complementary approaches to the Divine that characterize the 'Way of the Sufi'.

Here is an important piece, the short lyric titled 'यी गव ज़हूर' (This is the divine becoming manifest) :

अल्लाह तुॅ हू हू छुम दर मनय,
बुॅ क्याह वनय यी गव ज़हूर।
अऽम्य अऽश्कुॅ नारन ज़ाऽजनम तनय,
बुॅ क्याह वनय यी गंव ज़हूर।
रिदंन गिदुंन प्यव दरशनय,
ज़िन्दुॅगी लऽबुॅरव वुछुख नूर।
नूरस सूर गव पर्तव प्यनय,
बुॅ क्याह वनय यी गव ज़हूर।
आऽबिद तुॅ ज़ाऽहिद छि अथ निश ज़े'नय,
वाऽहिद तमिकुय छु शेख मनसूर।

अऽछव बोज़रव कन वुछनय,
मुकामि महमूद सपदी ज़हूर।
रफतार गुफतार तथ जायि छुनय,
बऽ क्याह वनय ती गव ज़हूर।
बो' सिर शसं फऽकीरो वनय,
सर त्राव पथ दर मख्मूर,
सुय अचि़ यस तति बर मुच़रनय,
बुॅ कयाह वनय यी गंव ज़हूर।।

The words 'Allah' (God) and 'hoo hoo' (referring to God)
Are engraved in my mind,
How can I convey
This is the Divine becoming manifest?
The fire of love has consumed my body,
The unfettered mystics (*rindas*)
Attained vision playfully as they experienced
illumination,
Of which the merely devout or the ascetics have no idea;
Moses had a vision unbearable
As the 'fiery' glow struck him on the mount Sinai,
The one excellent example of the *rinda*
Is Shiekh Mansur-ul-Hallaj,
Who pronounced 'I am Truth'
Even without any initiation into spiritual *gnosis*;
When you attain his elevated state,
You hear with the eyes and see with the ears;
(an experience transcending sensory perception)
Visualize Mohammad's spiritual height
At which conversation and movement stop;
O Shams Faqir, I'll reveal to you the secret :
Bow to the (feet of the) intoxicated mystic,
For he alone enters the realm of blessedness
To whom the gate is thrown open;
How shall I convey
This is the divine becoming manifest?

There is a significant mention in this poem of the unorthodox Persian mystic Mansur-ul-Hallaj who, asserting his innate divinity, declared "I am Truth" — a "heresy" for which he paid the penalty of his life. In the eyes of the poet, Mansur was an extraordinary mystic, a *rinda* not tied to any dogma, a true and bold lover of Truth. Shams Faqir also pays his tribute to the Prophet of Islam, praising his exalted spiritual stature; he speaks of the Prophet's supreme state of awareness transcending the senses. In the concluding lines, the poet talks about the principle of divine grace — that he alone enters the "realm of blessedness" who finds the gate "thrown open".

We shall now consider the poem titled 'बऽ केंहनय कस वनय पानय' (What shall I designate as Nothing?) It is a significant poem involving, in a subtle way, the *via negativa* motif that corresponds to the Upanishadic *neti neti* (not this) principle. The title, as a sentence in Kashmiri, is ambiguous; it could be interpreted as "I being 'nothing', how shall I designate myself?" or "Oh my self, what shall I designate as Nothing?" The 'nothing' corresponds to the *sunya* of the *Trika* system (associated with Kashmir Shaivism), not to be confused with the 'void' of the Buddhists. The first verse of the poem, given below, also brings in the *via affirmative* motif : positive assertion of the higher Self :

बऽ छुस केंहनय रव्वद पानय,
बऽ केंहनय कस वनय पानय।
वुछ्म ओरुँ केंह नुँ योरुँ केंह,
बऽ केंहनय कस वनय पानय।।

I am nothing but Myself,
What should I designate as Nothing?
I saw nothing on this side nor on the opposite,
What should I designate as Nothing?

In the verse that follows, the poet suggests what he considers the surest means to Self-realization :

कनन थव कन सऽही रठ मन,
वऽमी सपदरव द्वन आलमन।
बनरव आऽरिफ यज़दानय,
बऽ केंहनय कस वनय पानय।।

Listen to the inward music of the ears,
Keeping your mind in the right key;

> You will be aware of the two worlds — seen and unseen,
> What should I name as Nothing?

The verse actually prescribes a technique of meditation that closely resembles the Indian yogic practice — turning all one's attention inward and listening to the unstruck sound or the 'voice of silence', keeping the mind steadily poised. As the aspirant perseveres in this practice, he attains self-awareness as well as an awareness of the worlds unseen — all leading to the attainment of Supreme Consciousness in which the seeker realizes his identity with the Universal Self.

In this verse, we hear a clear Sufistic note throwing back to the Persian mystics :

> फना सपदिथ फना फाऽनी,
> बका बाला छु रुबाऽनी।
> ति गव वाऽसिल एहसानय,
> बऽ केंहनय कस वनय पानय।।
> Attain annihilation of the little self,
> Followed by continuity of the soul in life Divine —
> Favoured with the entry into the realm of blessedness,
> What should I call Nothing?

Sufism, like Vedanta, lays emphasis on the conquest of the little self as the means to spiritual elevation. Both talk of annihilation of the 'ego' or 'I-ness' as the prelude to union with the Divine. The concept of 'fana' (annihilation) has different connotations for the Sufi and the Vedantist. Union for the former does not mean total 'absorption' of the individual soul into God but its continuity in divine life — even after the mortal coil has been given up by the seeker. For the Vedantist, 'union' means final merger of the individual soul with God or the supreme Soul. The above verse obviously falls in line with Sufism or Islamic mysticism. Shams Faqir's use of the Persian words 'fana' (annihilation), 'baqa' (continuity) and 'vaasil' (securing what remains behind) shows the poet's acquaintance with the writings of the Persian mystics, thus giving us an idea of his literary background and the sources of his inspiration.

Here we have another verse from the poem under discussion, in which Shams Faqir gives us an account of his own total absorption into the Divine — a state in which there is no trace of the little self and the *aarif*/yogi attains a state of equipoise conducive to spiritual illumination :

बॖ थाह दिथ आलॖमे गाऽबस गोस,
दऽरिथ केंहनय तॖ क्याहताम ओस।
बॖ रूदुस गाऽबि गाऽबानय,
बॖ केंहनय कस वनय पानय।।
I plunged into the realm Unseen,
Finding nothing tangible as my ground
Though I felt 'something' as supportive,
I was totally lost to myself,
What should I designate as Nothing?

Shams Faqir's outlook as a man of religion is very broad, no doubt, but at the same time, he is consistently devout too as a Muslim, and as such he does not forget paying his homage to the Prophet :

अवल आऽखुर छु नूरि महमद,
ज़हूर तहुन्दॖय हदो लाहद।
हयातुन्नऽबी छु ताबानय,
बॖ केंहनय कस वनय पानय।।
The light of Mohammad abides
From the beginning to the end,
It pervades the finite and the infinite;
The Prophet's life is all effulgent,
What should I name as Nothing?

The concluding lines are replete with self-confidence, conveying the poet's conviction of his innate divinity — a positive awareness of his complete identity with God :

बऽ रव्वद शमस बऽ रव्वद सिकंदर,
बॖ रव्वद सरमद तॖ रव्वद रवावर।
बॖ रव्वद आज़ाद सुलयमानय,
बॖ केंह नय कस वनय पानय।।
I'm myself Shams (sun),
Myself Alexander,

Myself the Eternal,
Myself the sun :
I'm myself Suleman the Free,
What should I call Nothing,
When I am all by myself ?

The implication of this verse as a whole is that the Self is all-inclusive; nothing else is there besides or beyond it. It is all-in-all. And Shams Faqir also feels identified with this Self as Universal and all-embracing. Here he is almost echoing Mansur's assertion : "I'm Truth". This assertion is no different from the Upanishadic truth 'अंह भ्रह्मोस्मि' (I am Brahman) or 'शिवोंह' (I am Shiva), the doctrine professed by the Shaivites.

What follows hereinafter is a short lyric which stresses divine immanence, exhorting the aspirant to undertake an earnest quest of the indwelling self — the One without a second. The poem is titled 'हर म्वखुँ सुय नो'न द्राव' (He has manifested Himself everywhere), the word 'हर म्वरव' being ambiguous. According to the Kashmiri Hindu tradition, this is the name of the mountain believed to be inhabited by Lord Shiva. In the contextual sense, the word means 'everywhere'. Here is the text of the poem :

दुॅय त्राऽविथ वुछतन कुनये,
हर म्वरवुॅ सुय नो'नये द्राव।
सरुॅ करतन कुन पय कुनये,
हर म्वरव सुय नो'नुये द्राव।
फिकिरि हुॅज़िं रज़ि गछ़ि लमुनये,
ज़िकरि सूॅत्य लबुॅहन शाह।
कुजिं तुॅ कुल्फस वर गछ़ि ह्युनये
हर म्वरवुॅ सुय नो'नये द्राव।
अऽशकुॅ दऽरियाव सनि रवो'तुॅ सो'नये,
डुंग दिथ रवार दुर बे बहा।
लाल बाज़ारुॅ ह्यो'तुम म्वलुॅवुनये,
हरम्वरवुॅ सुय नो'नये द्राव।
कथि म्यानि गछ़ि मानि बोजुनये,
ज़ानि सुय यस असि आगाह।
अछ़ अंदर गरुॅ छु पनुनये,
हर म्वरवुॅ सुय नो'नये द्राव।

शमस फकीर छुय परुँ छ्यो'नुये,
छुसनुँ दो'गुन पथ ब्रोंह कांह।
यी सरुँ गोम ती मे वो'नुये,
हर म्वरवुँ सुय नो'नुये द्राव।।

Giving up duality, look for the One
Who has revealed Himself everywhere;
Realize how God's word
Brought forth all that He pervades,
Pull with the rope of contemplation
Aided by repetition of the Name,
You will attain the Supreme;
Twist the key firmly to open the lock,
The Lord will appear for sure,
Dive deep into the fathomless ocean of love
And emerge with the priceless pearl;
Ponder the meaning of what I say —
Only the enlightened ones will grasp it;
Get into your own 'dwelling',
You will see the Lord everywhere;
Shams Faqir is all by himself,
There is none beside him — behind or in front,
He said what he has experienced :
"I saw God as all-pervading."

In the poem reproduced above, we find Shams Faqir talking throughout about the Unitive experience — best known to the mystics. The experience ties up with the poet's grounding in Islam — a thoroughly monotheistic religion. The terms 'fikir' and 'zikir', conveying (as linked here) 'thoughtful remembrance of God' accompanied by the 'repetition of the divine Name', are frequently used by Shams Faqir in his poems elsewhere too. In the present poem, we come across two images/figures that deserve special attention. The expression 'कुज़ तुँ कुलुफ' (the lock and the key) thus functions as an image suggesting the strenuous spiritual effort that the seeker must put in to unravel the divine mystery — to get at the "heart" of life's mystery that becomes possible through contemplation on the Divine. The other figure used is that of 'दुर' (pearl) that stands for God or Self in Persian mysticism — the word, in fact, suggests the beloved as being invaluable to the seeker. The diver has to dive deep into the sea to seize the 'pearl'; likewise the *aarif* or yogi has to dive deep into the fathomless ocean of love to attain the Divine. The Vedanta philosophy, recommending yoga, also lays stress on the aspirant's cultivating the "inward gaze" through intense meditation to experience "illumination" — encountering the "Blue Pearl" as the fruit of deep introspection accompanied by devotion. Shams Faqir is, however, speaking here of the 'diver' and the 'pearl' strictly in the Sufistic vein.

We will now look at the poem titled 'मानॅुं रे'निये' पान बदलाब' 'O highly respected lady, transform yourself'. There is a plural voice suggested by the honorific use of the word 'अऽस्य' (we) used in the poem — a choric voice, as it were, directed to the listener, a female (the lady addressed). These are the introductory lines addressed to the lady :

नेरी वे'सिये अऽस्य दिमोस वऽनिये,
मानॅुं रे'निये पान बदलाव।
युथ नय आलॅुविथ त्रावरव कऽनिये,
मानॅुं रे'निये पान बदलाव।
अऽशकॅु बाज़रस द्रायरव नऽन्यये,
मो'लॅुनाऽव्यतन सोदागर।
तति मंदछान छिय चंदॅु छे'निये,
मानॅुंरे'निये पान बदलाव।
माशि माऽरिथ वुछमरव गाशिनये,
दीद अयान कर चॅु दीदार।
दीदॅु रो'स्तुय कया वुछे अऽन्यये,
मानॅुंरे'निये पान बदलाव।

Come forth, friend,
Let us look for the Beloved;
You, highly respected lady,
Transform yourself
(to gain the desired prize);
Don't be remiss
In throwing the stone away,
You've come into love's market
Bare and exposed,
Where the merchant will

Set a price on your beautiful form;
The pocketless fight shy there,
You, the honoured lady,
Should soon transform yourself;
I saw you early in the morning
When you had slept long;
Have a clear vision of the Beloved
With your eyes wide open,
For what can one see
Bereft of the eyes?
You, the honoured lady,
Transform yourself.

Here are some significant lines that occur in the poem further onward :

शाहस सॅूत्य छकय मो'ज़रे'निये,
योरनय नाहकय पिंडार।
अमि नारुॅ सॅूत्य दज़रव आरमे'निये,
मानॅुरे'निये पान बदलाव।
युथनय परमानॅु आसनय छे'निये,
सोदहस छुय रव्वदाह रवऽरीदार।
पारसंग कड गाड़ॅु हांज़ऽनिये,
मानॅु रे'निये पान बदलाव।

A maidservant attending
Upon the king,
You've got conceited for nothing;
The conceit will scorch you,
Female cultivator;
You, honoured lady,
Transform yourself;
Take care lest you should use false weights,
Know that you've to transact business with God;
O you fisherwoman,
Set your balance right
(To ensure it weighs accurately)
You, honoured lady,
Must undergo a transformation.

Shams Faqir is sounding a note of caution in the above lines, alerting the lady, a spiritual aspirant as she is, about the possibilities of pitfalls ahead and the dangers with which the path is beset. The concluding lines are noteworthy :

आगुँ साऽबस ज़ाग गछ़ि हे'निये,
बागस छिय नाग फम्वार।
गोशन थो'प थव होश थव नऽन्यये,
मानुॅरे'निये पान बदलाव।
माऽरयफत्कुय प्यालुॅ गछ़ि चो'नये,
आऽर्यफन निश्य सीरि असरार।
म्वरव्तुॅ पादन अऽस्य थो'वय थऽन्यये,
मानुॅरे'निये पान बदलाव।
शमस फऽकीरन वऽन्य मानुॅरे'निये,
मानि बोज़न बीनादार।
माजि प्रुॅछ़ प्रुॅछ़ वलय राजि रे'निये,
मानुॅ रे'निये पान बदलाव।

You should look for the Master,
The garden he inhabits
Abounds with springs and fountains,
Seal your ears, remain alert and receptive,
Transform yourself, O you honoured lady;
Drink a cupful
Of what the *aarifs* (gnostics) taste,
They know the secret of secrets;
We'll anoint with butter
Your pearl-like feet, O you honoured lady;
Shams Faqir sang this piece in your praise,
The enlightened will get at the meaning;
Come forth, O queen, with your mother's consent
And undergo a transformation.

That Shams Faqir speaks of mystical experiences with authenticity — having tasted them himself — can be inferred from many verses one comes across in his poems. Here I quote from the poem 'मो'त माशोक याद प्योम' 'I remembered the ardent beloved' to substantiate what I have maintained :

बोज़ अऽशकुन दोद यारुॅ गोम,
मो'त माशोक याद प्योम।
मयरवानुॅ मज़ लोलुॅ मय चोम,
मो'त माशोक याद प्योम।

अऽम्य क्रालन बानुँ थुर्य स्यठा,
रंगुँ रगुँ तथ आऽनथ क्या।
साऽर्य प्वरवतुँ छिय बऽय द्रास ओम,
मो'त माशोक याद प्योम।

दिलुँ के दर्वाजुँ किन्य चास,
अर्शिचि जो'यि पय हो वुज़्योम,
मो'त माशेक याद प्योम।
गरि पनुँने मेराज कऽरिथ,
शमस फऽकीर छुय रवराज।
छुस केंहनय कया सनुँ वुछोम,
मो'त माशेक याद प्योम।

Listen friend, I am love-sick,
The memory of the Beloved haunts me,
Having drunk of love's wine at the tavern;
The potter made pots of varied hues
All well-baked but me,
What splendour emanated from the One
And what is His name?
I raised myself from the multitude
As if by the rope,
I'm haunted by the memory of the Beloved!

. . .

Entering through the portal of my heart,
I emerged into the land of Oneness,
The celestial stream gushed out within me;
Attaining *Meraj* (divine ascent) at home,
I earned the tribute — of being called Shams Faqir,
Nothing as I am, I perceived the Indefinable,
Haunted am I by the memory of the Beloved !

In the above verse, we have convincing evidence of Shams Faqir's awareness of what true spirituality consists in — as regards the inward transformation that the mystics experience. He has surely tasted 'love-sickness' that is spiritual and not rooted merely in the senses. He talks of the 'tavern' and the divine 'drink', of mystic 'intoxication' and 'ecstasy' in line with the Persian masters in the background. The term 'Meraj' (reminiscent of the Prophet's ascent to the abode of God) used by the poet here with reference to his own spiritual attainment also throws light on his moorings as an Islamic mystic.

Before bringing this section to its close, let us look at the introductory stanza of the poem titled 'मसुक असरार सन्योम जिगरस' (Mystery of the divine drink haunts me) :

बऽ चोवनस मस तुँ सपनुस मस,
मसुक असरार सन्योम जिगरस।
कलय वालुँ सर वंदय कदमस,
मसुक असरार सन्योम जिगरस।
वुछुम साकियस मलर्यन मस,
क़रान पयमानुँ पूरुँ जामस।
दुर ये'म्य रवोर सु छुय मस मस,
मसुक असरार सन्योम जिगरस।
पनुँने नयि कन द्युतमस,
मनुँचे तारि साज़ वायस।
राज़ि दिल प्रुँछोम ज़ीरुँ बमस,
मंसुक असरार सन्योम जिगरस।
ये'मे नूरुँ तन लऽजुँन आदमस,
सुय नूर फो'लिथ द्राव आलमस।
अऽशकुँ सूँत्य ज़बान आयि कलमस,
मसुक असरार सन्योम जिगरस।

I was served with wine
And got intoxicated,
The mystery of the drink
Haunted my soul;
O cup-bearer, I shall offer my head
At the altar of your feet;
The liquor-shop has vessels
Brimful with wine,
The Master serves glasses in full measure;
The diver who got the pearl (from the sea-bed)
Is all intoxicated;
I listened to my flute
And played on the string within,
I sought the heart's secret
From the rise and fall of the note;
He who gave man a frame touched by light

Manifested himself and blossomed forth
In the universe around;
Love made the pen eloquent,
The mystery of the wine haunts me still;

The cup-bearer designated by the word 'कलवाल' (the 'wine merchant') is to be seen as none other than God in terms of the symbolism built into the verse. Another analogy introduced is that of the 'diver' and the 'pearl' (that we have come across earlier too). Obviously, the act of diving into the sea and seizing the pearl, calls forth courage, determination and concentration from the diver. This suggests the intensity and vigour of the spiritual seeker's effort that he must put in for attaining his goal. Here is the concluding verse of the poem :

शमस फकीरो नोश कर मस,
होश थाऽविथ रोज़ बर बामस।
दर हरमस वाऽतिथ कोर कुन नमस,
मसुक असरार सन्योम जिगरस।

Taste, O Shams Faqir,
The divine drink,
Be alert and attain heights;
Having reached the Harem (ladies' apartment),
Which way should I bow?
The mystery of the drink haunts me still!

Even after attaining heights, the *aarif* (gnostic or spiritual seeker) has to remain alert in spite of his 'ecstasy' and 'intoxication'. This is what Shams Faqir wants to convey in the concluding stanza. The divine mystery continues to perplex the spiritual seeker till last. Such assertive statements made at the end of Shams Faqir's poems leave us in no doubt about his personal experience of the Mystic Way.

## PART II

As stated at the start of this chapter, in this section I shall focus on four poems — two select poems each of Swami Govind Kaul and Shams Faqir. The Kashmiri text of each poem would be reproduced in full, followed immediately by mine translation. Having attempted an overview of the lyric verse of the two poets in the preceding section, it will be a fruitful exercise now to examine and discuss the four specific poems in some detail. This will help further to find out how the cultural streams represented by the two poets chosen for this study have interacted — resulting in the assimilation and fusion of related or parallel concepts and images in the verse of each poet.

I begin with Swami Govind Kaul's poem 'गथ करू शमहस लाग परवानय' (Hover around the candle-light), which is reproduced below :

गथ करू शमहस लाग पर्‌वानय,
शमह बऽनिथ पानुँ पानय गछ़।
तीज़ म्यूल तीज़स वुछ मंज़ ध्यानय,
सिरिये ओत वुछानय गछ़।
ग्वो'ट चो़'ल फो'ट तीज़ द्राव चमकानय,
शमह बऽनिथ पानुँ पानय गछ़।
प्राणह पवनुँ च्यथ नब साफ सपदानय,
च़ऽन्द्रमुँ छुय ज़ोतानय गछ़
रिन्दुँ पाऽठ्य गिदंबा शुनि मैदानय,
शमह बऽनिथ पर्‌वानय गछ़।
मलहो दज़ियो तीजुँके आनय,
शो'द कर मन बरफानय गछ़।
सनियो सूतय बनियो ज्ञानय,
शमह बऽनिथ पानुँ पानय गछ़।
डुंगुँ दिथ सो'दरस रवार दुरदानय,
दमुँलो दम दिवानय गछ़।
दुरि उरफॉ तोल पूरि परमानय,
शमह बऽनिथ पानुँ पानय गछ़।
बिजली रोशन गयि प्रथ खानय,
जूनुँ डबि प्यठ डालानय गछ़।
पानि मंज़ सपद्यो चरागानय,
शमह बऽनिथ पानुँ पानय गछ़।

Become moth-like and hover around the candlelight,
Thus consumed by the flame, get transformed into light,
Watch 'light' mingling with 'light' in meditation,
Gaze steadfastly at the sun;
Darkness having vanished, effulgence bursts forth,

Become the candlelight yourself;
The vital air cleanses the mind
Watch (now) the moon shining bright,
Like the *rinda*, divert yourself in the realm of *sunya*
And become the candlelight;
Purged by the fire, get illuminated,
Your mind rendered immaculately 'white' as the snow;
Absorbed in Him, you will attain knowledge supreme
As the Sadguru Bhagavaan bestows grace on you,
Collect all the bounty you have been endowed with
By the kindly Master, the Almighty Lord;
O you diver, remain steadfast in diving,
And collect pearls from the sea-bed;
Weigh carefully the pearls of *urfaan* (*gnosis*)
And become the candlelight yourself;
Light shoots forth from all sides,
As you watch the moon from the balcony atop,
Water is aglow (under the illuminated sky),
Become the candlelight yourself;
Bear the pain of love's fire, burn up your ego therein
And attain experience-grounded knowledge ('vigyaan');
Gain self-recognition and don't get mystified,
O Govind, join those in the sphere indescribable,
Become the candlelight,
Having attained self-knowledge.

The poem begins with the images of 'moth' and 'candlelight' that have been used frequently and popularised by the Persian poets, also adopted by many Indian poets in Urdu verse. The images have likewise been used in appropriate contexts by a number of Kashmiri poets in both Sufi verse and in love lyrics. It is interesting to note that Govind Kaul employs them at the very start of an important religious lyric that is meant to convey a spiritual instruction to the seeker or initiate — to get totally absorbed in the thought of the Beloved. In terms of the analogy of the 'moth' hovering around and getting burnt up in the 'flame', the spiritual seeker is advised to shed his ego completely *i.e.* achieve 'annihilation' of his little self, a sacrifice that alone can ensure his fulfilment in divine love and guarantee his communion with the Divine. The aspirant is reassuringly exhorted thus :

> Watch 'light' mingling with 'light' in meditation,
> Gaze steadfastly at the sun;
> Darkness having vanished, effulgence bursts forth,
> Become the candlelight yourself;

Onwards, Govind Kaul makes a significant use of the term 'rinda' in these lines, bringing the term 'sunya' also into focus :

> 'Like the *rinda*, divert yourself in the realm of 'sunya',
> And become the candlelight.

As mentioned earlier, 'rinda' is a Persian word meaning the 'true lover', a mystic who is not tied to this or that dogma but is absolutely free to explore Truth for himself. He is the ideal *aarif* (gnostic) who pursues the Beloved with single-minded determination and braves all difficulties on the path undeterred. Govind Kaul has adopted the vocabulary of the Sufis — 'moth', 'candle-flame' and 'rinda' — in the poem here that is devoted to the practice of yogic meditation. He is aware that the words 'aarif' and 'rinda' can safely be used to suggest an accomplished 'yogi' who is compared in the Hindu scriptures to the *Rajhans* (King-Swan), believed to have the ability of sifting 'milk' from 'water' — suggesting the ability to discriminate between what is 'Real' and what is 'illusory or false'. The term 'sunya' suggests ethereal regions beyond the earthy sphere, where all multiplicity of forms merges into the 'void'. The Sufis use the term '*laa makaan*' to suggest that God is formless — not confined but 'free' and 'infinite'. The term also conveys that God's throne or Abode is "unhoused" void or 'sunya' as the Hindus conceive of it too. Further onwards, these significant lines occur :

> O you diver, remain steadfast in diving,
> And collect pearls from the sea-bed;
> Weigh carefully the pearls of *urfaan* (*gnosis*)
> And become the candlelight yourself.

The words 'diver', 'sea-bed' and 'pearl' in the above lines are noteworthy. We have already discussed their use in the verse of

Shams Faqir in Part I. We find Govind Kaul using them confidently in the present poem on meditation. What the poet means here, as the Persian Sufi poets also do in their poems, is that the spiritual seeker, engaged in meditation, searches for Truth — that is of a rare or surpassing value, and as such appropriately comparable to a 'pearl'. The seeker can, accordingly, be compared to the 'diver' who holds his breath, plunges into the deep sea and emerges from water with the pearl in his hands. The yogi, with his eyes shut and the breath held in control, looks within — he plunges into the *Mansarovar* (mind's lake) to have a direct encounter with the Divine (that indwells us). The diver's seizing the invaluable pearl from the sea-bed conveys analogically that the *aarif* or yogi attains communion with the Divine. Govind Kaul uses the expression 'pearl of Urfaan'; it means the rich reward in terms of God-realization that the practice of *irfaan* or yoga promises the spiritual 'diver' who plunges into the 'unknown' and seizes the 'pearl Divine'.

In the lines that follow, we have a poetic description of what spiritual "illumination" is like — reminding us of similar accounts of the experience given by Shams Faqir in some of his poems through the extensive use of the word 'noor' (spiritual glow or halo) :

> Light shoots forth from all sides,
> As you watch the moon from the balcony atop,
> Water is aglow (under the illuminated sky),
> Become the candlelight yourself;

The concluding lines convey a hint of Govind Kaul's first-hand experience of the transcendent, what the mystics mean by a direct "encounter with the Divine". The heights he talks of suggest what is implied by the 'Ascent of self' in Kundalini yoga, corresponding to Shams Faqir's occasional use of the word 'Meraj' when he either directly refers to or has in the back of his mind Prophet Mohammad's "journey to the abode of God" mentioned in the *Koran*, or when he talks about his own transcendental aspiration and its fulfilment. Govind Kaul too aspires in these lines for transcendental heights :

Gain Self-recognition and don't get mystified,
O Govind, those who attained heights,
Join them in flight,
Beyond those heights is the sphere indescribable,
Become the candlelight, having attained self-knowledge.

Here is the text of the second poem of Govind Kaul that too we shall examine in some detail before we turn to the other poet :

ह्रदयिकि दर्वाज़ुॅ अछ़ कर पर्वाज़,
छुय वज़न साज़ ज़ीरुॅ बम तुॅ लोलो।
हर दमुॅ होश थव सरुॅ कर यि आवाज़,
अथ मंज़ छिय ज़ुॅ आलम तुॅ लोलो।
ओ'म शब्दुॅ गाश आव ओ'मुय छु जहाज़,
खस गगन कऽरिथ ओ'म तुॅ लोलो।
साऽल लामकानन कर बन चुॅ शाहबाज़,
हंसन सॅूत्य दि कदम तुॅ लोलो।
सत ग्वरुॅ दीशस वाति कांछ़ा शाहबाज़,
सुय वाति यस छुॅ प्रेयम तुॅ लोलो।
ज्ञान प्राव याद थाव माज़स मो माज़,
सतंन खोच़ान यम तुॅ लोलो।
गोवं'न्दुॅ सत ग्वरो होवुय भोवुय चे' राज़,
परमात्मा चुॅय उत्तम तुॅ लोलो।

Enter through the heart's door and soar high,
You'll hear a melody marked by rhythmic rise and fall;
Remain ever-watchful and recognize the sound :
It comprehends, at once, the two worlds,
The syllable 'Om' brings forth light,
It truly serves as the ship;
So chant 'Om' and ascend to heaven,
Hawk-like soar to the uppermost reaches of
'unhoused space'
Walk in step with swans;
Thus the goal won't seem distant,
And as an Atman, you will soon reach your abode;
Rare is the individual who attains
To the Sadguru's country,
Love alone serves him as the means here;
Achieve *gnosis*, bearing in mind

That you shouldn't be lured by 'flesh',
Even death is afraid of the saints;
O Govind, the Sadguru revealed to you the secret :
That you yourself are the Parmatman supreme.

This poem too is concerned with the attainment of self-knowledge (spiritual *gnosis*), and the means suggested are all that is comprehended in *Surat Sabda yoga*. The yogi regulates and controls his breath; he turns all attention inward, thereby catching and listening to the "melody" of the soul. He also directs his "gaze" to the "point" of light between the eyebrows. With sustained practice he not only hears what the mystics call "unstruck" sound or music but also experiences "illumination" in the head. We find similar accounts of "light" and "sound" given in the poems of Shams Faqir (as indicated in Part I). Beyond the experience of "anahat" (unstruck music) and of spiritual illumination, Govind Kaul brings in here the metaphor of 'flight' (as we also came across in the foregoing poem). These are the relevant lines from the present poem under discussion :

Enter through the heart's door and soar high,
You'll hear a melody marked by rhythmic rise and fall;
Remain ever-watchful and recognize the sound :
It comprehends the two worlds;
The syllable 'Om' brings forth light,
It truly serves as the ship;
So chant 'Om' and ascend to heaven,
Hawk-like soar to the uppermost reaches of
'unhoused space',
Walk in step with the swans;

The idea of spiritual ascent is made explicit through the word 'Om' likened to a 'ship' and the mention of 'swans'. Swans can fly to the upper reaches of outer "unhoused space" and are credited with the "ability" of sifting milk from water as the myth goes. They serve as symbols for the accomplished yogis who have attained God-realization through the grace of the Sadguru. Hence Govind Kaul's assertion of equality of status with "swans" ("walk in step with swans"). Shams Faqir also has used the word "razahonz" (swan) in several poems; it is a variant of the word "razahans" : used by Govind Kaul. Both are derived from the word "rajhans" (King-swan), which is of Sanskrit origin. Likewise, the images of 'moth' and 'candlelight' also occur in the verse of both the poets. This interfusion and exchange of vocabulary drawn from diverse cultural streams exemplifies the intermingling that takes place in literature when two or more communities interact socially.

Let us now come to Shams Faqir's two poems. Here follows the text of the first titled 'ज़ान मिलु नाव भगवानस सूॅत्य' (Recognize God)

ज़ानुॅ वुॅनि ज़ान कर प्राणस ज्ञानस,
ज़ान मिलुॅनाव भगवानस सूॅत्य।
पूज़ायि करनि गऽयि मंज़ कर्मुॅ वानस,
धरमुॅ शास्तुॅर निस बुत रवानस।
को'र ललि यिकुॅवटुॅ आकाश प्राणस,
ज़ान मिलुॅनाव भगवानस सूॅत्य।
सो'दुॅ माऽल्य वदुना को'र पाऽन्य पानस,
दिवुर मंगि कया दिवुर वटस।
ललि त्रोव ज़ल नो'ट मजं पो'तुॅल्य रवानस,
ज़ान मिलुॅनांव भगवानस सूॅत्य।
छ़लुॅ गऽयि ललुॅ मऽच़ शुरायार रवानस,
पिलुॅ तमि को'र ज़गि तार तरनस।
ज़ान मिलुॅनांव भगवानस सूॅत्य।
सबक तति रुदुय तस अबख छानस,
राज़ दाऽन्य तऽम्य लऽज़ वाऽरानस।
ललि ओस निलुॅवठ ललुॅवुन पानस,
ज़ान मिलुॅ नाव भगवानस सूॅत्य।
व्पदीश करनि गऽयि नुन्दुॅ रे'शानस,
ज़ान मिलुॅनाव भगवानस सूॅत्य।
छे'पि छेपिरस गिदुंन शाह हम्दानस,
ज़ान मिलुॅ नाव भगवानस सूॅत्य।
शमस फऽकीर नाऽमी परकांठस
छ़ाय वुछुॅतुॅ मा छय रौ सिरियस,
छ़ाय ओ'बुर लाऽगिय रवऽच आस्मानस,
ज़ान मिलुॅ नाव भगवानस सूत्य।

O you enlightened one,
Recognize the vital air and attain *gnosis*
To realize God;
Real worship is performed
In life's workshop itself :
What the holy scriptures truly mean
By 'the house of idols',
Lalla achieved the fusion
Of her vital air and ether,
And thus realized God;
Sodabhai (on the other hand) got lachrymose,
What would he ask of the stone image?
Lalla dropped the pitcher of water
Inside the house of idols
And attained God-realization;
Intoxicated as a mystic, she contrived
To bathe at the confluence of 'sixteen rivers',
And she built a 'bridge'
Across the ocean of temporal existence;
She knocked off the Devil's head
And gained self-recognition;
The 'unskilled carpenter',
Having built the palace in wilderness,
Learnt a lesson from Lalla,
She had to bear with the stone
Her mother-in-law kept concealed
In the plate of rice served to her,
(she stood to gain from this austerity)
Lalla went to Nunda Rishi's
To teach him her doctrine,
What the *rinda* mystics call *gnosis* (irfaan)
She played 'hide and seek' with Shah Hamdan
And had a direct 'encounter' with God;
O, you "learned" Shams,
The sun doesn't have a shadow;
Lalla ascended to heaven like a cloud,
Realize God (as she did).

This poem is, in fact, Shams Faqir's extended tribute to the spiritual qualities and attainments of the celebrated Kashmiri mystic poet, Lal Ded. Aware of her religious background and her upbringing in a Shaivite Kashmiri Pandit family, Shams Faqir conspicuously uses Kashmiri words of Sanskrit origin, derived from the Hindu scriptures, while paying his poetic homage to the noted 14th century woman mystic (Lalla). The words/phrases include terms such as *praan* (vital air), *jnaan* (knowledge), *aakash* (ether), *karmavaan* (meaning 'life's workshop' in the poem, elsewhere it generally means 'performer of good actions').

To begin with, the poet addresses the spiritual seeker, asking him to comprehend the functioning of the 'vital air' and attain knowledge in order to perceive the Divine, that would eventually lead to his union with Him. Then he turns straight to the spiritual attainments of Lal Ded — saying that her worship consisted in what she performed in 'life's workshop' itself — that is no different form what our scriptures truly mean by the 'house of idols'. The world is inhabited by human beings and other creatures, who too are, in a sense, 'idols' — when we talk of worship performed in life's workshop.

Shams Faqir calls attention specially to Lalla's spiritual skill in bringing about the union of 'vital air' and *chidakash* (ether of consciousness). Lalla didn't approve of stone-worship, which one of her *vaakhs* conveys explicitly. Shams Faqir alludes indirectly to that *vaakh* while mentioning 'Sodabhai', a Brahman, as engaged in the futile exercise of idol-worship. He also alludes to the miracle attributed to Lalla — how the water contained in a pitcher that she was carrying on her head retained the shape of the pitcher even after the vessel broke into pieces. A few of the other details of her life are also mentioned. A specific reference is made to the harsh treatment that Lalla suffered at the hands of her mother-in-law — she would keep a stone concealed in the plate of rice served to her everyday, until her father-in-law overheard one day Lalla revealing to an inquisitive lady that "she (Lalla) has to bear (the tyranny of) the stone throughout". Shams Faqir alluded to the well-known fact of Lal Ded's having made the saint Nunda Rishi, as a baby, to suck his mother's breast (having initially refused doing so as he was born). It was through this contact with the baby (having first made it suck milk from her own breast), that Lalla is believed to have spiritually initiated the future saint. Other details of her life also are mentioned — her taking a dip into the sacred water "at the confluence of sixteen rivers" that had a religious significance. Also, her spiritual association with Shah Hamdan, a noted Musilm saint, is also mentioned in the poem. Shams Faqir further makes a pointed reference to one more *vaakh* of Lal Ded in which she used the expression "अबरव छान" (unskilled carpenter), implying a person who doesn't know how to value the human tenement as the "राज़दाऽन्य" (palace) that "houses God". Finally, he compliments the spiritual achievement of Lalla in these words : "छ़ाय ओ'बुर लाऽगिथ रवऽच़ अस्मानस" ("she ascended to heaven like a cloud").

Now let us take up the other poem of Shams Faqir also chosen specifically for this section. Here follows the full text of the poem titled 'बो'बावय सीरि असरार' (I'll reveal to you the secret of secrets) :

बो' बावय सीरि असरार यिनो आसरव वुबाऽली,
मे' वुछ हर शायि सु यार, छुनो कांह मो'य ति रवाऽली।
दमाह अकि मे गयम कल मे बूज़ दिलुॅक्यन परन तल,
छु साजुॅ नाज़ अफज़ल छे' ज़ीरस बम ति चाऽली।
चुॅ लाय मंज़ वहदतस थाह गछी मोलुम शहन्शाह,
रिदंय छुख मरतुॅ यक्जा गिंदान गछ़ खो'रदुॅ साऽली।
चुॅ वस सनि सऽदरस सो'न महीत क्या ज़ानी ओ'न,
सहल छा मानि बोज़ुन ति बोज़न गाटाऽली।
फना जामय चऽटिय द्राव, अऽच़िथ मंज़ दीदुॅ नुॅय द्राव,
गछी मालूम पनुन नाव बऽगय पगमानुॅ रवाऽली।
सजूदस मंज़ मे' ड़्यूठुम, वजूद शहूद गव गुम,
सु सिर मूजूद रूदुम छिना तथ जामुॅ नाऽली।
मे' सपदुन ओरुॅ निदा बऽ सपदुस आऽन मूसा,
मे' बोव नऽबयन मुफसल, बऽ सपदुस आऽनि मुरसल,
पे'यम मे जुल्फ हाऽकंल गऽयम हर सोयुॅ नाऽली।
वनय क्या अम्युक सूद मऽरिथ आशक जिदंय रूद,
चुॅ कर शमसो यि कथ बूद छुरवय आमुत सवाऽली।
I'll reveal to you the 'secret of secrets',
Heed it well and don't remain indifferent;

I saw that Friend everywhere,
He indwells what is even infinitesimal (an iota);
Once I felt an urge to listen
To the heart's inward music;
I heard a melody surpassingly sweet
With its measured rise and fall.
Plunge deep into the realm of unity,
You'll know the Emperor;
If you're a *rinda* (a true lover),
Die a total death, engaged in the game
From childhood itself.
Dive deep into the sea,
What do the blind know of the circumference?
The meaning is not easy to grasp,
Only the wise comprehend it.
Tear off the garments of mortality,
And lose yourself in the deeps of the eyes;
You will discover the name
Along with the measuring cup (emptied of the drink).
I saw Him in my acts of kneeling down,
When both existence and attributes disappeared;
That experience stayed with me as the secret,
Bare of any garments.
Moses-like I got the call from above,
Saw the Light resplendent,
And was shown the way
By the Almighty.
The Prophet revealed all to me,
And I verily became a divine messenger;
I got trapped in chains — the Beloved's curly hair
Spread all-around myself;
How should I convey the import of what I experience?
The lover dies into life eternal,
O Shams, unravel the mystery
If you've come to this world
Charged with a mission.

This is among Shams Faqir's famous poems and has become very popular among the lovers of Kashmiri poetry as a lyric sung to the accompaniment of music. The title is significant : Shams Faqir wants to take the listener into confidence and reveal to him the secret touching upon the Divine, that he describes as the "secret of secrets". As a Sufi poet, he refers to God as the "Friend" — suggesting that the relationship between God and the seeker is intimate, based on deep love. The poet affirms that he "saw the friend everywhere", inhering in the minutest particle. Here he is obviously talking about the immanence of the Divine.

Then Shams Faqir reveals another spiritual experience — of having heard the "inward melody" that thrills the mystic (or yogi) engaged in deep meditation. The poet mentions this experience in other poems too, as we noticed in some of the poems examined in the foregoing section.

Onwards, the poet directs the addressee — the spiritual aspirant as the initiate — to plunge "into the realm of oneness". Islam as a monotheistic religion lays the utmost emphasis on the oneness of God. True to his faith, Shams Faqir reiterates this cardinal tenet of Islam; compares the divine Master to an Emperor, seeing him as the sovereign Lord of this universe. As in several other poems too, he uses the term 'rinda' for the unfettered mystic herein. Such a mystic "dies into spiritual life"; he realizes the Self through the conquest of his little self.

The poet directs the spiritual seeker to plunge into the "sea" to fathom its depth and to reach out to the "infinite", which is inaccessible to those who are not perceptive and, as such, are comparable to the "blind". The various "steps" mentioned in the poem would lead the aspirant to his spiritual goal. Resorting to the use of "wine" imagery, the poet mentions the "measuring cup" as having been emptied of the content. What is thereby suggested is that mystic "intoxication" goes hand in hand with the experience of self-awareness. Shams Faqir claims to have become aware of God's presence through his acts of kneeling down — in which state all sense of objective existence is transcended and all attributes disappear; nothing remains there to "witness". He further claims to have got direct inspiration from the Unseen, that made him experience "illumination"; he specially attributes this to the Prophet's grace. What he realized in essence is that the true lover of God attains immortality through the annihilation of the little self. He believes it has been his life's mission to investigate the divine mystery and that the 'secret of secrets' has been imparted to him by Prophet Mohammad. He has now become a love-mystic "trapped in the beautiful locks of hair of the Sweetheart", an expression conceived in the erotic vein in line with Sufism — suggesting spiritual fulfilment.

# 9

# Some Observations on Bhavani 'Bhagyavaan' Pandit's *Mana Pamposh*

BHAVANI 'BHAGYAVAAN' Pandit's achievement as a poet is formidable. She is a remarkable poet of the first rank and I have no hesitation in maintaining that she can be set beside the major Kashmiri poets such as Shams Faqir, Ahad Zargar, Samad Mir, Mehjoor, Master Zinda Koul and others. Before the volume of her Kashmiri poems titled *Mana Pamposh* was brought out in the year 1998 in Devnagri transliteration (now also available in the State Govt. approved *nastalik* script), her poems had reached only a small section of Kashmiri Pandits including the devotees of Swami Govind Kaul and her own admirers. Some of Swami Govind Kaul's poems from the volume *Govind Amrit* have been recorded in a cassette (available in the market). A poem of Bhagyavaan bearing the title 'च़ऽजिम गटुँ दूर सिरियन त्रोव प्रकाश' (वलय वन हाऽर्‌य मुच़र बर ताऽर्‌य फो'ल गाश) is also recorded in the same cassette, all poems having been sung by Arti Tiku.

Undoubtedly, Bhagyavaan is highly gifted as a poet. Her son maintains in the preface to the volume *Mana Pamposh* that she had no literary antecedents and that judged from the worldly point of view, she was illiterate though she had all the makings of a woman of knowledge, implying that she had an inborn genius. Again, he observes of her that she was an "embodiment of knowledge and devotion".

However, a thoughtful reader, who is aware of the corpus of Kashmiri mystical and devotional poetry, including the works of our Bhakti and Sufi poets, will not fail to catch the echoes of some of these poets in the *Mana Pamposh*. Judging by the evidence of what Bhagyavaan Pandit has assimilated from both her predecessors and her favourite contemporaries (some of whom were her possible models too) through aural culture — hearing poems recited or sung in chorus at religious congregations and on festive occasions — I have no doubt in my mind that she owes a lot to the rich tradition of Bhakti and mystical poetry in Kashmiri as our other notable poets also do. I shall try to indicate this through the textual evidence hereinafter as I examine specific lines from some of her poems here and there for illustrative support. Bhagyavaan's main inspiration has been her own Guru, the saint-poet Swami Govind Kaul, who in turn has carried forward the tradition of Bhakti poetry in Kashmiri started by the poets Parmanand and Krishan Joo Razdan as the pioneers in the background. Most of the *Mana Pamposh* poems are rooted in Bhagyavaan's devotion to Govind Kaul — whom she adores as father, friend, guide, Govind (the deity), Master and Beloved.

There is a section of poems in the *Mana Pamposh* devoted to the praise of Krishna, a sequence of poems on 'लोल' *(lole)*, what the Kashmiris understand as love in its human and divine form, and a few poems are addressed to the divine Mother. A sizable number of poems could legitimately be characterized as Songs of Self — in which Bhagyavaan talks of 'असरारि खुदी' (the secrets of selfhood), throwing back to Mansur-ul-Hallaj and other Persian poets who talked of 'irfaan' or spiritual *gnosis* as also of *Mahabba* (love). Interestingly, here and there in the book, we come across pieces composed in Hindi of a sort as we also find in the masters of *Bhakti* verse like Parmanand and Krishan Joo Razdan. This is both an intriguing and amusing feature of the volume.

There are pervasive literary allusions in the *Mana Pamposh* and we have enough evidence in the book of what in the modern critical parlance is described as inter-textuality — we especially find specific lines and phrases from Lal Ded and Shams Faqir integrated into the text of some poems in a slightly altered but recognizable form. Further, it is probable that Bhavani Pandit too had scaled spiritual heights as her Guru, Swami Govind Kaul, had done. However, Govind Kaul, in my considered view, is a saint first and then a poet; poetry served him as a medium of expression to convey his experiences of a direct "encounter" with the Divine. There is a lot of brain-work too in his poems and much of his poetry embodies his message as a spiritual teacher. Though quite a number of his poems have a true lyrical touch and some, as such, can be sung to the accompaniment of music, a lot many others constitute versified "wisdom". Bhagyavaan I consider a poet first and last, though she is saintly at the same time. As a poet she certainly excels her master, Govind Kaul, whom she intensely loved and adored.

The hall-mark of good poetry is *flow*, and the ease with which the poet communicates fine perceptions depends on his or her command of the medium *i.e.* the language he or she employs. Poetry comes naturally to a genuine and seasoned poet as "leaves to a tree". But that is not enough; spontaneity has to be matched by 'artistic control'. In the case of Bhagyavaan, we notice that this quality is evident in most of her poems. While she sings under an inward compulsion, her words fall into shape and flow at a measured pace uninterruptedly. And she can press words into service to communicate delicate shades and nuances of thought accompanied by deep insights as an accomplished 'Metaphysical' poet. Yet, in the main, she is a mystical poet using image and symbol to convey lofty emotions and passions "whetted by thought". She mostly draws upon the traditional vocabulary of the lyric as used by Kashmiri mystical poets, but she is also capable of forging new compounds and novel collocations of words, which shows that she is creative rather than merely conventional as a poet. Her metaphors and similes are drawn from real life having a direct bearing on the various occupations of householders in a rural setting. Repetition of words, images and concepts in her poems does not show her to disadvantage because she is innovative and enlivens the words and epithets earlier used by utilizing them in fresh and appropriate contexts.

What follows now are a few illustrations from the *Mana Pamposh* in support of some of the observations I made on the poet, her art and her concerns. First of all, I quote these lines from poem No. 8, immediately followed by my translation :

तन मीज्य तने, मे' यार वुछ हनि हने,
वुछिहन गोविन्दुँह कोलुय, वो'व तऽम्य प्रेमुक ब्योलुय,
सुय लोनि यस लोल बने, मे' यार वुछ हनि हने।

(Poem No. 8)

Bodies came in contact, I saw the Friend in
every fragment,
I wish to see Govind Kaul, who sowed the seed of love;
He alone will reap (the harvest) whose love is deep
and intense.

Here the poet depicts union with the beloved Guru, described as the Friend, in terms of physical contact between bodies, as a seemingly "profane" image in a sacred poem. However, that precisely gives the devotional lyric a mystical touch.

There are numerous allusions to Lal Ded in the *Mana Pamposh*. The following lines, for example, are evidently reminiscent of Lalla *vaakh* :

न्यबरय दो'पनम अन्द्रय अचुन,
दिह दारिकाये नचुन छुम।
सम चथ समन्द्रस तऽरिथ,
मे' शक्ति पातुॅय कऽरिथ गोम।। (Poem No. 4)

लल द्यदि थो'वुम तो'न्द्रह बऽरिथ,
मन्सूर काऽठिस गऽरिथ गोम।
भाग्यवान रुज़य ज़िंदय मऽरिथ,
मे' शक्ति पातुॅय कऽरिथ गोम।। (Poem No. 8)

The first line of the first piece (from Poem No. 4) recalls Lalla's famous *vaakh* stressing inward meditation on the Self, based on the instruction she had got from her Guru, Sedamol : to turn inward (अन्दर अचुन). Bhagyavaan elaborates the meaning by saying that she had to explore all the dimensions and recesses of the inner world of "दिह दारिका", the body's "mansion", inhabited by the Self. Having received the Guru's grace she tasted divine "nectar" and was thus able to cross the "ocean" of temporal existence. In the second verse (again from poem, No. 4) Lalla's name is directly mentioned. As the legend goes, Lalla came out unhurt from the baker's oven, wearing garments of "divinity". Reference is also made in the lines to Mansur-al-Hallaj and the heavy price of his "head" that he had to pay for asserting his own divinity : "I am Truth". Then Bhagyavaan reveals what the Guru's grace means to her — it involves "dying" into (spiritual) life, (ज़िंदय मरुन), implying the pain and agony an aspirant has to undergo until he achieves conquest of the little self.

The following verses remind us of Shams Faqir and Lalla :

ज़ानॅुरे'न्य ज़ानकऽर प्राणह ज्ञणानस,
मानॅुरे'नि दो'पनस मान करह बो।
पुशि रे'नि मालॅुकरि पोशि वे'मानस
करय जानानस होतय हो।। (Poem No. 79)

मार पेच शूभ्या मंज़ ज़ोलानस,
कार तूस मंज़ शोरॅुखानस बो।
सबक प्रॅुछ़िया अबक छानस,
किनॅु वनॅु पनॅुनिस पानस बो।। (Poem No. 99)

The expressions 'ज़ानॅुरे'नि' (a knowledgeable woman), मॉनुरे'नि' (a self-reliant woman), 'प्राणह ज्ञान' (Knowledge of the vital air), 'पोशिरे'नि' (flower-woman) and 'अबक छान' (unskilled carpenter) used in these verses echo the vocabulary originally used in Shams Faqir's poems titled 'ज़ान मिलनाव भगवानस सॅूत्य' and 'पानॅुरे'निये पान बदलाव'. Obviously, Bhagyavaan has used the expressions in appropriate contexts, which also indicates that she is familiar with the poems she has somehow drawn upon, consciously or unconsciously. She certainly must have had a good grasp of what these words and expressions mean in their original contexts and has employed them effectively to communicate her message. The term 'अबक छान' was used by Lalla in one of her *vaakhs* and Shams Faqir used it later in his poem titled 'ज़ान मिलनाव भगवानस सॅूत्य' devoted to the praise of Lal Ded. Bhagyavaan says of herself in the second line of the second verse 'कारतूस मज़ं शोरॅु रवानस बो' (I am a cartridge in an ammunition factory). I am reminded of a poem of Emily Dickinson's in which she says "my life had stood a loaded gun" until a hunter "identified" and "carried me away". In the light of the similarity of the two metaphors "cartridge" and "loaded gun" — stretching the comparison a little further — we could interpret Bhagyavaan's line as meaning that before she entrusted herself to Govind Kaul's spiritual care, she had the required potential of a true aspirant for grace. In the hands of the Master, she acquired "wings" and equipped thus, she attained spiritual heights.

In the following lines, we notice a marked influence of *tasawuf* implying sufism and the refrain 'जानानॅुं मसाऽ रोश' (beloved, don't feel angry) of a song of Rasul Mir (lingering in my mind) occurs as the initial phrase in the second line :

> शब्बानॅुं प्याला चोम, ताबानॅुं वुछ नुन्दॅुबोन,
> जानानॅुं मसाऽ रोश, चथ आम लोलुक होश।
> वन चूरि कऽमिस न्यूम, अल्लाहतय ओ'म
> कथ प्यठ मे' छिम नाखोश, चथ आम लोलुक होश।

The occurrence of the words 'शब्बानॅुं' (at night), 'ताबानॅुं' (effulgent), 'जानानॅुंह' (beloved), 'चथ आम लोलुक होश' (I drank 'nectar' and gained awareness of love), 'अल्लाह तय ओ'म' 'Allah' and 'ओ'म' (Om — sacred symbol of the Hindus) in this verse immediately suggests to the reader that it has been composed in a Sufistic vein.

Bhavani 'Bhagyavaan' Pandit is very potential as a 20th century Kashmiri woman poet who has, no doubt, attracted some critical attention since her *Mana Pamposh* was published posthumously a couple of years back. I hope she receives adequate scholarly attention with the passage of time.

# 10

# A Re-Appraisal of Lal Ded

REAPPRAISING LAL Ded as a saint-poet and mystic is the need of the hour. Perhaps this task has to focus first on exploring what the genuine poetic outpourings or *vaakhs* of the great saint are (to be sifted from the spurious ones). Then a reinterpretation of the genuine utterances is to be attempted with a view to removing a number of misconceptions and erroneous notions about Lal Ded, some of them obviously based on deliberate distortions and even lies spread to serve a vested interest. All this will call for rigorous research — that is a challenging task in view of our present inaccessibility to the relevant and some indispensable materials lying unused in the State Research Library, that was years back shifted to the Kashmir University campus at Hazratbal, Srinagar.

In spite of the severe handicaps of Lal Ded scholarship, fresh research studies on the saint-poet can take off from the pioneering work in the background accomplished by such scholars as Bhaskar Razdan, Grierson and Barnett, Sir Richard Temple and Pt. Anand Kaul. To my mind, Prof. Jayalal Kaul's *Lal Ded*, a subsequent publication, is a monumental little volume that can serve as a guide-book to the prospective researchers. Compact and packed as it is with documentary details, it has to be tapped with care as a rich resource, being highly useful as a secondary source-material. Professor Kaul has also done a pioneering job in raising sensible and legitimate questions about the authenticity of Lalla *Vaakh* — how best to establish it through a stylistic study of the utterances as they have come down to us by word of mouth. His intelligent grasp of what linguistic change over a period of time, in its bearing on the *vaakhs*, involves in a cross-cultural context is praise-worthy. Some of the crucial observations he has made further on the so-called evidence of various influences on Lal Ded are valuable too. And his forceful rebuttal of the claims some scholars have made about the fusion of various schools and creeds in her *vaakh*, as if consciously attempted by her, deserves to be specially complimented. His total rejection of the evidence put forward by a couple of scholars that Lal Ded at a later stage of her life came under the decisive influence of Islam, followed by her conversion to the new faith, is based on sound and convincing arguments.

Prof. Jayalal Kaul's outstanding contribution to Lal Ded scholarship in the book titled *Lal Ded* has been followed by another accomplished work on the saint-poet authored by Prof. B.N. Parimoo, which too is a significant contribution in terms of his detailed literary translation and interpretation of the *vaakhs*. Its chief merit lies in the chapter-wise sequencing of the verse-sayings aimed at demonstrating Lalla's spiritual ascent to the plane of supreme consciousness and her union with Parma Siva as a yogini. Both Prof. Parimoo and his predecessor, Prof. Jayalal Kaul, have maintained that Lalla followed the Saivite technique of meditation based on Kundalini yoga.

Subsequent works on Lal Ded brought out in the past three decades or so include Nilakanth Kotru's *Lal Ded : Her Life and Sayings* published in 1989, a special 'Lal Ded' number of the *Koshur Samachar* brought out in the year 1971 and Prof. R.N. Kaul's *Kashmir's Mystic : Poetess Lal Ded alias Lalla Arifa* published in 1999. Nilakanth Kotru too has attempted his own English translations of the *vaakhs*, falling in line with the vaakh-sequence adopted by Jayalal Kaul before him. His meanings and explanations are plain and simple, reflecting, at the same time, a good grasp of the doctrines of Kashmir Saivism. As regards Prof. R.N. Kaul's recent book on Lal Ded, it has some novel features that cannot escape the attention of the thoughtful reader. It is readable and enjoyable in view of its literary charm and lucidity of expression. The interpretation of the *vaakhs* points very much to a perceptive and assimilative mind behind the book — inasmuch as the content of the *vaakhs* is made intelligible to the average reader, appealing, at the same time, to the scholar through the author's beauty of expression. The book would have gained further in value if the author had provided adequate details about the essentials of *Trika* or *Kashmir Saivism* and mysticism in general in his account of Lalla as *Kashmir's Mystic* (which is the main title of the book).

The special number of the *Koshur Samachar* mentioned earlier is a very useful source-material for the Lal Ded scholar who cannot, in the prevailing circumstances, have an easy access to the materials available in the State Research Library. Besides providing English translations of Lalla's verse-sayings in a separate section, the journal contains useful and learned articles in English and Hindi contributed by many competent writers from our community (Kashmiri Pandits) and also by some well-known writers like Abdul Ahad Azad, Amin Kamil and Prof. Rehman Rahi. It also contains two short write-ups in English contributed by Swami Laxman Joo and J. Rudrappa.

I should like to mention two more materials on Lal Ded before I switch on to the other related aspects of the topic of this chapter. I was able to lay my hands on the small volume titled *Lalleshwari : Remembered by Swami Mukhtananda* published in 1981. The Preface by Swami Prajnanand and the Introduction by Joseph Chilton Pearce, both thoughtfully written, are valuable as informative pieces on Lal Ded and her sayings. Then follow English renderings of the sayings in the form of poems attempted in the free-verse pattern. These poems capture the essence of the *vaakhs* without observing accuracy in keeping close to the form and content of the original text. They could be described as "transcreations" rather than translations. Joseph Chilton Pearce justifies this feature by observing that "A true translation is always a re-creation".

The other book I acquired very recently was published in early 1999. It bears the title "*Voice of Experience*" : *Lall Vaakh of Lall Ded/ Lali Shori of Kashmir* and contains English translations of 154 *vaakhs* attempted by the author, B.N. Sopori. The *vaakhs* are grouped under five headings chosen as the titles of individual chapters — 'Sadhana', 'Adventure in Space', 'Fortitude', 'Precepts' and 'Discourses with Guru (Master)'. In the Foreword, the author himself, as translator and commentator, describes his particular approach to the study of the *vaakhs* — involving scientific terms and concepts such as 'vibration', 'frequency', 'wave-length' etc. which, interestingly it seems to me, are drawn from his professional vocabulary as a former employee of the Department of Telecommunication. Since he is not a man of any special literary expertise, he has not been able to develop his ideas into a coherent and systematic theory sustainable throughout the study. He manages somehow to communicate intelligibly in English though his command of the language is faulty at places. All the same, he seems knowledgeable about the import of the *vaakhs* in terms of actual yogic practice. As he informed me himself, he plans to bring out a second volume as a sequel to the present one, which will contain another 150 *vaakhs* or so. I wonder if all the *vaakhs* the author has collected are authentic as Lal *vaakh*. The present volume has sold well despite what I see as its shortcomings. The author's attempt is a laudable one.

That Lalla was a rare genius — as a saint and poet in one — is disputed by none, and is acknowledged by all the Kashmiris, Hindus and Muslims alike. It is essentially through the *vaakhs*, which she uttered as direct outpourings from her heart rather than as consciously wrought poetic compositions, that Lalla became very popular as a saint-poet in Kashmir. As Professor Jayalal Kaul very aptly observes, there was no polarization between Kashmiri Hindus and Muslims in her time; the *vaakhs* made a tremendous impact on the collective psyche of the two communities. Perhaps most Muslims being only fresh converts to their new faith were as receptive to the wise sayings of the saint-poet as the Hindus who then must have still been in the majority as the natives of the Valley. Even after the latter got reduced to a minority in consequence of conversions, Lalla continued to be held in reverence as 'Lal Ded' by both the communities. She was also called 'Lalleshwari' by one community and 'Lalla Arifa' by the other, showing that both thought very highly of her spiritual attainment in accordance with their religious perceptions. If a Muslim hailed her as an 'Arifa', he did not mean to convey that she had been influenced by Islam in any remarkable way or had accepted a new faith. Later, some Muslim scholar made deliberate distortion of facts in asserting that Lalla had experienced inward "illumination" only after coming into contact with Sayyid Hussain Somnani and had then got converted to Islam. This wishful "myth" can't stand the test of reason and must be exploded. It has, however, done the mischief : I recall having read in a secondary source-material on Lal Ded that the saint-poet has been mentioned as a convert to Islam in some encyclopaedia. If Muslim scholars draw a parallel between Rabia and Lalla as love-mystics, this seems a befitting comparison and should be acceptable to us. But to distort history and try to perpetuate a lie about Lalla's faith should be rebutted with convincing arguments as Prof. Jayalal Kaul has already done on the basis of his sound Lal Ded scholarship.

Significantly, it is Lalla's younger contemporary, Nunda Rishi or Sheikh Noor ud-Din Wali, acknowledged by the Kashmiri Muslims as well to have been blessed by her at his birth, who has paid her this befitting and glowing tribute :

तस पद्मापोरिचि लले,
तमि गले अमृत पीवा।
स्वह साऽन्य अवतार ल्वले,
त्यथुय मे वर दितो दीवा।
That Lalla of Padmanpora (Pampore) — She drank
Her fill of divine nectar;
She was indeed an *avtaar* of ours (dearly loved)
O God, grant me the same boon!

There are three crucial sacred terms used in the Kashmiri text of the tribute that are obviously derived from our *shastras : deeva* (God), *avtaar* (incarnation) and *var* (boon). The words confirm that Nunda Rishi held Lalla in great esteem and looked upon her as a saint of remarkable achievement, having all the qualities of a divine incarnation. Evidently, he aspires to emulate her, craving to have "his fill of nectar" too as a boon from God. Keeping in view the content of the verse quoted, the responsive reader when informed of the following remark about Lalla made by Sir Richard Temple in his book titled *The Word of Lalla* (C.U.P., 1924) will hardly give any credence to it (the remark) but reject it as a piece of misinformation :

> Lalla is said to have been influenced by the great national patron saint of the Kashmiris named Noor-ud-Din Wali of Tsrar-i-Sherif.
>
> (See p. 3 of Richard Temple's book)

Prof. Jayalal Kaul, quoting the remark in his book titled *Lal Ded,* makes his observation on it in these words :

> As every Kashmiri, Hindu or Muslim, sees it, the truth is the other way round. Besides, Lal Ded should have been sixty, if not more, when Nunda Rishi was born.
>
> (Quoted from p. 72 of Jayalal Kaul's *Lal Ded)*

Yes, the real truth is that as a saint, Nunda Rishi was greatly influenced by Lal Ded. It was his unqualified veneration for the saint-poetess that had a great impact on the devout Muslims, his followers. That explains why for several centuries Kashmiri Muslims have continued to own her, delighting in memorizing and quoting her sayings as Kashmiri Hindus do, singing the *vaakhs* on appropriate occasions — festive events such as marriage ceremonies and at cultural functions. Another important tribute to the spiritual genius of Lal Ded has been paid by Shams Faqir in his poem 'ज़ान मिलुँ नाव भगवानस सूँत्य', discussed in an earlier chapter at some length.

On the basis of the internal evidence from the *vaakhs*, the thoughtful reader is left in no doubt about Lalla's spiritual moorings as a yogini : her Saivite upbringing in a Kashmiri Brahman family. We have unmistakable clues in some of Lalla's *vaakhs* about her initiation into yoga at the hands of her Guru,

स्यदुॅमोल (Sedamol), who was an accomplished *Siddha* as a follower of the Saivite path. The very first *vaakh* (from among many *vaakhs*) in which Lalla talks of her initiation into spirituality and of the remarkable effect of the *Guru mantra* on her, convinces us that she immediately experienced "illumination of the Self ". She had no reason to roam any more in search of a spiritual guide :

> ग्वरन वोननम कुनुय वचुन,
> न्यबरॅ दो'पनम अंदर अचुन।
> सुय गव ललि वारव तुॅ वचुन
> तवय ह्यो'तमय नंगय नचुन।।
> The Guru gave me but one precept,
> "From without turn inward",
> It came to me "Lalla" as God's word;
> I started roaming nude.

The *vaakh* explicitly conveys that Lalla experienced instant spiritual transformation and was thrown into a state of ecstasy on receiving the Guru's word. Elsewhere she says "वुछुम पऽडिंत पनॅुनि गरे" (I found the all-knowing Self within — in the sanctuary of my own heart), "वुछिम शिव तुॅ शक्ती मीलिथ" "I saw Siva and Sakti conjoined in eternal embrace" and "तवय वाऽचुॅस प्रकाशस्थान" (That's how I attained the abode of Light). A tone of confidence and self-assurance, based on a sense of spiritual fulfilment and an awareness of the ultimate Truth, is clearly reflected in these utterances of Lal Ded. We are convinced that she has got to the root of the matter and attained self-realization. Her affirmative statements, such as those quoted, confirm her Hindu faith throughout (call it Saivite if you see it as a distinct cult within *Sanatan Dharma*). The fact is that she had no reason to seek further direction or spiritual succour from any visiting divine or preacher belonging to a faith other than her own. All the so-called evidences given by the Muslim scholar to prove her conversion to Islam is nothing but an unacceptable tissue of lies.

I should like to mention a few scholars from our own community who have made some observations on Lalla that don't seem tenable. They seem to have supposed or imagined that she played the role of a committed social activist, a professional preacher or teacher of spiritual values and brought about fusion of diverse creeds and schools of thought. Forgetting that Lal Ded didn't compose her *vaakhs* as professional poets compose and publish their verses today, they draw their own inferences on which they base very facile and untenable views as if Lalla meant to preach and propagate a philosophy of her own through her *vaakhs*. Here are the two examples that Professor Jayalal Kaul has questioned in chapter 5 of his book *Lal Ded* :

(i) She brought about a "synthesis of the two philosophies" (The *Trika* and Islamic Sufism) and this synthesis "was given to the world in poetic sermons by the wandering ministrel through the rest of her life" (See *Daughters of Vitasta* by Prem Nath Bazaz, Pumposh Publications, New Delhi, 1959, p. 129).

(ii) "The order she founded was an admixture of the non-dualistic philosophy of Saivism and Islamic Sufism" (*See A History of Kashmir* by P.N.K. Bamzai, Metropolitan Delhi, 1962, p. 498).

Again, in the view of Daya Kishen Kachru "Lalleshwari took the best of Islamic thought and fused it best with her own creed". (See Daya Krishen Kachru, "The Light of the Valley" *Koshur Samachar*, 1971 — Lal Ded Number, p. 7.) This view is also questionable, especially the way it is worded.

Lalla's *vaakhs* convey a message of peace and harmony and one can see that she owes it as much to her educational background in a Saivite Kashmiri Brahman family as to her spiritual enlightenment based on her own *sadhana*. There is a definite impress of the Saivite thought and terminology on her *vaakhs*. Whatever her background, there is also evidence in the *vaakhs* of a state of awareness and of an outlook far transcending cults. Her teaching is, in fact, in tune with our *Sanatan Dharma* that is exceptionally catholic and all-embracing, acceptable as much to the emancipated Hindu as it should be to the liberal Muslim. It is her direct "encounter" with the ultimate Truth as a true yogini or mystic that explains why Lalla *vaakh* appeals to men of all shades of religious thought (inasmuch as all religious paths lead to the same goal). When scholars read her *vaakhs* with pre-conceived notions, they interpret them to convey that Lalla aimed at achieving a fusion or synthesis of Vedantic philosophy and Islamic Sufism, as if with a conscious purpose (reflective of her outlook as a thinker and intellectual).

Professor Jayalal Kaul has been consistent in his description of Lal Ded as a Saivite yogini. In this connection, he has been at pains to clarify in what ways *Trika* and *Vedanta* are distinguishable as non-dualistic philosophies. In particular, he characterizes *Shankara Vedanta* as illusionist and praises the Saivite philosophy of Kashmir for its view of the world as Real. As a student of the *Gita* and on the basis of my reading of some of the *Upanishads* (in English translation), I don't find *Vedanta* altogether distinct from *Trika*. Both philosophies are rooted in the *Vedas* and are complementary to each other. If according to *Trika* the world is Real, a manifestation of the *Swarupa*, doesn't Lord Krishna affirm the same truth in the *Gita*?

> बहूनां जन्मनामन्ते ज्ञानवान मां प्रपद्यते
> वासूदेवः सर्वमिति स महात्मा सुदुर्लभः
>
> [sloka 19, chap 7]
>
> At the end of many births (of striving), the knowing one makes Me his refuge, realizing that Vasudeva is All. A great soul of that type is rare to find.

So we see, as the Lord tells us in the *Gita,* "वासूदेवः सर्वमिति" (All is Vasudeva), implying that God inheres in what we see as the external world, which is as such Real — a manifestation of God. This is what *Trika* also emphasizes. In the *Sivastotravuli*, Utpaldeva — celebrated Kashmiri Saivite philosopher and poet — gives equal importance to seeing Siva as विश्वमय (immanent in the world) as well as विश्वोतीर्ण (transcendent or beyond the phenomenal world). As a devotee of Siva, he wants to have शिवाभास (consciousness of the Supreme Self) in the wakeful state — while experiencing the world through the senses, and not merely when he is absorbed in meditation. If there were no compatibility between *Saivism* and *Vedanta*, Abhinav Gupta (famous Kashmiri Saivite philosopher after Utpaldeva), would not have attempted an interpretation of the *Gita* in terms of the *Trika* philosophy.

A word about Sankaracharya, who is branded an illusionist by some Saivites. We must not forget that he is also credited with being the author of the Sanskrit work titled *Saundarya Lahri*. What is *Mayavaad* for the *Vedantin* assumes the form of *Shaktivaad* in the book mentioned as Shankara's point of view undergoes a change. In a Sanskrit poem attributed to him, he uses the line "चिदानंद रुप: शिवोहं शिवोहं" as the refrain — a statement that a Saivite believes to be very true of the Self. I feel that the Lal Ded scholar must avoid seeing the saint-poet as an exponent of only a particular school of thought — *Trika*. So long as Lalla is a poet (and she is so pre-eminently), she cannot afford to be rigorously doctrinal as a systematic philosopher. No doubt, many of her *vaakhs* have the preacher's tone. She is a seeker too in a number of the *vaakhs*; her poetry is mystical as the poetry of aspiration as well as of fulfilment. If we over-stress Lalla's being a Saivite poet, we then overlook her catholicity. In one of her *vaakhs* she says clearly that she sees *Siva* as no different from *Kesava*. How true she sounds when she says "अभ्यासॖ्ूके गनिरय शास्तॖुर मऽठिम" (I forgot the *sastras* as my spiritual practice gained in depth and intensity). And as Lalla's practice advanced, as she went up the ladder of meditation and crossed all the hurdles — negotiated the *chakras* — her utterances became spontaneous as mystical outpourings, coming straight from the heart. What interestingly cannot escape our attention is that even when she has the preacher's tone in some of her *vaakhs*, she is not overtly didactic; we don't see a "palpable" design in the whole body of her verse-sayings. That explains why her poetry is soul-stirring.

Finally, it is the *vaakhs* of Lal Ded — that are aphoristic and, as such, replete with wisdom — on which her great popularity as a mystical poet largely rests. And she is a great poet precisely because she is intensely spiritual and, conversely, she is highly spiritual because she is gifted with an extra-ordinary poetic sensibility. The *vaakhs* bear testimony to Lalla's genius as a saint and poet in one. What the American literary critic, Helen C. White, remarks about the mystic poet is unreservedly applicable to Lal Ded as a poet :

> It is not a strange hybrid of poet and mystic who writes a mystical poem. It is not a man who writes first as a mystic and then as a poet. It is not even a mystic who turns over to the poet who happens to dwell within the same brain and body the materials of his insight to be made into a work of art by the competent craftsman. It is rather that the same human being is at once poet and mystic, at one and the same time from the beginning of the process to the end. (*The Metaphysical Poets* : *A Study in Religious Experience,* 1936; rpt., New York, p. 22.)

# 11

# A Note on T.S. Eliot's *Four Quartets*

THE FOUR Quartets have received enough critical attention as poems of deep religious significance, articulately Christian in inspiration and also intensely personal. One cannot, however, just label them devotional or loosely characterize them as mystical in the light of the ideas we owe to Eliot himself — he did not think highly of devotional poetry inasmuch as it leaves out "major passions", and was not quite happy about the indiscriminate use of the word 'mysticism' in this age, when it is particularly identified with sheer emotionalism. The mysticism that he would accept as valid is not incompatible with dogmatic religion and demands, to use his own words, "the most terrible concentration and askesis".[1] He spoke approvingly of poetry which is significantly concerned with religious doctrines, at once embodying lofty thought and profound emotions. The Four Quartets do come up to this standard.

The mystical element in the Quartets has been discussed by critics, its connections with the Christian and neo-Platonic traditions traced, and the poet's debt to oriental mysticism widely talked about. The general impression that one gets from the relevant critical studies is that the images and motifs that the poems largely employ are recognizably Christian. In this brief chapter, I want to discuss two things : first, how far the language of mysticism used in *Four Quartets* is not just typically Christian but shares universal characteristics, and secondly, whether Eliot's assimilation of the mystical concepts that he owes to his reading is sound enough, backed up by any evidence of his own experience of the Mystic Way, to convince the reader that he compels comparison with any of the great mystical poets belonging to the tradition he followed. Or else, is he too cerebral and academic a poet to be seriously considered mystical?

Ours is an age of extreme uncertainty and doubt, obviously not very conducive to the growth of religious poetry. The unprecedented advancement in the field of science and technology that we have witnessed during the 20th century has alienated man from the Divine and, in consequence, rendered devotional piety into an unattractive theme for poetic treatment. In this context, it is significant that Eliot emerged as a great writer of our times, acclaimed as such not merely because of his modernism, which is revealed both in his thematic concerns and his revolutionary poetic technique, but also because of his commitment to Christian values. That he found inspiration in Christianity became evident in his writings, notably in 'Ash Wednesday' and the *Four Quartets*.

Relatively speaking, the *Four Quartets* make easy reading. They are not riddled with the difficulties which bedevilled the reader of *The Waste Land* years back when enough critical commentaries or annotations on the poem were not available. In the *Quartets* we notice a positive assertion of Christian values; the Christian note, however, is subdued and the speaking voice is very human in appeal, which explains why the non-Christian reader also finds them enjoyable and valuable. The four poems, on the whole, carry a message of hope and reassurance for man in spite of the insistent awareness of the human predicament that accompanies it. Eliot sounds personal though he has not given up the impersonal mode of description or narration that he stuck to in all his works. His wide reading in different literatures, including the sacred writings of the East and the West, informs the text of the *Four Quartets*. The scholarly allusions and echoes enrich the poems without making strenuous demands on the reader.

The *Four Quartets* read as poems of meditation; the speaker in them draws upon memories and associations which serve as starting points for serious contemplation on the meaning and significance of human life and experience. Questions of abiding importance that have engaged the minds of great sages and philosophers throughout the world are woven as leading motifs into the fabric of the poems — relating to Being and Becoming, time and eternity, heaven and hell, sin and redemption, etc. Blended with these motifs are some basic and vital mystical concepts that Eliot has drawn from various sources; they are absorbed into the texture of the poems, presented as images and symbols, such as the 'rose garden', the 'still point' and the 'point of intersection', which speaks of Eliot's own artistic ability and also establishes his debt to the tradition he valued so much. Apart from what he owes to Dante as his master, lines and turns of phrase echoing St. John of the Cross, St. Julian of Norwich and the unknown author of *The Cloud of Unknowing* are easily traceable in the poems; in one of the poems, the *Gita* is alluded to and one can also sense in it assimilation of the Upanishads in some degree. The two ways of spiritual life — *via negativa* and *via affirmativa* — deserve particular mention as the two leading and important motifs of the *Four Quartets*; these two complementary mystical approaches, it needs to be pointed out, have been followed universally.

Eliot makes a striking use of the imagery of darkness in the *Four Quartets* which he directly owes to St. John of the Cross. The imagery is rooted in the negative Christian concept of the 'Divine Dark' or the 'Cloud of Unknowing' traceable to neo-Platonism. The concept acquired an extended meaning in 'The Dark Night of the Soul' which St. John of the Cross chose as the title of his celebrated work on mysticism. In his view, the soul has to go through a state of deprivation, divesting itself of all worldly desires, in order to attain union with the Divine. The following lines from *Burnt Norton* illustrate Eliot's use of the 'dark night' theme :

> Descend lower, descend only
> Into the world of perpetual solitude,
> World not world, but that which is not world,

Internal darkness, deprivation
And destitution of all property,
Desiccation of the world of sense,
Evacuation of the world of fancy,
Inoperancy of the world of spirit;
This is the one way, and the other
Is the same, not in movement
But abstention from movement; while the world moves
In appetency, on its metalled ways
Of time past and time future.

As mentioned in an earlier chapter St. John of the Cross, in fact, prescribes a technique of meditation through the mystical concept of darkness — what he calls going up the 'ladder of contemplation', consisting in total evacuation of the mind as a prelude to the soul's illumination followed by its final union with the Divine.

Let me now refer to another specimen of verse from the *Four Quartets* which employs a mystical motif, and involves a language use which is characteristic — the language is odd in a sense, violative of normal logic but not of grammar. The lines are from *East Coker*, directly modelled on St. John of the Cross; they dwell on the 'negative way' and involve the language of paradox that accords with it :

To arrive where you are, to get from where you are not,
You must go by a way wherein there is no ecstasy.
In order to arrive at what you do not know
You must go by a way which is the way of ignorance.
In order to possess what you do not possess
You must go by the way of dispossession.
In order to arrive at what you are not
You must go through the way in which you are not.
And what you do not know is the only thing you know
And what you own is what you do not own
And where you are is where you are not.

In the 19th century, Francis Thompson used similar language of paradox in the following key-passage of his poem entitled 'The Mistress of Vision' :

Learn to dream when thou dost wake;
Learn to wake when thou dost sleep;
Learn to water joy with tears,
Learn from fears to vanquish fears,
To hope, for thou dar'st not despair,
Exult, for that thou dar'st not grieve;
Plough thou the rock until it bear;
Know, for thou else couldst not believe;
Die, for none other way canst live.
When earth and heaven lay down their veil,
And that apocalypse turns thee pale;
When thy seeing blindeth thee
To what thy fellow-mortals see;
When their sight to thee is sightless;
Their living, death; their light, most lightless;

The two passages that I have cited are logically odd (but grammatically in order), marked by "violence" of a sort which, in effect, serves to awaken perception, making the addressee see oddness in what passes for the normal and seek truth in the reverse direction.

"Game of Love" or "Love Chase" is a familiar theme in the eastern and the western mystical literature alike. The Reality behind appearances is apprehended by most mystics as a personal god and is pursued with passionate love. The seeker establishes an intense relationship with the Divine — that of the son to the parent, or of the servant to the master or of the lover to the beloved representing the three well-known forms of mystic devotion. Thus, the spiritual quest is presented as a love adventure in St. John of Cross's poem titled 'Obscure Night of the Soul' — secret pursuit of the Divine is confined to the psychic world of the aspirant. The account given in the poem rings true and the reader is very powerfully affected by the sheer compulsive quality of the verse, though the idiom is simple and the images familiar.

Among the Metaphysical poets of the 17th century, Crashaw, Vaughan and Herbert notably, in their own ways, do move us by virtue of their mystical awareness accompanied by devotional feeling and intense expression. The later poet Blake is a category apart; he is thoroughly mystical and yet heretical. The language of Wordsworth's Nature mysticism is universally acknowledged. Francis Thompson's *Hound of Heaven* is a masterpiece of linguistic resourcefulness. His senior contemporary, Patmore, writes in a vein of voluptuous mysticism; his prose work titled *The Rod, The Root and The Flower* is a treasure of mystical insights. The devoutly religious Hopkins is among the greatest innovators of mystical language (though Eliot would not rate him highly).

Coming to the *Four Quartets*, I should reiterate that the mystical element in the poems owes itself largely to what Eliot has read of the mystical writers who were his favourites. There is no doubt that he has a good grasp of the Christian mystical theology and a feeling for whatever his assimilative mind has seized upon. Added to this, he is a master craftsman who knows how best to exploit his material and shape it into a work of art. Capable of metaphysical speculation, he could be likened to Donne, the poet he admired and about whom a critic has rightly observed :

> The immediate sense of God was not for him. Vaughan, Blake and Francis Thompson were seers or mystics in a sense in which Donne never was. But, he shared their desire.[2]

My reading of the *Four Quartets* does not convince me that Eliot had experienced the dark night of the soul as, for instance, Herbert had "when he felt cut off from any contact with the Divine Master".[3] Eliot is a poet of vision and an accomplished manipulator of language, no doubt, but as to his standing as a mystic poet, I must confess my reservations.

## NOTES AND REFERENCES

1. Quoted from Eliot's essay 'Religion without Humanism' in Kristian Smidt. *Poetry and Belief in the Work of T.S. Eliot* (London : Routledge and Kegan Paul, 1961), p. 200.
2. Joan Bennet. *Five Metaphysical Poets* (1964; rpt., Cambridge : Cambridge University Press, 1971), p. 136.
3. Lord David Cecil, ed. *The Oxford Book of Christian Verse,* p. xix.

# 12

# Nunda Rishi : A Brief Introduction

WE HAVE discussed Lal Ded's pre-eminence as a Kashmiri saint-poet of consequence in the two chapters devoted exclusively to her. She is held in special esteem by the Hindus and Muslims of the Valley. This holds equally true of the saint-poet Nunda Rishi alias Sheikh Noor-ud-Din Wali of Chrari Sherif, Badgam (Kashmir), hailed as Sheikh-ul-Alam by the Kashmiri Muslims, who look upon him as the founder of the Rishi order among them; he is specially venerated as "Alamdari Kashmir", implying the "standard-bearer of Kashmir". His Hindu admirers in Kashmir, preferring to call him Nunda Rishi, mention this name with deep respect; occasionally one hears some of these admirers referring to the saint as "Sahazanand" too. Born in or around the year 1475 A.D, Nunda Rishi exhibited the signs of an extraordinary saint right from the days of his childhood. His parents, Sheikh Salar-ud-Din and Sodermaji, were converts to Islam; Sodermaji did not bear a child for many years and it is believed that through her intense prayers she was blessed with the birth of a child that was named Nunda. It was the fine traits of character that he exhibited as a boy, his precociousness and, above all, his spirit of self-abnegation that very much pointed in advance to his future eminence as a saint-poet.

It is widely believed in Kashmir that as a babe Nunda Rishi refused to suck milk from his mother's breast. Legend has it further that Lal Ded, who was by then advanced in age, made a surprise appearance at Nunda's home and spoke these words to the babe :

यिनँ मन्दुँछोख नुँ चनुँ छुख मन्दछान
When you didn't shy away from being born
(into this world),
Why do you feel shy of being breast-fed?

With these words of gentle admonition uttered by Lal Ded, the baby immediately sucked milk from her breast. When Nunda grew up to be a well-known saint with a great following, he paid this befitting tribute to the memory of Lal Ded in these lines (quoted earlier too) :

तस पदमा पोरुँचि लले,
तमि गले अमर्यत पीवा।
सो' साऽन्यति अवतार ल्वले,
त्युथुय मे' वर दितो दीवा।।
That Lalla of Padmapur,
She had her fill of divine nectar;
A beloved *Avtar* of ours too (we would fondle
in our laps),
O God, bestow a similar boon on me.[1]

What is significant in this *shrukh* (meaning a *shloka* or verse-saying) is that the Sheikh conceives of Lal Ded having partaken of divine nectar and thus become adorable as an incarnate Goddess. Holding her in very special regard, he wished to emulate her as his model. Though a Muslim, he is not averse to the Hindu belief in the *avtarhood* of Lal Ded. He is thus in perfect accord with the Hindus of the Valley inasmuch as they hail the saint-poetess as Lalleshwari (Lalla, the Goddess Incarnate). The Rishi order founded by Sheikh Noor-ud-Din Wali evolved in the Valley itself after the advent of Islam. It acquired an indigenous character and constituted a "brotherhood" reminiscent of the order of monks called "Buddhist Sanga", with its cultural roots in the Rishi tradition of the Hindus in the distant background. Even before Nunda Rishi openly renounced his domestic life (at the age of 32 years) and embarked upon his spiritual mission, he was least inclined towards worldliness and had the marks of an ascetic given to meditation. He had the makings of a 'Rishi' — a Sankrit term of immense cultural significance, meaning a spiritual seer who models his life on the Vedic standards.

In view of the early death of his father, Nunda Rishi had to depend upon his mother, Sodermaji, and her two step-sons for his sustenance as a youngster. His step-brothers chose to commit thefts and burglaries; they tried to induce Nunda to join them in their reprehensible business. Nunda Rishi eluded them somehow and outwitted them too, frustrating their designs to make him an accomplice in their crimes. Obviously, cut out for sainthood, he remained untouched by evil. One day Sodermaji took her son to the village religious teacher, the Maulvi. She urged him to introduce Nunda to the Arabic alphabet. The teacher wrote the Arabic letters on a tablet, repeating for the boy each letter with proper articulation. He then directed Nunda to read the alphabet as he had been taught. The boy just pronounced for the Maulvi the first letter "Alif". Beyond "Alif" the young defiant learner would not proceed, however hard the teacher tried to induce him to obey the instruction — through persuasion, admonition, threats, etc. The enigmatic boy offered a logical explanation for stopping at the letter "Alif" itself: the letter stands for the oneness of God, and this is the highest knowledge one can and need attain. All else is redundant. The teacher got dumbfounded hearing this explanation and admitted that the boy did not need any tutoring. It is said that later in life, when Nunda Rishi had taken to the path of asceticism, he had an encounter with a Brahmin who considered the Sheikh unfit for the path on the ground that he was "unlettered and uneducated". Nunda Rishi's retort to the Brahmin was his admission that he had got no formal education. In spite of this shortcoming, however, the saint claimed that he had "experienced the presence of God" and also realized "divine unity". Describing the sky, earth, moon, fire, wind and food as the "gifts of God", he convinced the Brahmin of his natural wisdom and didn't waver in his decision to keep to the path of renunciation.[2]

Most biographical and other details about Nunda Rishi have come down to us through "Noor-namas or Rishi namas". These works suffer from several inadequacies and all that they say cannot be taken as wholly authentic, especially the account of the miracles attributed to the saint. All the *shrukhs* in Sanskrit that the saint-poet is credited with having composed have, it seems, been deliberately left out by the authors of "Noor-namas". The fact is that although the Sheikh hadn't received any formal education, he knew Sanskrit and the language had made a great impact on him : as is reflected in his appropriate use of the Sanskrit words or words of Sanskrit origin that one comes across in the *shrukhs*. Such words far outnumber the Persian words used by the saint-poet.

As a saint whose parents were converts to Islam, Sheikh Noor-ud-Din alias Nunda Rishi towers over many of his ilk as far as his spiritual stature is concerned. Among the Kashmiri saints, he stands out as a model of purity, penance, asceticism and moral virtue. A great admirer of the Prophet as an adherent of Islam, his actual religious practice and his pronouncements in the form of *shrukhs* show amply that he can be classed with other great saints in the country professing different faiths, who have influenced generations of followers. Perhaps true to the Indian tradition of sainthood, he preferred to live single all his life, wedded to spirituality and to the ideal of social service, led a simple life, partook of vegetarian food, donned a woollen *loachh* (a Kashmiri *pheran*, its borders stretching upto the feet and its slceves being long), and practised penance and meditation. He lived in caves at several places, spending a decade or so at a place, and remained occupied with his mission as a preacher of spiritual values. As a follower of Islam, that stresses *tableeg* (propagation of faith) and encourages *proselytisation*, he didn't hesitate to convert non-Muslims to Islam, choosing some of them as his disciples. Yet he consistently preached amity among divergent faiths; accordingly he preached harmony between Hindus and Muslims as the inhabitants of the Valley. All through he practised piety, self-control and non-violence. He preached universal brotherhood and non-violence on the basis of his perception of divine unity, in which all diversity is comprehended.

Before we examine some select *shrukhs* of the saint-poet in question in order to have a clear and precise idea of his message, it is feasible to consider briefly how he stands in comparison with his important spiritual predecessor, Lal Ded. Is he to be classed with her as a mystical poet? Perhaps not, not at least in the full sense of the word 'mystical' as distinguished from the word 'religious'. As the mystical verse examined in the foregoing chapters has revealed, such verse invariably provides a hint of the poet's direct *experience* of the Divine : an awareness of something deeply felt which ordinarily defies expression but is conveyed suggestively through image and symbol, and through other linguistic devices. Lalla's utterances in bulk satisfy this criterion while Nunda Rishi's only occasionally approach the standard. The *vaakhs* of Lal Ded and the *shrukhs* of Nunda Rishi, no doubt, share several similarities as aphorisms composed in verse-form; but the content of the *shrukhs* is largely didactic, the preacher's tone being marked in them. However, those *shrukhs* which express the Sheikh's spiritual anguish, his disenchantment with worldliness in general and his aspiration for deliverance from the ills of this temporal world, do move us by virtue of their lyrical appeal as pieces of self-expression. Leaving them apart, it is only in a small number of the *shrukhs* that we perceive the mystical touch too, but even such utterances do not match Lalla's *vaakhs* in mystical depth and intensity. Yet in some *shrukhs*, here and there, Nunda Rishi too engages our hearts through loftiness of introspection and devotional intensity. On the whole, his message impresses *believers* as a teaching that is valuable and cherishable.

We now come to select *shrukhs* of the saint-poet Nunda Rishi. Here is the one that he addresses to his two stepbrothers to convey how wrong of them it is to commit the sins of housebreaking and stealing :

आँगन नाद करान हूनू,
बायो मे'कुन तो'ह्य शुनितव।
यऽम्य ये'ति वो'वुय तऽम्य ततिलूनू,
हूनू छु करान वव बा वव।।

The dog is barking in the courtyard, conveying :
"O Brothers, pay heed to me;
What one sows here reaps there (in the world hereafter),
The dog's bark means — sow you (and reap)".

This *shrukh* reminds us of the Hindu belief in the law of *karma* according to which our actions — good and bad — bring forth the results that determine our future destiny in the lives to come. Obviously, the *shrukh* cautions us to refrain from doing evil and, instead, perform virtuous deeds. For a Muslim, the reward of good actions performed is promised as his or her entry into "heaven" after death. The Hindu belief, however, goes a step further and envisages man's deliverance from the cycle of births and rebirths through *nishkaam karma* (disinterested pursuit of action) backed up by self-knowledge — that consists in seeing the witnessing self as not involved in any activity. The *shrukh* in question, as it is worded, appeals to both Kashmiri Muslims and Hindus in spite of their divergent thinking on man's ultimate goal : as the attainment of "heaven" and "mokhsha" (liberation from the cycle of births and rebirths) respectively.

As maintained before, Nunda Rishi had firm belief in the oneness of God even as a youngster and looked upon the realization of this truth as the end of all knowledge. In the *shrukh* that follows, the Sheikh reaffirms what he had meant to convey as a boy through his insistence on repeating only the letter "Alif" of the Arabic alphabet and having nothing to do with any of the remaining letters :

कुनिरय बोज़रव कुनिनो रोज़रव,
अऽम्य कुनिरन कोताह द्युत जलाव।
अकॅुल तॅु फिकिर तोर को'त सोज़रव,
कऽम्य मालि च्यथ ह्यो'कुय सु दऽरियाव।।

If you practise oneness (in life), you'll lose your identity,
Behold how the one shines resplendently!
Neither your intellect nor mind can comprehend this,
My dear, who can drink that deep stream (of knowledge)?

We come to know from these lines of Nunda Rishi's his understanding of God's transcendence; he is aware of the limitations of the human mind and intellect as the instruments of higher knowledge : of how difficult it is for the seeker to attain God-realization through self-conquest as the *only* means to this end. The saint-poet is close here to the mystical perception of the Real seen as something beyond phenomena.

Having failed to persuade Nunda Rishi, as a boy, to obtain tuition from the Maulvi, Sodermaji got him engaged as an apprentice to a weaver, but he again disappointed her at the end of the day, having watched the loom involved in the process of weaving. The boy bluntly refused to pick up the trade to earn a living that he was not interested in. He summed up the "message" of the loom in a few *shrukhs*, two of which are reproduced below :

> ओता छु दपान द्यू कन दारि,
> मुक छु दपान मो बर पछ़।
> खाव छय दपान च़मू कबरे,
> मालि माजि दो'पनम हो'नरे गछ़।।
> The reed prompts one to listen carefully,
> The shuttle cautions us not to trust blindly;
> The wooden sandal tells you "shrink in the grave"
> My mother sent me to learn weaving (as a craft).

The Sheikh, gifted with innate wisdom, was not satisfied with the explanation offered by the weaver : how the alternate upward and downward movements (closely resembling those of the cyclist working the wheels through his feet on the paddles as we can watch today) help him in accomplishing his task. He drew an esoteric meaning from the working of the loom — the right foot pressing the earth hard and shunning it in the act of moving up and the left doing otherwise, coming back to the Mother Earth. The point is elaborated in this *shrukh* :

> आदम व्वपदोवुम मे'च़े,
> मे'च़ि हऽन्दी कार गऽन्डिथ क्यथ।
> साऽर्‍य न्यामच़ व्वपदाव्यन मे'च़ी,
> रनान मे'च़िव्यन बानन क्यथ,
> जुव च़लि नीरिथ मो'र म्वच़ि मे'च़े,
> मे'च़ी मे'च़ गछ़ि मीलिथ क्यथ।।

Man was born of earth,
Cast out of clay, he got his human frame;
Earth itself is origin of all bounties,
We use earthenware to cook our food,
Life is gone, the body is absorbed into earth again,
And this absorption is for our weal.

The Sheikh further expounds the loom's "mystery" : that the shuttle, resembling man, enters through the gate of birth. As man's "thread of life" is exhausted, he leaves through the gate of death.[3]

We come across many *shrukhs* that depict the saint-poet as engaged in deep self-introspection. Such *shrukhs* are tinged with melancholy : a sense of frustration pointing to the Sheikh's awareness of the spiritual path being beset with obstacles. And the greatest hurdle on the path is 'doubt' contending with one's faith, that lurks Satan-like within the aspirant's mind. This is hinted at in the following *shrukhs* involving introspection or self-analysis on the part of the spiritual seeker (the persona identifiable invariably with the saint-poet himself) :

करॅ क्याह क्याह करॅ हनि हनि दीह गोम,
पाप गाऽम चऽर्य तुॅ कति व्वबरॅ।
म्यूठ तुॅ मो'दुर रवे'य रवे'य वेह रव्योम,
दाह गोम पानस तुॅ क्याह करॅ।।

What am I to do, my body has wasted away by inches,
My sins have piled up and how can I grow spiritually?
I overate sweet dishes, that turned poisonous for me,
No one else is to blame but myself for my bad plight.

The image of despair and desolation is kept up in the *shrukh* below. It suggests the psychological condition of the spiritual seeker going through the agony of separation from the Beloved, an experience of extreme spiritual anguish :

स्वन्दरी कामुॅ दीवुन च़ाव गोम,
यावुन पान गोम पोशन मो'तू।
सगंरुक शीन तुॅ व्वलुॅरुक वाव गोम,
मुहित ठग गोम अकुॅहतू।

वो'लगि बतस कनुॅ तुॅ तोह गोम,
गऽरीबस दोह गोम वहरस यो'तू।।

I became a victim of love :
A beautiful woman captivated by Cupid,
All my youth I got infatuated with flowers;
I suffered as a mountain buried under snow;
Or as the Wolur (a big lake) lashed by a storm;
I felt miserable as if robbed of all I had,
A dish of fine rice ('volag') turned for me into chaff and unhusked grain;
The day lengthened into a year for me, poor Nunda !

The *shrukh* that comes next sounds like a *vaakh* of Lal Ded; it too conveys deep spiritual anguish :

नफसुॅ म्याने च़ीरिवि अगो,
दिच़मय दगो फो'लहम नुॅ ज़ांह।
पानय म्याने हथ मन शो'ठो,
पाप छिय पोठान द्यन किहो रात।।

O my little self, hard as a knot in wood,
That wouldn't break however hard I hit it,
O my ego, swollen as a log of wood weighing a hundred mounds,
Your sins are piling up day and night;

What this conveys in brief is that the ego or little self is unyielding, not pliable. All our efforts to tame it do not succeed. The task of bringing our little self under control is really formidable and a big challenge.

Here is another *shrukh* that reminds us of a Lalla *vaakh*; addressed to God, there is a tone of earnestness and urgency in it :

गऽहऽलि वनुॅ ज़न पे'यम गतय,
बो'ति ओ'पुय मो'ठुम सूहम तार।
चुॅ वुछख अन्दुॅ यो'द मे' अथुॅ कुस रटे,
बार रव्वदाया पाप ने'वार।।

It is as if I lost my track in a pitch dark forest,
A fool as I am, I forgot 'Soham', 'the sacred word'
That would have served me as a ferryboat;
If you remain aloof unmindful of my plight,

Who else will come to my help?
O God, absolve me of my sins.

The next *shrukh* also has the tone of a Lalla *vaakh*; it is an aphorism that spiritual seekers must value as helpful in *sadhana* :

जुव नेरि ब्रोठं लूब नेरि पतॅु
गछ़न द्वन जॅु वतॅु तॅु पे'यि शुन्याकार।
यिदिरव ब्रोंठ तियी पतॅु,
बार रवव्दाया पाप निवार।।

Life will be out, then only greed will go,
As the two fall apart, the void will emerge;
What you give now will serve you hereafter,
Oh God, absolve me of my sins.

The *shrukh* that follows now has in it a fine blend of spiritual terminology drawn from Arabic (letters of the alphabet) and sacred Muslim names, and from the *shastras*, as used by Lal Ded in several of her *vaakhs* :

दाल गोम मीलिथ अऽलिफस तॅु हयस,
अऽम्य हयन को'रनम बयस नाश।
शऽशिकल त्रो'परुॅम अहदॅुकिस पयस,
मीमॅु रो'स अहमद लो'बुम राश।
शे'यि वनॅु फ्यूरुस मोयस मोयस,
अदॅु पर मो'क्ल्योम तॅु को'ड़ुम वाश।।

'Daal' got suffixed to 'Alif' and 'Hai',
And the 'Hai' destroyed my fear;
I focused the sixth sense on the One,
And attained the One — Ahmad minus the letter 'meem':
A treasure of joy for me;
I roamed the six forests through, every inch,
Then, overcoming all obstacles, I felt relieved.

In this *shrukh*, Nunda Rishi brings in three letters of the Arabic alphabet — 'Alif', 'Hai' and 'Daal'. These three letters make up the word 'Ahad', a divine name that symbolizes one God. The saint-poet also mentions the letter 'meem' which occurs in the word 'Ahmad'; if we knock out the English letter 'm' from 'Ahmad', corresponding to the letter 'meem' of the Arabic alphabet, we get the word 'Ahad' that stands for God. The saint-poet also makes an appropriate use of the terms 'शऽशिकल' (sixth sense) and 'शे'यिवनुँ' (six forests) which Lalla too has employed in her *vaakhs*. In line with her, as his spiritual predecessor (who had blessed him at his birth), he claims to have attained union with God after negotiating all the six *chakras* (spiritual centres) and making full use of the sixth sense in reaching Him (as Lalla too talks of her union with Shiva).

In the following *shrukh*, Nunda Rishi uses terms and concepts that are crucial to Islamic mysticism involving *Irfaan* (spiritual *gnosis*) and to Kashmir *Saivism* of which Lal Ded has been the best exponent as a saint-poet :

ला इल्लाह इल्–अल्लाह सऽही को'रुम,
वुही को'रुम पनुन पान।
वो'जूद त्राऽविथ मूजूद सो'रुम,
अदुँ बो' वोतुस लामकान।।

I verified the Quoranic teaching "There is no god but God"
And burnt up my little self,
Going beyond the manifest, I meditated on the Eternal,
Thus I attained the Spaceless.

The term 'लाभकान' ( the spaceless ) used in this *shrukh* is matched by the term 'प्रकाशस्थान' (the Abode of Light), the ultimate goal of *sadhana*, that Lalla claims to have attained in one of her *vaakhs*.

Here is another *shrukh* of Nunda Rishi that merits our attention :

सुछुनुँ वुछान कीलस तुँ कालस,
सु छुय वुछान हालस कुन।
ज़िकिरि हख पर ज़्यव दिथ तालस,
राजुँ होंज यियी ज़ालस कुन।।

He (God) does not judge you by your ability to argue or examine ideas,
He marks your present spiritual condition;
Repeat mentally the divine Name with your tongue held against the palate,
Then the King Swan will be drawn towards the net.

Herein Nunda Rishi uses the Sufi term 'ज़िकिर' which means chanting the name of God, but he qualifies this by insisting on silent meditation (with one's tongue held against the palate). This corresponds to the practice of *ajapa gayatri* or repetition of the *gayatri mantra* without chanting or whispering it as followed in some forms of yogic meditation (the tongue held against the palate). The other term used is राज़ुँहोंज (king swan) that we find in Lalla *vaakh* too mentioned as 'राज़ुँहंस' and Lalla speaks of her spiritual goal attained through 'हंसुँ गथ' (The Way of the Swan). What the two saints claim to have attained through their spiritual practice is the ultimate goal in the shape of union with God.

Let us look at the following *shrukh* that speaks of the saint-poet Nunda Rishi's deep spiritual distress :

प्रऽनिस बदनस मलिनू दाग गोम,
सु ज़ाग गोम नीरिथ बाग अन्दरय।
तति हारुँनि गरमी पोह तुँ माग गोम,
सु फाह गोम नीरिथ हरुँ बन्दय।।
My fair body got stained with dirt,
The bird (I cherished) deserted the garden;
Midsummer turned into chilly winter for me,
And warmth left my body — the city of the Lord.

This *shrukh* makes use of several images that suggest spiritual drought. Readers familiar with the poetry of Wordsworth and Coleridge, on coming across this *shrukh*, will be reminded of the almost analagous themes of the two English poems 'Immortality Ode' and 'Dejection Ode' involving meditations on the "declining powers of the imagination". The fair body stained, the absence of the song-bird from the gardern, the chill of extreme winter and the loss of warmth from the body conceived as the dwelling-place of the Lord — all these images cumulatively present a vivid picture of the saint-poet's state of mind, projecting an important phase of the spiritual journey. In Christian mysticism, as we have seen in chapter 2, this phase is referred to as the "dark night of the soul". And there are corresponding descriptions given in the Hindu and Sufi accounts of the spiritual adventure. In this phase, the mystic experiences loss of joy and cheerfulness; his soul feels pangs of separation from the Beloved. This experience of pain, however, augurs well for the mystic, who has only temporarily lost the joy of "illumination", holding for him an immediate prospect of the unitive experience *i.e.* union with God.

The *shrukh* reproduced below shows Nunda Rishi's knowledge of the Hindu scripture *Ramayana* and his catholicity in making allusions to it to justify his own conduct as a spiritual seeker :

नर बेछू नारान बेछू
ईश्वर बेछू अथॅू ह्मथ कम्पाल।
डडंक वनुक राजॅु राम बेछू
असि गऽरीबव ति ब्यूछ तॅु क्याह छे' गाल।।
'Nar' (man) begged and so did 'Narayana',
The Lord himself begged with a bowl in his hand;
Rama, the King, begged in Dandakvana,
If the poor ones, we, also beg, wherein lies disgrace?

The two *shrukhs* that follow are comparable to the *vaakhs* of Lal Ded in both content and tone :

वनन पऽज़्य तॅु वॉदर आसान,
गगर ग्वफन बरान वास।
यिम पांच़न वकतन अख मल कासन,
निशि आसन बाऽच़न तिमय छिय खास।।
Monkeys and apes inhabit the forests,
And rats occupy caves;
Those who cleanse themselves of *one* impurity
five times a day,
And lead household lives,
Are the most refined.

यऽम्य ह्यो'त तहऽन्दि बरॅु तल ज़ागुन,
तस पनॅुन्य शरबत पानय चावी।
छिस पाऽथॅुर ब्यो'न ब्यो'न अकुय मागुन,
सुय यस टूठ सुय अदॅु प्रावी।।
One who lies in wait, looking for God at the door,
Will be served nectar by Him with his own hands,

Various are the plays staged, but the Stage-Manager is one,
He prospers who is blessed by Him.

The *shrukhs* of Nunda Rishi examined in this chapter show that they have value for the spiritual aspirants across cultures and creeds — as moral sayings and as practical hints on treading the spiritual path. Studying them with loving care must be rewarding for the religiously inclined.

## NOTES & REFERENCES

1. For the biographical details of the saint-poet Nunda Rishi and the authentic text of the *shrukhs* utilized in this short chapter, I have largely depended upon the source material in the shape of the research-oriented volume titled *Nunda Rishi : Unity in Diversity*, tr. and Introduction by Prof. B.N. Parimoo, J&K Academy of Art, Culture and Languages, Srinagar, 1984. I have also mainly consulted the same material in connection with my English renditions of the saint-poet's *shrukhs*, at times even adopting the English translations attempted by Prof. Parimoo — a fact I am mentioning here with due acknowledgements to him.
2. See B.N. Parimoo. *Nunda Rishi : Unity in Diversity*, J & K Academy of Art, Culture & Languages, 1984, pp. 19-20.
3. *Ibid.*, pp. 34-41.

# Select Bibliography


**SECTION A**

Arberry, A.J. *Sufism : An Account of the Mystics of Islam.* London : George Allen & Unwin Ltd., 1950.

Bryant, M. Darrol. *Religion in a New Key.* New Delhi : Wilney Eastem Ltd., 1989.

Buckley, Vincent. *Poetry and the Sacred.* London : Chatto and Windus, 1968.

Cassirer, Ernst. *Language and Myth.* Trans. Susane K. Langer. London : Constable & Co., 1946.

Dhar, A.N. *Mysticism in Literature.* New Delhi : Atlantic Publishers and Distributors Ltd., 1985.

Gardner, Helen. *Religion and Literature.* London : Faber and Faber, 1971.

Ghose, S.K. "Mysticism" in *The New Encylopaedia Britannica.* Vol. 12, 15th Edn. Chicago : Encyclopaedia Britannica Inc., 1977, pp. 786-93.

Grierson, Sir George & Barnett, Dr. Lionel J. *Lalla Vakayani.* R.A.S. Monograph, Vol. XVI, London, 1920.

Hodgson, Phyllis. *The Fourteenth Century English Mystics.* Longman's Green & Co., 1967.

Hussain, Itrat. *The Mystical Element in the Metaphysical Poets of the Seventeenth Century.* London : Oliver & Boyd, 1948.

Inge, W.R. *Christian Mysticism.* London : Methuen, 1899.

James, William. *The Varieties of Religious Experience.* New York : The Modern Library, 1929.

Kaul, Jayalal. *Lal Ded.* New Delhi : Sahitya Akademi, 1973.

Kaul, R.N. *Kashmir's Mystic : Poetess Lal Ded alias Lalla Arifa.* New Delhi : S. Chand & Co., 1999.

Kotru, Nilakanth. *Lal Ded : Her Life and Sayings.* Srinagar : Utpal Publications, 1989.

Martz, Louis. *The Poetry of Meditation.* New Haven : Yale University Press, 1954.

*Nunda Rishi : Unity in Diversity*, Tr. & Introduction by B.N. Parimoo. Srinagar : J&K Academy of Art, Culture and Languages, 1984.

*Oxford Book of English Mystical Verse, The.* Ed. D.H.S. Nicholson and A.H.E. Lee, 1917; rpt., Oxford : At the Clarendon Press, 1962.

Parimoo, B.N. *The Ascent of Self.* Delhi : Motilal Banarsidass, 1987.

Raina A.N. *Zinda Kaul.* New Delhi : Sahitya Academi, 1974.

Rice, Cyprian O.P. *The Persian Sufis*, George Allen & Unwin Ltd., 1964.

Rudrappa, J. *Kashmir Saivism.* Mysore : Prasanga University of Mysore, 1969.

Shah, Idrics. *The Way of the Sufi.* Australia : Penguin Books, 1974.

Singh, Darshan. *Spritiual Awakening.* Swami Kripal Publications, Virginia 22427 and 2 Canal Road, Vijay Nagar, Delhi-110009 (India), 1982.

Smith, Margaret. *Readings from the Mystics of Islam.* London : Luzac and Co. Ltd., 1950.

Spurgeon, Caroline, F.E. *Mysticism in English Literature.* 1913; Reissued, London : Kennicat Press, 1970.

Temple, Sir Richard. *The Word of Lalla*, C.U.P., 1924.

Underhill, Evelyn. *Mysticism : A Study in the Nature and Development of Spiritual Consciousness*, 1911. Paperback edn., New York : E.P. Dutton & Co., Inc., 1961.

Wilson, Colin. *Poetry and Mysticism*. London : Hatchinson, 1970.

*Yogi and the Mystic : Studies in Indian and The Comparative Mysticism*. Edited by Karl Werner. London : Curzon Press Ltd., Riverdale, The Riverdale Co., 1989.

White, Helen C. *Metaphysical Poets, The : A Study in Religious Experience*. Rpt., New York, 1936.

Zaehnar, R.C. *Mysticism : Sacred and Prophane*. London : O.U.P., 1973.

Zukav, Gary. *The Seat of the Soul*. New York : Simon & Shuster, 1990.

## SECTION B

### (Materials in Urdu/Hindi/Kashmiri)

*Reshyaat*. Edited by Mohd. Yousuf Teng, Jammu; J&K Academy of Art, Culture and Languages, 2nd edn., 1992. (Urdu)

Kaul, Swami Govind. *Govind Amrit*. Introduction by Somnath. Bombay : Swami Govind Kaul Ashram, 1975. (Hindi/ Kashmiri)

Kaul, Zinda, *Smaran*. (Parts I & II). The Rosary as Token of Love. Explanatory Engish translation by the author, Srinagar, 1951.

Pandit, Bhavani 'Bhagyavaan'. *Mana Pamposh*. Introduction by Somnath. Bombay : Published by the Pandits, 1998. (Hindi/Kashmiri)

# INDEX